AF477814

Franz Greß, Jackson Janes (eds.)

Reforming Governance

Lessons from the United States of America
and the Federal Republic of Germany

Campus Verlag · Frankfurt/New York
PALGRAVE · New York

REFORMING GOVERNANCE
Copyright © Franz Greß and Jackson Janes 2001

PALGRAVE, 175 Fifth Avenue, New York, N.Y. 10010

First published by PALGRAVE, 175 Fifth Avenue, New York, N.Y. 10010.
Companies and representatives throughout the world. PALGRAVE is the new global imprint of St. Martin's Press LLC Scholarly and Reference Division and Palgrave Publishers Ltd. (formerly Macmillan Press Ltd.)
Printed in Germany

ISBN 0-312-23982-3

Library of Congress Cataloging-in-Publication Data

Reforming governance. Lessons from the United States of America and the Federal Republic of Germany / edited by Franz Greß and Jackson Janes.
p. cm.
Includes bibliographical references and index.
ISBN 0-312-23982-3 (cloth)
1. United States – Politics and government – 20th century. 2. Germany – Politics and government – 20th century. I. Gress, Franz. II. Janes, Jackson.

JK271 .C395 2001
320.43–dc21

2001031547

Die Deutsche Bibliothek – CIP-Einheitsaufnahme

Ein Titeldatensatz für diese Publikation ist bei
Der Deutschen Bibliothek erhältlich
ISBN 3-593-36742-4

Printing office and bookbinder: Druckhaus »Thomas Müntzer«
Printed on acid free paper
Printed in Germany

Besuchen Sie uns im Internet: www.campus.de

Reforming Governance

Nordamerikastudien

Eine Schriftenreihe des John F.-Kennedy-Instituts der Freien
Universität Berlin, des Zentrums für Nordamerika-Forschung (ZENAF)
der Johann Wolfgang Goethe-Universität Frankfurt am Main und des
Instituts für Anglistik und Amerikanistik an der Humboldt Universität
zu Berlin.

Für das John F.-Kennedy-Institut herausgegeben von:
Willi Paul Adams (Geschichte), Winfried Fluck (Kultur),
Carl-Ludwig Holtfrerich (Wirtschaft), Heinz Ickstadt (Literatur),
Hans Joas (Soziologie), Knud Krakau (Geschichte) und
Margit Mayer (Politik)

Für das ZENAF herausgegeben von:
Volker Albrecht (Geographie), Michael Bothe (Rechtswissenschaft),
Christa Buschendorf (Amerikanistik), Christian F. Feest (Ethnologie),
Franz Greß (Politikwissenschaft), Olaf Hansen (Amerikanistik) und
Hans-Jürgen Puhle (Politikwissenschaft)

Für das Institut für Anglistik und Amerikanistik von:
Renate Hof (Literatur und Kultur) und Günter Lenz (Literatur und Kultur)

Band 14
Herausgegeben vom ZENAF

Franz Greß is a Professor of Political Science at the Johann Wolfgang
Goethe-University, Frankfurt/Main., Germany. Besides teaching in the
Department of Social Science, he is also an active member at the university's
Center for North American Studies, where he has served several times as
Executive Director. *Jackson Janes* is Executive Director of the American
Institute for Contemporary German Studies at the Johns Hopkins University
in Washington.

Contents

II. Federalism and Devolution

III. Fiscal Transfers and Local Government Reform

IV. Concluding Remarks

Contributors

Preface

This volume presents contributions by leading experts from the USA and Germany dealing with concepts and experiences related to the modernization of government at the national, state and local level. Concentrating on structural questions, which concern the organization and framework of the political-administrative process, it explores the recent developments in both countries and examines ideas for future developments as well. The focus is on questions concerning the reform of government and administration, decentralization and devolution, and the financial transfers in both federal systems as interlinking features.

This volume is organized around the presumption that the United States and Germany share significant similarities as transatlantic partners. Both socio-political systems, being modern industrialized societies, are responding to many of the same challenges by offering a more efficient and a more responsible administration. On the other hand, there exist important differences in the value systems and with regard to government action. This includes the concept of the state itself; e. g. in its relation to society and to the market, the structures of intergovernmental relations, and the differing institutional arrangements in a parlamentarian and presidential system.

The topic "Changing Governance" has special political and practical relevance when we consider the background of the current political discussion in Germany, which in the past few years has had to deal intensively with factors such as "globalization" and progressing European integration. These factors have shown the need for almost constant reform of governmental activities, e. g., the establishing of the program "Moderner Staat - Moderne Verwaltung" on Dezember 1, 1999 by the Schröder Administration. In this context concepts and developments in the United States concerning "reinventing government" have been of special interest for the German political and scholarly community.

The same is true for the reconstruction of the relations between the federation and the *Länder*/states in both political systems. The fiscal and jurisdictional consequences of changing intergovernmental relations, focusing on the degree of competition and the scope of decentralization, are prominent features in the public debate in the USA and Germany.

Here is also the place to say special thanks to The German Marshall Fund of the United States and the Robert Bosch Foundation, which generously funded the project of an American-German exchange on this subject, including a groundbreaking transatlantic conference in May 2000. For the support of our work at that stage we also would like to thank the U.S. Consul General Mr. Edward B. O'Donnell and the staff of the Amerika Haus Frankfurt am Main. The publication gives credit to Mrs. Sara Hoefler of the staff of the Center for North American Studies and Mr. Matthias Hannes of the Department of Social Sciences of the Frankfurt University who shared some challenging experiences with the editors. Last but not least, special thanks to Michael Roth, Member of Parliament (MdB) who helped in getting the project from rhetorics to results.

Franz Greß   Jackson Janes
Frankfurt am Main   Washington, D.C.

Perspectives of a New Relationship between Government and Society:
Transatlantic Conflicts and Commonalities

Karsten D. Voigt

Since the founding of the Federal Republic of Germany, the transatlantic partnership has been one of the fundamental pillars of German foreign policy alongside the European unification process in the European Union. It has brought Germany peace, prosperity, and reunification. The maintenance and strengthening of its transatlantic ties will be consistent with German objectives and interests in the future as it has been in the past.

At present, the transatlantic relationship is undergoing a sea change caused by two global developments: on the one hand, the bipolar world is changing into a more complex reality which can be represented adequately neither by a unipolar nor a multipolar world view. On the other hand, now that the world is no longer threatened by the Soviet Union and its marxist-communist ideology, Europe's factual and psychological dependence on U.S. protection has been lessened.

At the same time, new technologies are changing our societies in fundamental ways. The Internet and the so-called New Economy are revolutionizing our economies, the globalization process is making national borders less relevant, but also undermines the protective function of the state. Globalization is reflected, among other things, in a multiplication of the forces active in the transatlantic relationship: individuals, enterprises, organizations, associations, and communities operate and communicate ever faster and cheaper across the Atlantic. This leads to more points of contact, but at the same time also to greater friction. Increasing communication leads not only to new cooperation, but also highlights differences in cultures and values.

The United States is the only remaining global power and has been left without an equal rival for the first time in its history. It is world-wide the only country capable of long-term global projection of military power. It has

the strongest economy in the world, which has been enjoying an almost decade-long boom. It is the nation most easily in a position to impose its own
concepts as world-wide rules, if necessary all by itself. It is true that in the
cultural field, many Europeans continue to feel superior to the United
States; but this has long ceased to be justified. For quite some time, the
United States has set the standards not only for the masses, but also for the
cultural élites. Its global role is based on a unique synthesis of economic
strength, world-wide cultural leadership, and military superiority.

Germany is now unified and is not being threatened by any of its European neighbors. On the contrary, it is surrounded only by friends and partners. Thus Germany finds itself in the best position internationally since at
least 1618, when the Thirty Years' War started. In comparison to 1989, there
are more than one million fewer soldiers stationed in Germany, and almost
all nuclear weapons and the majority of foreign soldiers have been withdrawn. Domestically, too, Germany has changed more since reunification
than many Germans realize. For instance, over the last ten years, Germany
has become the second-largest country of immigration in the industrialized
world after the United States. Politically, these changes are symbolized by
the government's move from Bonn to Berlin. All this contributes to the fact
that Germany's image and role in Europe have changed, too.

The European Union is in the process of developing a common approach
as an actor on the world stage. Although it will not be as powerful by far as
the United States, especially in military terms, it will at least have the potential, primarily regarding its economic, trade, and monetary policies, to play
in the same league. In the last decade, Europe has made enormous progress:
in 1993 it achieved the single European market, in 1995, the accession of
Austria, Finland, and Sweden, and in 1999 the introduction of the euro.
Thus Europe speaks with one voice, as the United States has so often demanded, at least in monetary matters. Now Europe is getting ready to master
the next challenges, such as the deepening of integration and a new round of
enlargement for which there are now 13 candidates. This will lead to the EU
being able to rightfully speak for Europe as a whole - with the exception of
the European members of the Commonwealth of Independent States.

In this transitional phase, controversial issues like "bananas", "genetically
altered products", "data protection", "home schooling", "death penalty", and
"American unilateralism" are making headlines in the Euro-Atlantic relationship. There is talk of a "new transatlantic lack of understanding" or

"continental drift". To be frank, for me these conflicts do not place our common interests and values in jeopardy. They are simply an expression of the increasing closeness of the transatlantic relations that have developed between us to the point where they are now almost a domestic matter. However, these problems should be cause for us to take a sober and calm look at the issues about which we differ and those we have in common, in order to be able to assess them and deal with them.

- In the United States, the right to free speech is the inviolable "first among equals" of the American basic rights. Our history has taught us to develop a concept of the defense of democracy ("militant democracy"), which under certain circumstances allows and demands a restriction of free speech for the enemies of democracy. Thus Article 18 of the Basic Law provides that in case of an abuse of the basic right to free speech, that right can be withdrawn.

- At present, the transatlantic differences are becoming particularly clear with regard to right-wing extremism. The spread of neo-nazi ideas via Internet is possible in the United States, but in our country it is a criminal offense. The Internet allows undesirable propaganda from the United States to be accessed easily elsewhere, too. This example shows how globalization (in this case the Internet) can undermine the protective functions of the European governments.

- In America, interference with property rights is considered a violation of a specific freedom. In contrast, we consider the obligations attached to the ownership of property an irrenounceable basic value of our freedom-based system. The different weight given to property rights becomes clear even in U.S. foreign policy, for example, in the extraterritorial Helms-Burton Act. Every American considers expropriation illegal, and at least immoral, and consequently, investments in expropriated assets (according to the Helms-Burton Act) are held to be immoral. By the same token, the recognition by the reunified Germany of the expropriations that took place during the first years of the Soviet occupation is meeting with a total lack of understanding in the United States.

- In addition, there are differences in the concept of the freedom of religion, which is legally protected in the United States. While on the one hand, the separation of church and state has been strictly observed from the country's inception, everyday life and politics in the United States have a strong religious component. Religious formulae and avowals of faith can be found everywhere, for instance in the construction of shopping malls in the shape of the cross, or the definition of the United States as the "Promised Land", as well as missionary elements in the American election campaign and in U.S. foreign policy.

In Europe, the secularization of the society is much farther advanced than in the United States. The belief in God, life after death, and attendance of religious services in Europe, in contrast to the United States, has declined considerably. Religious remarks or avowals hardly ever occur in public life in Europe.

These two different approaches collide on the issue of the treatment of the Scientology Organization. While in the United States the idea of freedom of religion is defined very broadly, similarly to that of the freedom of speech, the government in Germany has an obligation to protect its citizens against threats to democracy emanating from organizations even if these claim to be religiously motivated.

A relatively new issue is that of home schooling. While - especially religiously motivated - parents are allowed in the United States under certain conditions to teach their children at home, Germany, for historic and social reasons, has compulsory education.

- The French Jacobin concept of the state, as well as the traditional role of government in German politics, stands in stark contrast to American individualism. In America, the individual is autonomous, and groups form only through the will of individuals. Therefore the roots of American solidarity, i.e. philanthropy and volunteerism, can be traced back to individualism.

A case in point in this context is the problem of data protection. While in Europe government is responsible for protecting the privacy of its citizens against uncontrolled transfer of personal data, the United States has so far relied on the individual responsibility of its citizens as well as on self-regulatory market forces. The solution to this problem that was finally found by the United States and the European Union demonstrates, on the one hand, the cultural differences, and on the other hand the ability to arrive at viable compromises in spite of these differences. The American concept for providing a level of data protection equal to that of the European Union is a mixture of private-sector self-regulation and legal provisions.

Another example concerns genetically altered products: the United States sees in these products a possibility for overcoming possible food shortages and leaves it up to the consumer whether or not to accept the product. Europe places primary importance on protecting the consumer. The European rejection of genetically altered products, however, in the opinion of many Americans far exceeds consumer protection and is motivated by economic protectionism and anti-technological ideologies in Europe.

- Due to the country's history, violence plays a somewhat different role in U.S. society than in Europe. On this side of the Atlantic, the idea that the government has the exclusive right to use force has prevailed, while in the United States the right to bear firearms has been raised to the level of a mythical constitutional right. The issue of punishment also belongs in this framework. The fact that the idea of retribution plays a much larger role in U.S. criminal law than the goal of helping the criminal to retake his place in civilized society is attested to not only by the death penalty. In contrast to Europe, a much larger percentage of the population is in prison in the United States. At the same time, the structure of the prison population reflects considerable social problems: 46% of the inmates are African-Americans.

- While Europe, in a realistic assessment of its own potential, has since 1945 been relying primarily on multilateralism as a tool of its foreign policy, the United States, in its undiminished and still growing military, political and cultural self-confidence as the "Promised Land", practices a selective internationalism. In cases where multilateral approaches - which most Americans also prefer - appear to them to be impracticable, the United States still has the option to go it alone.

All these differences should not and cannot blind us to the fact that they are more than offset by our common values. Frequently the differences within the United States and within Europe are more serious than those between the two shores of the Atlantic. Europe and America share a common cultural and intellectual history. They share the same basic values and have a very similar understanding of representative democracy, human rights, the rule of law, and a free market economy. Their cultural affinity persists. America and Europe have structurally comparable civil societies. The differences I have pointed out refer less to differences in values than to different priorities of values. Here, too, these differences are nothing new. The Atlantic Community has never been a perfect community of values. In spite of largely shared interests there have always also been considerable conflicts, even during the period of the Cold War.

The reason that these differences are felt more keenly today is not only to be found in the problem of increased closeness. It is the increased and justified American self-confidence that many Europeans find hard to take. This self-confidence expresses itself, in spite of the American tolerance, in a tendency to try to transfer American values and systems to other societies. In addition, globalization is frequently equated with Americanization. It is true that the wave of globalization shows clearly American features: the Internet and the New Economy were invented in America, and in Euro-Atlantic enterprises, English is the lingua franca as a matter of course. However, it must also be remembered that America has become the undisputed leader in the globalization process simply because it was prepared to make painful changes earlier than most of the European countries.

This criticism also reflects a European weakness. It must therefore be Europe's goal to continue its consistent development towards becoming an equal partner. This requires an increase in its efforts to measure up to global competition. Europe cannot successfully and permanently safeguard its identity through protectionism and isolation, but only through modernization and greater openness.

Only together, within a close partnership resting on two pillars, can Europe and the United States globally protect and uphold their concepts of freedom, democracy, the rule of law, and human rights. Only together can they tackle the problems of the twenty-first century, namely the containment of security risks in the broader sense, especially the prevention of the further proliferation of weapons of mass destruction and their delivery systems, migration, environmental threats, international terrorism, and organized drug trafficking, and ensure regional stability.

The increasing mutual economic integration will contribute to the strengthening of common values. Global corporations today are in reality mostly basically Euro-Atlantic enterprises. It is Europe as a whole, and not Asia, that is the largest investor, employer, and - with the exception of Canada - the largest trading partner of the United States. Every twelfth American employee works in an enterprise led by Europeans. In return, American enterprises employ more than three million European workers. In economic terms, Europe and America are certainly not drifting apart - in spite of existing conflicts of interest.

In short: Although differences between Europe and the United States regarding the priorities of their values do exist, their common values far exceed these differences. The differences have become more a matter of public attention because the transatlantic partnership is increasingly assuming a quasi-domestic character. Economic, social, and cultural discussions and decisions in the United States are the subject of domestic debates in Europe. The differences by no means justify the talk about a cultural divide between Europe and the United States. The difficulties we are experiencing are the typical symbols of a period of transition. We are actually witnessing the birth pangs of a new Atlanticism.

I. Reinventing Government

Introduction

Volkmar Schultz

The topic of this chapter is government and administration reform in a transatlantic context. The bottomline of the presentation of facts and arguments is the following: The basic problems in this area are the same on both sides of the Atlantic, even if different types of advancement have been made in America and Europe.

The state has expanded its activities into too many fields. The fact that both, resources and governmental efficiency are lacking, should lead us to reflect upon how the exercise of these tasks could be improved.

A new division of functions between government and society is necessary that will give citizens more responsibilities. There is a need for more opportunities where initiatives of the citizens can develop.

The creation of a framework for the development of individual freedom and security of citizens is therefore one of the central responsibilities of the government. Internal security, legal protection, and the fiscal administration were main tasks and will remain so in the future as well. This concentration on central areas will lead to the following: Areas, that are not directly governed by the state, must be taken over by other societal groups. The state simply regulates the framework in these fields. In service areas like the postal service, telecommunications, and transportation, a transatlantic community is already a reality or is just about to undergo the final stages of transformation.

The state and its administration must accept its citizens as partners, and no longer treat them as "subjects". That means more service, shorter distances, faster decisions, and new forms of dialogue. The government has a lot of catching up to do in this area in order to effectively team up with the citizens. New information technology, which has become a matter of course, must be implemented in communications between the citizens and the state. This also makes the governmental decision making process more transparent.

However, the state must not only concentrate on central areas and improve communications with its citizens. Moreover, it must become more efficient in dealing with the limited resources it has at hand. This is important not only at times when the budget has to be balanced, however. It means that the government must make a commitment to use tax money in a meaningful and efficient manner. Modern management methods, such as controlling, must be introduced in public administrations. Phenomena like "surplus fever" and stiff hierarchies are simply out of place today, and do nothing but hurt the image of the state. Citizens are not willing to cooperate with inefficient administrative agencies. Therefore, modern management methods, which contain both priority and resource management, are a key concept to government and administration reform, that will bring progress for both the state and the society.

Once again: Modern, achievement oriented and democratic societies are also dependent upon governmental bureaucracies. However, these bureaucracies – the example of the "transformation states" in Central and Eastern Europe makes this especially clear – must consider themselves as service providers.

Changing Governance in Comparative Perspective: Traditions and Opportunities

Richard Lehne

Interpreting differences in public policy between Germany and the United States is an especially problematic aspect of comparing governmental patterns and practices in the two countries. What should citizens or political actors conclude when German and American institutions react in dissimilar ways to global economic trends, the decisions of the World Trade Organization, or the emergence of the Internet? Scholars conventionally attribute divergent national reactions to parallel events to significant differences in either values or interests. Ronald Inglehart, for example, traces national differences in governmental policies to variations in the emergence of modern and postmodern values in the various countries,[1] and Raymond Vernon admonishes investigators comparing interactions between government and business in Europe with those in the United States to keep in mind "the radical differences in national values" that are present.[2] At the core of political scholarship in both countries is another prominent analytic tradition that identifies governmental policies as the result of contests among competing interests and factions, and recent theorists have enhanced this interest-driven understanding of policy differences by appraising the coalitional and rational-choice dimensions of group behavior.[3]

Historical Institutionalism

In addition to values and interests, political analysts can also explain differences in national policy by examining the character and history of a country's major institutions.[4] The circumstances in which institutions were created and the ways in which they developed have a lasting impact on a realm's governmental practices and policies. As a methodology, historical institutionalism scrutinizes a nation's basic societal structures, its formal in-

19

stitutions, and its informal rules and procedures.[5] Institutional factors are seen to be influential because they define a country's political process, structure relations among contending groups, shape the strategies of political actors, and privilege some interests at the expense of others. In his assessment of the importance of institutional relationships in German economic history, Colin Crouch dismisses the political significance of "disembodied sentiments" and insists that values "can be a major influence on behavior only when they are embodied in institutions."[6]

Historical institutionalism emphasizes three features of a nation's institutional arrangements. First, governing institutions often constitute the basis of continuity in a country's public policies.[7] During his investigation of national policies for railroad development, Frank Dobbin found that "nations read reason into existing state institutions."[8] National political success produces a collective understanding of the social order, and the traditions of the political order subsequently structure a country's responses to its policy challenges. The principles that shaped the political order in France, Britain, and the United States reappeared in these countries' industrial policies for the rail sector. "When nations face new policy dilemmas", Dobbin discovered, "they design new institutions around the principles of existing institutions."[9] The second hallmark of a nation's institutional history is the importance of the sequence of its institutional development. The creation of a societal institution reflects a commitment to certain organizational arrangements and the rejection of others. Older institutions are shaped by their purposes and resources, but newer institutions must also accommodate the established structures of their organizational environment. Ira Katznelson explains the relative prominence of socialist traditions in continental Europe and the United States by noting that political parties emerged at different points in the societal development of the two regions.[10] While political parties originated in the United States in an agricultural era, membership-based political parties in Europe were defined in response to the upheavals of the industrial revolution, organized around workplace communities, and committed to the agenda of the unionization movement. Third, institutionalists also acknowledge that historical events and relationships are sometimes the product of accidents or coincidences. Rather than driven by major societal forces, some developments occur simply by chance. Gerhard Lehmbruch's analysis of German reunification explains the easy adoption of West German institutional arrangements in some sectors of the Eastern economy but not others on the basis of purely coincidental developments such as the early confirmation of property rights in the East for the members of collective farms.[11] Contemporary proposals to reform governmental patterns and practices in Germany and the United States are elucidated by investigating the history of institutional developments in the two countries and by appraising the continuity in the relevant policies, the sequence of institutional development, and the significance for the prospects of reform of purely coincidental events.

Patterns of National Development

The United States was founded as a democracy at the end of the eighteenth century, fashioned an industrial economy in the second half of the nineteenth century, and then created the large bureaucracies of the administrative state in the early decades of the twentieth century. The United States was not a democracy at the end of the eighteenth century according to today's standards. Societal circumstances then were seldom included in an understanding of democracy. Women usually could not vote, voting was sometimes limited to property owners, and slaves did not vote, but from the beginning the United States was a country where the broad patterns of public preference were significant for the conduct of public affairs.[12] *The Federalist Papers*[13], the commentaries on the Constitution that were published when ratification was being debated, can be read as testimony to the centrality of public opinion for the new governmental system. The political system was based on the consent of the public, and the basic task of the drafters of the Constitution was to design political institutions that could accommodate the dynamics of public preferences. There was an acute awareness of the dangers and dilemmas of the public mind, but from the start the political system rested on the importance of public preferences.

The emergence of an industrial economy in the second half of the nineteenth century in the United States was both an economic and a social revolution. Within a generation, most Americans went from working on land they owned to working for someone else. They went from being independent artisans to being members of a "labor force".[14] One distinctive feature of industrialization in the USA was the prominence of large companies. Unlike

Unlike Great Britain where industrialization was based on the activities of small firms, the characteristic feature of U.S. industrialization was the emergence of huge corporations that conducted economic activity on an unprecedented scale.[15] American railroads were, for a time, the largest economic organizations in the world.[16] In the late 1880s, when no U.S. manufacturer had more than two thousand employees, the Pennsylvania Railroad employed fifty thousand workers. By the time the federal government came to employ fifty thousand civilian workers, some individual railroad companies had more than one hundred thousand employees.

These firms grew up in a society where the role of the national government was quite circumscribed, and they largely set their own course. Most companies did not need national licenses to conduct their business, the national government did not provide them capital, it was not a major market for their products, and it did not help them sell their goods internationally. At the same time, companies recognized the importance of public opinion. Large companies represented unprecedented concentrations of wealth and political influence, and their activities had disrupted established social and community norms. Corporate leaders knew that their firms were regarded as illegitimate institutions by a substantial portion of the public. In 1890, the United States Congress enacted the country's basic competition policy, its fundamental anti-cartel law, and companies attributed this action to public hostility toward large corporations. Fearing that their position was vulnerable to political attack by an antagonistic citizenry, corporations sponsored welfare programs for employees and launched systematic public relations efforts to enhance their public acceptance.[17]

Large national administrative agencies in the United States were mostly a creation of the twentieth century.[18] The United States Constitution does not mention bureaucracies or administrative agencies, but it may be even more telling that there is essentially no discussion in American political theory of the role of administrative agencies. There is no U.S. counterpart to *Staatstheorie* in the classic German sense. In American political theory, the basic task of administrative officials is to carry out the wishes of elected officials. Members of Congress are authorized to make policy, and administrative agencies implement their judgments. Major agencies of the U.S. administrative state were founded after the priority for public preferences had been established and after the patterns of corporate behavior were defined, and, as a result, administrative agencies have never won the esteem in the United

States that are afforded in the European tradition. The sequence of development in the United States recorded first the inauguration of democratic practices; major corporations emerged after public preferences had already captured a primacy in public affairs but when national administrative agencies had only limited significance; and large national government bureaucracies were a twentieth century invention that appeared when public and corporate patterns of behavior had been defined.

The sequence of institutional development in Germany was essentially the opposite of what transpired in the United States. Germany first developed the institutions of state administration, then became an industrial nation, and subsequently forged its democratic traditions. Lutz Raphael traces the origins of the modern Prussian-German administrative state to the fiscal reforms and the creation of a standing army by the Hohenzollern dynasty in the second half of the eighteenth century.[19] While exploring relations between rights and administration, Raphael uses the subtitle "Herrschaft durch Verwaltung" to emphasize the growth of state authority through a combination of functional assignments and theoretical training. Klaus-Henning Rosen stresses even more strongly the relevance of the eighteenth century administrative heritage for contemporary governance:

> The transformation of the absolutist state of the 18th century, the authoritarian state of the 19th century into administrative state of the 20th century was not the result of a revolutionary process but of an evolutionary one which allowed the state as an institution to preserve and maintain its unbroken prestige. From this the conclusion can be drawn that administration in Germany is traditionally based on the authoritarian principles.[20]

Industrialization in Germany roughly coincided with industrialization in the United States, and it was shaped by government policies that facilitated access to capital, technology, infrastructure development, and foreign markets.[21] Local German rail networks were built early in the nineteenth century, and these networks were then linked to provide a national rail system that could serve national markets. The need to pool capital stimulated the development of the banking sector, and vast demand for railway equipment assisted the emerging coal, iron, and machinery industries. By the start of the twentieth century, Germany had become a world leader in such classic industries as coal mining, steel production, chemicals, electrical products, and machine tools. German democracy, in large measure, was not a deeply rooted societal phenomenon until the twentieth century. The liberal democratic norms of the Basic Law combined traditional and innovative organizational practices, provided flexibility for the nation's evolving political orientations, and still respected the conviction that the state is more than the sum of its parts.

The contrasting sequences of institutional development in Germany and the United States are not simply curiosities from a dusty past. They continue to play a vital role in a broad array of governmental patterns and practices in both countries. The consequences of the patterns of institutional development are evident in the priority afforded public and administrative preferences in Germany and the United States, the structure of governmental programs, and the relationships between government and the economy.

Consequences of Institutional Development

Institutions, Peter Hall points out, are "usually more consequential than their creators intended."[22] Fashioned in response to a particular set of problems in specific circumstances, they then survive for decades or centuries with consequences that ripple out into domains of society that are distant in time and place from their origins. Organizations are sometimes influential because they structure the goals and incentives of political actors,[23] but the discussion here emphasizes the consequences that result from the fact that institutions in each era structure the community's capacity to discharge societal functions and provide public services.

The sequence of institutional development has been highlighted in many analyses of the emergence of the welfare state.[24] In the United States, the patterns of institutional influence were in part a consequence of federalism. Stephen Skowronek has noted that federal administration in the nineteenth century possessed few organizational resources, and, as a result, policy strategies that required little federal action appeared in numerous policy areas.[25] States and charitable organizations were active in the early provision of welfare services, and conflicts between the states and the national government accompanied most initiatives for social service reform. A critically important aspect of nationalizing welfare functions was the need to organize bureaucratic machinery that could administer the new programs while protecting the interest of the beneficiaries and compromising the concerns and national and state governments.[26]

Since industrialization in the United States preceded the development of national administrative agencies, corporations also played a large role in the provision of social services.[27] U.S. companies began to provide health care to workers after the Civil War.[28] Some firms found it in their interest to have a healthy workforce, and other enterprises operated in unsettled areas where medical care was not otherwise available. During the Progressive Era, proposals for government-sponsored universal health insurance were widely debated, but they were opposed by doctors who feared third parties would influence their medical decisions, firms which worried that employees would have more justification to avoid work, and unions which concluded that government-sponsored benefits would undermine worker loyalty to unions. During the 1920s medical costs rose, and private health insurance gained in popularity. Corporate health insurance plans expanded during World War II when employers needed to attract qualified workers but were barred by wartime controls from raising employee salaries and when insurance companies recognized that contracts with large employers held down administrative costs. National government programs to finance health care for the aged and through the states for the poor were enacted in 1965, but at the end of the 1990s two-thirds of all non-elderly Americans still received health care through voluntary employer-sponsored programs.

The American Express Company created the first U.S. corporate pension program in 1875. In 1916 an amendment to the federal tax code allowed companies to deduct payments to retirees from the income tax base, and after 1919 donations to employee pension funds could also be deducted. The enactment of the Social Security Act in 1935 did not replace employer pension programs but supplemented them. With people retiring earlier and living longer, and with the federal income tax drawing an increasing share of private savings, retirement expenditures both by companies and through the Social Security system grew rapidly. Government regulation of employment retirement programs began with the passage of the Employee Retirement Income Security Act (ERISA) in 1974. This legislation increased the stability of private plans and guaranteed that retirees would receive the benefits to which they were entitled, and government regulation of the plans was tightened by additional legislation in subsequent years. The sequence of institutional development has left the United States not with unified national structures for its health and retirement programs but, instead, with a heritage of fragmented organizational arrangements that blended federal, state, and corporate structures in a complex, perhaps chaotic, manner.

The consequences of institutional development are also apparent in the bureaucratic structures that support the administration of governmental programs. The principles of federalism have prevented the emergence in the United States of unified personnel systems for governmental service that define a common set of responsibilities for each position, a standard pay scale, and clearly-stated retirement benefits.[29] While the national government determines the standards for each of its major personnel systems, state governments have the authority to create their own personnel structures based on their own requirements, judgments, and preferences. Each state will define in its own way the qualifications for being hired, the salary and health care benefits associated with each position, the standards for salary increases and promotions, the professional obligations for various posts, and the benefits former employees will receive during retirement. The training, pay scales, expectations, standards, careers prospects, employment restrictions, and benefits defined by each state will differ from those of the federal government and of other states. The qualifications for being an environmental official in Alaska, for example, are a world away from the qualifications required for appointment in Massachusetts or in the federal service. When examining U.S. social policies and organizations, you usually do not find the unified national systems for providing benefits that are more common in Germany. You are more likely to discover a confusing array of programs, structures, and practices that probably no not fit together perfectly. The absence of unified programs and personnel systems compounds the difficulties of reaching national agreement on contentious issues and complicates the process of governmental reform.

The historical legacies of institutional development also help explain the distinctive features of relations between business and government in the United States and Germany. In the United States, huge corporations were established at a time when the national government had a limited impact on the economy and only later came to regulate their conduct while in Germany administrative agencies were significant societal institutions well before the industrial revolution, and governmental policies helped shape the industrial economy and nurture the new companies. Thus, it is not surprising that contemporary commentators normally find cooperation between business organizations and government in Germany while they stress adversarial, sometimes hostile relations between businesses and government in the United States. David Vogel summaries relations between business and government in the United States in these terms: "The most characteristic, distinctive, and persistent belief of American corporate executives is an underlying suspicion and mistrust of government."[30] Vernon finds that the ties of U.S. managers to the federal government are "more opportunistic than ideological", and he concludes that the managers have a "disposition to keep the government at bay except when they felt that it could serve their interests as entrepreneurs."[31] The U.S. government also had an ambivalent attitude toward business, Vernon reports, being less supportive of corporate expansion abroad than European governments and quicker to challenge corporate conduct and impose sanctions.[32] Volker Schneider has also traced differences in regulatory behavior in the two nations to contrasting patterns of institutional development.[33]

The consequences of the different sequences of institutional development are also visible in the status afforded public preferences in the two countries. While there was an acute recognition of the dilemmas and dangers of public opinion in the United States from the start, there has generally been an acceptance of the legitimacy of public preferences and an awareness of the need for institutions to somehow accommodate those preferences. Recent proposals have called for reforms in the activities of a variety of German institutions, but U.S. institutions, whether they be political parties, universities, government agencies, or businesses, devote more attention to public preferences in their procedures and operations. Administrative agencies allow for public comments in their proceedings, political parties allow citizens to select candidates through primary elections, and universities seek to build support for their operations among alumni, voters, and corporate leaders. Even the term populism in the United States is not always a negative word. It reflects the belief that people who are not well educated, who do not have impressive positions in the society, and who live in difficult circumstances deserve a respectful hearing for their views. The status afforded public opinion in the United States, I believe, does not always serve the nation well. Public preferences have now become so important in the policy process that every major piece of congressional legislation, such as the endorsement of the WTO or the extension of permanent normal trade relations with China, is accompanied by efforts to mobilize public opinion, often on the basis of a television advertising campaign. A public policy issue, such as a change in the procedure for calculating the pensions received by Social Security recipients, would probably be accompanied in the United States today by televised appeals to generate expressions of support or opposition. From my perspective, the conduct of government in the United States would be more successful if its institutions were less directly responsive to public preferences, if its administrative structures were more coherent, and if the relations between its government and the private economy were less adversarial. Regardless of their desirability, I think these practices result from the early priority attached to public preferences in the United States, the limited regard for the traditions of the administrative state, and the sequence of development of the nation's institutions.

Conclusion

Sven Steinmo quite sensibly insists, "Neither institutions nor values nor economic interests for that matter by themselves provide adequate explanations for significant political outcomes over time...."[34] Obviously values and interests are influential, but it is not necessary and perhaps not constructive to interpret all policy differences between Germany and the United States as the result of diverse values or contrasting alignments of interests. Such a perspective attaches a greater sense of inevitably to diversity and disagreement than may be warranted. If differences in governmental patterns and practices are regarded as inevitable, there is little reason to analyze divergent approaches to common policy issues and little point in trying to discern constructive lessons from the experience of another impressive and influential nation.

This chapter has argued that numerous influential features of Germany and the United States emerge from the historical process of institutional development. While institutional practices are sometimes deeply rooted in a nation's values or interests, they may also be a simple historical legacy that has little foundation in contemporary society. If a governmental policy or practice crying out for reform results from deep-seated values or powerful interests, there may be little possibility of change, but if the program or procedure needing reform is based on nothing more than institutional practices from an earlier age, the renewed attempts to seek an innovative strategy for administrative and governmental reform will probably be rewarded.

Notes

1   Ronald Inglehart, *Modernization and Postmodernization*, Princeton, N.J., Princeton University Press, 1997; see also the classic Seymour Martin Lipset, *The First New Nation*, New York, Basic Books, 1963.

2   Raymond Vernon, *In the Hurricane's Eye: The Troubled Prospects of Multinational Enterprises* Cambridge, Mass., Harvard University Press, 1998, 123.

3   For an introduction to the enormous literature on this topic, see: David B. Truman, *The Governmental Process: Political Interests and Public Opinion*, New York, Alfred A. Knopf, 1951; C. Wright Mills, *The Power Elite*, New York, Oxford University Press, 1956; Ralph Miliband, *The State in Capitalist Society*, London, Weidenfeld and Nicolson, 1969; Frank R. Baumgartner and Beth L. Leech, *Basic Interests*, Princeton, N.J., Princeton University Press, 1998; Hans Peter Ullmann, *Interessenverbände in Deutschland*, Frankfurt, Suhrkamp, 1988; and Jürgen Weber, *Die Interessengruppen im politischen System der BRD*, Stuttgart, Kohlhammer, 1977.

4   See, for example, John W. Kingdon, *America the Unusual*, New York, St. Martin's/Worth Publishers, 1999, especially 7-10, 50-55, and 79-84.

5   This discussion is based on Kathleen Thelen/Sven Steinmo, "Historical institutionalism in comparative perspective", in Sven Steinmo et al. (eds.), *Structuring Politics: Historical Institutionalism in Comparative Politics*, New York, Cambridge University Press, 1992, 1-32; and Ellen M. Immergut, "The Theoretical Core of the New Institutionalism", *Politics & Society*, vol. 26, no.1/ 1998, 5-34.

6   Colin Crouch, "Co-operation and Competition in an Institutionalised Economy: The Case of Germany", in Colin Crouch/David Marquand (eds.), *Ethics and Markets: Co-operation and Competition within Capitalist Economies*, Oxford, Blackwell Publishers, 1993, 82.

7   See, for example, Peter A. Hall, *Governing the Economy: The Politics of State Intervention in Britain and France*, New York, Oxford University Press, 1986, chapter 9; and Fritz W. Scharpf, "Economic and Institutional Constraints in Full-Employment Strategies: Sweden, Austria, and West Germany", in John Goldthorpe (ed.), *Order and Conflict in Contemporary Capitalism*, New York, Oxford University Press, 1984, 257-90.

8   Frank Dobbin, *Forging Industrial Policy: the United States, Britain, and France in the railway age*, New York, Cambridge University Press, 1994, 26.

9   F. Dobbin, *Forging Industrial Policy*, p. 3.

10   Ira Katznelson, *City Trenches: Urban Politics and the Patterning of Class in the United States*, Chicago, University of Chicago Press, 1981.

11   Gerhard Lehmbruch, "Sektorale Variationen in der Transformationsdynamik der politischen Ökonomie Ostdeutschlands und Ihre situativen und institutionellen Bedingungen", in Wolfgang Seibel and Arthur Benz (eds.), *Regierungssystem und Verwaltungspolitik: Beiträge zu Ehren von Thomas Ellwein*, Opladen, Westdeutscher Verlag, 1995, 155-87.

12 One perspective on these issues is presented by Michael J. Sandel, *Democracy's Discontent: America in Search of a Public Philosophy*, Cambridge, Mass., Belknap Press of Harvard University Press, 1996.

13 Alexander Hamilton, James Madison, and John Jay, *The Federalist Papers*, Clinton Rossiter (ed.), New York, Penguin Books, 1961.

14 James Oliver Robertson, *America's Business*, New York, Hill and Wang, 1985, 175.

15 Alfred D. Chandler, Jr., *Scale and Scope: The Dynamics of Industrial Capitalism*, Cambridge, Mass., Belknap Press of Harvard University Press, 1990; and Mansel G. Blackford, *The Rise of Modern Business in Great Britain, the United States, and Japan*, 2nd ed., Chapel Hill, N.C., University of North Carolina Press, 1998.

16 Alfred D. Chandler, Jr., *The Visible Hand: The Managerial Revolution in American Business*, Cambridge, Mass., Belknap Press of Harvard University Press, 1977, chapters 3-5; and Thomas K. McCraw, *Prophets of Regulation*, Cambridge, Mass., Harvard University Press, 1984, 64-67.

17 Roland Marchard, *Creating the Corporate Soul: The Rise of Public Relations and Corporate Imagery in American Big Business*, Berkeley, Calif., University of California Press, 1998, especially 7, 21, and 41.

18 See Robert Higgs, *Crisis and Leviathan: Critical Episodes in the Growth of American Government*, New York, Oxford University Press, 1987; and Stephen Skowronek, *Building a New American State: The Expansion of National Administrative Capacities, 1877-1920*, New York, Cambridge University Press, 1982.

19 Lutz Raphael, *Recht und Ordnung: Herrschaft durch Verwaltung im 19. Jahrhundert*, Frankfurt am Main, Fischer Verlag, 2000, especially 17-18, 20, and 53-60; see also Wolfgang Reinhard, *Geschichte der Staatsgewalt: eine vergleichende Verfassungsgeschichte Europas von den Anfängen bis zur Gegenwart*, München, Beck, 1999, 15-27.

20 See the contribution of Klaus-Henning Rosen "Better Opportunities for Citizens", in this volume, 55.

21 Jeffrey Fear, "German Capitalism", Thomas K. McCraw (ed.), *Creating Modern Capitalism: How Entrepreneurs, Companies, and Countries Triumphed in Three Industrial Revolutions*, Cambridge, Mass., Harvard University Press, 1997, 135-82.

22 Peter A. Hall, "The movement from Keynesianism to monetarism: Institutional Analysis and British economic policy", in S. Steinmo et al. (eds.) *Structuring Politics*, 109.

23 See for example, Victoria C. Hattam, *Labor Visions and State Power: The Origins of Business Unionism in the United States*, Princeton, N.J., Princeton University Press, 1993.

24 See for example, Douglas E. Ashford and E.W. Kelley (eds.), *Nationalizing Social Security in Europe and America*, Greenwich, Conn., JAI Press, 1986, especially Christa Alternstetter, "German Social Security Programs: An Interpretation of Their Development", 73-97; and Henry Teune, "The Political Development of the Welfare State in the United States", 7-24.

25 S. Skowronek, *Building a New American State*, 1982.

26 Douglas E. Ashford, "Overall Introduction: Politics and Social Security", Ashford and Kelley, *Nationalizing Social Security in Europe and America*, xx-xxii.

27 Alfred D. Chandler Jr., "Government versus Business: An Americacn Phenomen", in John T. Dunlop (ed.), *Business and Public Policy* , Cambridge, Mass., Harvard Graduate School of Business Administration, 1980.

28 This section relies on Gregory Acs and Eugene Steuerle, "The Corporation as a Dispenser of Welfate and Security", in Carl Kaysen (ed.), *The American Corporation Today*, New York, Oxford University Press, 1996, 360-82. See also, P. Starr, *The Social Transformation of American Medicine*, New York, Basic Books, 1982; Jamilyn J. Field and Harold T. Shapiro (eds.), *Employment and Health Benefits: A Connection at Risk*, Washington, D.C., National Academy Press, 1993; and Edwin Amenta and Theda Skocpol, "Taking Exception: Explaining the Distinctiveness of American Public Policies in the Last Century", in Francis G. Castles (ed.), *The Comparative History of Public Policy*, New York, Oxford University Press, 1989, 292-333.

29 For background, see Donald E. Klingner and John Nalbandian, *Public Personnel Management*, 4th ed., Upper Saddle River, N.J., Prentice Hall, 1998; and David McKevitt, *Managing Core Public Services*, Malden, Mass., Blackwell, 1998.

30 David Vogel, *Kindred Strangers: The Uneasy Relationship between Politics and Business in America*, Princeton, N.J., Princeton University Press, 1996, 29.

31 R. Vernon, *In the Hurricane's Eye*, 124.

32 For documentation on the U.S. government's prosecution of Microsoft, see the Web sites of the U.S. Department of Justice's Antitrust Division, *http://www.usdoj.gov/atr* and the Microsoft Corporation, *http://www.microsoft.com/freedomtoinnovate/*.

33 Volker Schneider, "Corporatist and Pluralist Patterns of Policymaking for Chemical Control: A Comparison between West Germany and the USA", in Alan Cawson (ed.), *Organized Interests and the State*, London, Sage, 1985, 174-191.

34 Sven Steinmo, *Taxation and Democracy: Swedish, British and American Approaches to Financing the Modern State*, New Haven, CT.,Yale University Press, 1993, 201.

Reinventing Government:
The German Case[*]

Klaus König

I. An International Movement of Modernizing Government

The current international modernization movement is that of New Public Management which had its beginnings in the Anglo-Saxon world, found a partner in the "Reinventing Government" school in the USA and has now spread to continental Europe where it has also affected the legalistic bureaucracy of Germany in such forms as the "Neue Steuerungsmodell" ("New Steering Model"). It is furthered by international organisations – UN, World Bank, OECD – which communicate in the lingua franca not only of economic life but, in increasing measure, of state life as well, namely in English.

The current movement of state and administrative modernization has its reasons in the financial crisis experienced by the Western welfare states. Accordingly, it is, in essence, a matter of modernizing state and public administration economically. As the centrally planned economy has not proved to be efficient and the set of instruments employed by welfare-state-type fiscal policy appears to fail, the concepts of neoliberal institutional economics are expected to provide a new system of order for state and administrative services and performances.[1]

While, in the United States, a mixture of neoliberal economic theories, management techniques and popular business-motivation theories have influenced "Government Reinventing", it could be observed in Thatcherist Great Britain that the Public Choice approach was propagated top-down by political leaders, a school which – rejecting welfare economics – does not consider the state to be bound by public interests but instead declares every actor within the politico-administrative institutions to be a homo oeconomicus.[2] It is well known that Margaret Thatcher urged all her cabinet members to read the American economist William Niskanen when she took office in 1979.[3] In New Zealand top politicians and financial experts – of a Labour government in this case – designed their new state management and steering concept on the basis of a further institutional economics approach, namely the Principal/Agent-Theory.[4] Here, the role of principal is assigned to the politician. The administrators are given the agent's role.

Such institutional economics concepts call for a different kind of intelligence from the one implied in other places where proven administrative institutions are transferred across borders. Other than with institutional transfers, this is a matter of model thinking. Models are beyond the limits of strict empiricism, though they may be combined, as in institutional economics, with the attempt to supplement normative approaches to welfare economics by empirical science analyses of actual state action. The premises of the model are not statements that are made on constellations of downright observable, real conditions but notional constructions complying only in part, if at all, with reality.[5]

Its being rooted in different neoliberal economic theories and management doctrines is the underlying reason why New Public Management today is full of conceptional contradictions also internationally. Whereas the Public Choice Theory is intended to re-establish political control exercised by representative governments over bureaucracy, the new managerialism stresses the "managers' rights to manage". The intention is to institute the primacy of management principles over bureaucracy. While – for the economic approach – the very issue is how the budget-maximising bureaucracy is to be steered by the democratically legitimated political sector and, consequently, how to deal with the state's fundamental resources, namely public revenue, the idea behind the management approach is that the capacity of a complex organisation to fulfil its functions can be improved by management techniques de-bureaucratizing such organisation, making it leaner, making it use resources more economically, and improving its productivity. So, if, on the one hand, the bureaucracy problem is to be solved by political control of the bureaucracy which also acts managerially and, on the other hand, management is considered to be both the cause and the solution, this must result in a number of consequential contradictions. For economic liberalism, for instance, the important thing is providing mechanisms that protect from "imprisonment" in public programs or schemes. Managerialism, on the other hand, simply considers getting closer to the customers an absolute necessity. Practitioners of administrative modernization tend not to be troubled by such paradoxes. One can push them aside as being "theoretical". Or, if one sets a high value on conceptional foundations, one may select those aspects that "fit in well".

Where administrative modernization is not just reduced to the rhetorics of entrepreneurialism, clientele, market, competition, etc. concrete agendas of operationalized reform items are drawn up. By international comparison, three strategies can be identified in this regard. The first one still continues to be the strategy of shifting responsibility for social action from the public to the private sector or to the Third Sector. This encompasses subjects like the privatization of property and functions. Above all, functional privatization such as contracting-out with public-private partnerships is widely resorted to, complemented by deregulation, the cutdown of subsidies and social transfers, etc.

The second strategy, and in many places the one dominating at first sight, is the internal rationalization of state and administration. This begins with a performance-oriented restructuring of public services, mainly in the field of top-level positions. Another focus is budgeting, cost and results accounting, and controlling. As to the structural organization, there are preferences for agencies and segmented production units. With regard to the operational organization, mechanisms are preferred which are meant to attain the internal rationalization of administrative action through "client pressure". The ultimate idea is that, where privatization does not occur, quasi-markets and virtual competition will be established as functional equivalents winning for the state sector the market economy's assumed lead in terms of rationalization.

A strategy less favoured by rhetorics but de facto of great weight is the strategy of restrictive measures, of reductions, curtailments and downsizing. This strategy cannot simply be correlated with a stricter notion of economic efficiency in the relations between targets and means as well as benefits and costs. One has to resort to the old term of thriftiness in state and administrative matters which, in view of all the imponderables of the public weal, is intent on avoiding public spending wherever possible. A characteristic example of such avoidance strategies is the German "Sparpaket", i.e. a "package of economizing measures". Schemes and organizational structures are reduced, slimming above all the workforce, however. In the U.S. federal administration, for instance, where the staff originally totalled about 2.1 million civil servants, over 200,000 jobs have been pruned already.

New Public Management, despite a certain shifting of activity out of the sector such as contracting out, is more concerned with internal rationalization within the state sector. This middle position towards better public administration post Reaganism and Thatcherism is both better accepted by many administrators and their working and professional organizations and better suited to a form of modernization beyond party political differences from the social democrat and liberal-conservative camp.[6]

In spite of all global perception, administrative modernization takes place within the historical situation of national states; as a result, multifarious general settings in space and time terms play an important role, as the case may be. Out of this wide variety, three factors must be spotlighted from a present-day viewpoint, the factor to be referred to in the first place being the extent of the financial crisis in the welfare state concerned. The deeper the financial crisis from New Zealand via the United Kingdom and Germany to Japan, is perceived to be, the greater the readiness to interfere more deeply in the scopes of politico-administrative traditions.

The conceptional contradictions inherent in New Public Management, depending on the prevailing neo-liberal or liberal-social-democratic values as brought forward as the case may be by the governing parties concerned, allow the focusses to be determined primarily in the fields of privatization, deregulation and breaking away from "imprisonment" in public schemes or, on the other hand, a policy of protecting vested rights to be adopted and, beyond all Reaganism and Thatcherism, aiming not at less state but at public administration being improved by way of internal rationalization.

Finally, another factor decisive for the mode of administrative modernization is the degree of centralization in the state organization concerned. In highly centralized countries like the United Kingdom, a particular concept can be enforced top-down to the level of local government. In countries like the United States of America, there are a wide variety of activities ranging from the federal administration via the state administrations to the local governments. In this regard, even neighbors like New Zealand and Australia are different.

Compared with single reforms, the current modernization of public administration relates to such a complex range of problems in public matters that it requires a specific institutionalized intelligence of change. This applies as regards scientific advice, assistance from management consultants, the administration's own expert councils and committees and, not least, a specific government staff for modernization.

A fundamental rearrangement of state and administration in accordance with efficiency and effectiveness cannot be achieved by reform elites alone. Thus, it is plain, for instance, that efforts are made to approach broad groups, though not among the clientele so frequently referred to, but among the administrative staff itself. Examples of this are the Reinventing Laboratories in the U.S. federal administration, mobilization at local government level in Germany being another example.

Administrative modernization needs political leadership. This becomes evident from the reform efforts made by the former Labour government in New Zealand, from Thatcherism in the United Kingdom and also from the U.S. American case, limited as it is due to the split of rule between presidency and congress. One may not stake everything on the expectation that the propagation of automatic economic mechanisms or management models can replace the political will to improve efficiency and effectiveness in state and administration.

II. Modernization in a Decentralized Political System

1. Local Government

The New Steering Model is an example of model thinking in Germany. It is not meant to transfer administrative institutions as existing in the Dutch city of Tilburg to local German governments. For that, Tilburg is probably much too little representative of conditions in the Netherlands and, apart from this, one would have to take a much closer look at the general setting prevailing in the local authorities there. Instead, the New Steering Model is the construction of a local government steering concept that is considered reasonable and comprises components such as market orientation, opening up towards competition, customer and quality-oriented attitudes, target and result-oriented steering, self-management in decentralized units complemented by a centrally steered basic management, integrated responsibilities for subject matters and resources, at the same time delegating responsibility for results, etc. Yet reference to the case of the Tilburg municipality is illustrative of the fact that pragmatic model thinking, too, needs to deal with two reference issues, namely the empirical foundations and the theoretical approach

If the empirical foundations of the "New Steering Model" were only based on the example of Tilburg, they would appear to be a bit scanty. In this context, it must be noted that, even in the United States, it is criticized that the empirical material of the Reinventing Government disputation was quite scarce when considering that a whole nation's "big government" is right away to be turned upside down, with the entrepreneurial spirit directing the public sector. Now, one may reply that this was a step precisely into the future of a "new" administration, for which but few empirical findings are available. But this is no longer true today. For New Public Management has become an international modernization movement, and it is being said about one of our closest neighbors, namely the United Kingdom, that a "revolution" resulting in a "skeleton administration" has taken place.[7]

Many a designer of pragmatic models repudiates the suspicion of theoretical thinking. Nevertheless, whether reflected on or not, such models, too, do imply theoretical approaches. With the "New Steering Model", the important point is to delimit responsibilities between the political sector and the (service-rendering) administration. The role to be taken on by the political organs in this context is restricted to the following: determining management philosophy, the leadership structure, and the general setting for optimum administrative performances; defining targets on the basis of respective product definitions and giving orders for concrete services; assigning to the specific administrative departments the product budgets and the scopes of action allowing them to fulfil their tasks; and also continually monitoring the execution of tasks and functions and, in case of any deviations from the course, making the appropriate corrections.[8] The administration's role, on the other hand, is limited to fulfilling the pre-defined service orders in the form of concrete products, reporting continually to the political sector on the execution of such orders and any deviations there from as well as to assuming responsibility for results in this way.

It is perfectly evident that this construct contains rudiments of the Principal/Agent Theory[9]. The role of principal is allocated to the political sector.

The administrators are assigned the role of the agent. In a kind of order giving/order-taking relationship, the agent receives a remuneration calculated in accordance with definite criteria. The political sector, as the principal, gets the result produced by the agent's action. From this viewpoint, the "New Steering Model" may be said to have some hereditary defect. For it was because of its dysfunctionality that abolishing the dualism of (political) lordmayor and (administrative) city manager has recently been propagated.[10] Now, a city manager would fit perfectly well into the model. It is hardly a comfort in this context that the heads of administration in prize-winning New Public Management cities in New Zealand and the United States of America do not at all convey the impression on their German interlocutor that they are unpolitical agents; and, in fact, just as little as civil servants are responsible for traffic abatement in shopping streets give the impression that communal politics descended upon them only in the form of systematic and orderly products.

2. State Government

Influenced by a wave of local-level reforms and the tense budget situation, it is since the early 90s or middle of the 90s that endeavours have also been made at state or *Land* level to modernize existing administrative structures there according to the principles of efficiency and effectiveness. True, from an overall viewpoint, the extent of their reform efforts is somewhat smaller than at the local level. Yet it must be taken into account here that local authorities are more closely in touch with the problems confronting them, although the rhetoric of customer-oriented attitudes is appreciated in state or *Land* governments.[11] Viewed generally, however, the entire scope of modernization measures that are characteristic of the reform phase under the auspices of New Public Managements can be observed at state level as well.[12]

So far, the development of New Steering Models at *Land* level has proceeded furthest in the city states of Berlin and Hamburg. This is due, on the one hand, to their double position as both state and local administrative authorities and, on the other hand, to the existing metropolitan administration, which seems to allow approaches to a municipal concern model to be implemented more easily because, here, the state and local levels correlate directly with one another within a relatively transparent setting.

Finally, it must be stated that there is a certain asymmetry between West and East Germany, the both highly developed and expensive administrative authorities in the Western *Länder* getting more and more under rationalization pressure following the German unification, whereas large parts of the Eastern *Länder* still continue to be engaged in consolidating the very transformation of public administration and fundamental reforms. In this situation, it is in the Western states' administrations that elements of a New Steering Model meet with a much greater response than in the East German *Länder*, where, for the time being, the establishment of efficient administrative structures as well as their territorial and functional reforms fully engage politico-administrative powers.

3. Federal Government

The leitmotif of public sector administrative restructuring in the OECD states, the redefinition of both substance and modality of state action, also occurs in the discussion at federal level in Germany. Unlike the local level with its orientation to the New Steering Model, the federal government, in the 13th legislative period, stressed that there is no One Best Way. A summing up of the agenda of modernization at federal level, shows the three dominant strategies of administrative modernization, there too, namely privatization and deregulation, intra-administrative rationalization, and the policy of down-sizing.

The selling of federally owned assets has been a goal since the Christian Democratic/Liberal Coalition came to power. However, only in recent years have the advantages of private management and financing modi been emphasised and a privatization of public tasks been called for. Possible ways of privatizing individual service sub-sectors of the ministries, for example, have been tested in a number of pilot projects. On the basis of the experiences gained through these projects, the federal government decided, for example, that the Berlin ministries should no longer run their own printeries and no longer set up medical and social services. They were also ordered to privatize personal security services.[13] An additional pilot project investigates the field of personnel costs to determine possible synergy effects as regards

the co-operation between private agents and state administrative protago-
nists[14]. New forms of financing public investments have been met with great
interest particularly as means of financing transport infrastructure.[15] With
respect to shortening lengthy official testing examinations and licensing
procedures, the "Independent Expert Commission for the Simplification and
Expedition of Licensing Procedures" made suggestions on how petitioners
could take over certain procedural tasks that up to now have been handled
by an authority. The Commission further suggested that testing tasks be
handed over to and planning tasks be taken over by private agencies. The
federal government announced that by supplementing Specialised Law and
the Law Concerning Administrative Procedures with additional clauses as
regards auditing procedures, licensing and monitoring procedures should in
principle be opened up for substitutes on the basis of self-regulation.[16] The
suggestions of the "Independent Expert Commission for the Simplification
and Expedition of Licensing Procedures" and of the "Independent Commission for the Simplification of Legal and Administrative Procedures" were
decisive for measures taken for the deregulation and the simplification of
legal procedures introduced in the 13th legislative period.[17]

If one takes a look at the internal rationalization measures taken in the
federal administration, the generalizing impression of the federal government lagging behind in terms of modernizing public administration, a trend
which started in Germany in the early 1990s, can no longer be upheld. In the
early 90s, a number of subordinate executive authorities started initiatives to
increase the efficiency and effectiveness of administrative activities at the
same time that activities were increased at the *Land* level.[18] The extensive
reformatory activities in the portfolio of the Federal Ministry of Transport
may serve as an example: The Federal Office for Goods Transport, the Federal Office for Railway Traffic as well as the Federal Institute for Road Research were reorganised in such a way that their individual scopes of functions were restructured and that their structural organizations were tightened
by reducing the number of hierarchical levels.[19] An organizational and procedural re-orientation took place at the German Meteorological Service. As
a prerequisite for an increased customer orientation, for the establishment of
individual areas of responsibility as well as for the establishment of clearly
structured management relations, the Meteorological Service replaced the
traditional *Länder*-related office structure by a vertically oriented business
field structure. The internal management of the entire system is to be

achieved by a comprehensive Controlling. The external management by the Federal Ministry of Transport is to be exercised by setting up targets and quality control.[20]

The obligation to consolidate the budget as well as the vote of the German *Bundestag* of 20 June 1991 for the "Petition for the Finalization for Germany's Unity" resulted in increased modernization efforts on behalf of the ministries. To reduce the budgetary deficit, both the governmental statement of policy and the motto of a "Lean State" forced the federal ministries to act. The federal ministries have demonstrated an increased level of activity since the cabinet decision on "Reduction and Reshaping of Federal Authorities" of 7 February 1996[21], which initiated the implementation of a number of pilot projects based on suggestions by the budgetary department of the Federal Ministry of Finance and which forced the ministries to set up an organizational target structure. Meanwhile, the majority of ministries has on the basis of critical examinations of the scope of tasks – and, in individual cases, by ascertaining staff requirements – determined their organizational structure for the time during which the seat of government is moved to Berlin.[22] The organisational changes were to a large extent connected with a structural reshaping as a result of a concentration of tasks, of a handing over of tasks to the private sector, or the relocation of tasks on a subordinate level. They were further connected with efforts to standardize the management scope and with the establishment of alternative task structures such as working groups and project groups.

The extent of the ministerial restructuring efforts is relatively small compared to that of international models. Alternative concepts for task allocation and for management relations are being discussed due to suggestions from management consultant firms; however, these concepts are only rarely implemented. Although the introduction of new management and steering instruments via the creation of role models and the introduction of cost-performance analyses on the subordinate level does make progress (the new approaches for the allocation of resources in the Federal Office for Motor Traffic, the Federal Property Administration, the Federal Office for Safety in Information Technology or the Federal Statistical Office may serve as examples), only the Federal Press Office as federal superior authority has started to conduct cost-performance analyses since January 1, 1998.[23] Results of the pilot project "Controlling in the Foreign Service", which are due at the beginning of 1999, are awaited with scepticism as regards the prospects of success of optimising internal management structures in a federal authority, which is to a large extent subject to daily changes[24] in political agendas.[25] The Federal Ministry of Family Affairs, Senior Citizens, Women's Affairs and Youth plans the introduction of a strategic Controlling in form of a politically strategical, budget and program-related as well as political planning process.[26]

The fact that the ministries have to deal with the double burden of implementing the administrative reform on the one hand and of organizing the move to Berlin on the other hand has proven to be a reform hindrance. So far, no ministry has shown signs of a useful linking of different measures for organizational development, for an implementation of Controlling and cost accounting conceptions, for estimates on personnel requirements, for a setting of goals as well as for an allocation of staff and functions in Berlin and Bonn.[27] The existing outline directives concerning employment regulations, salary regulations and regulations concerning collective bargaining, which stand in the way of extensive efforts to render more flexible the organizational structure and staff allocation, have for the longest time been held responsible for hampering innovations.[28] A great discrepancy can be seen between the administrative demands and the available instruments if, for example, the administration is to be streamlined through an intensified use of information technology, yet at the same time the expenditures for the budgetary item "Data Processing Costs" are reduced by 5%[29]; or if the budget allows a more flexible distribution of money, yet possible financial savings are kept back as "efficiency yield" by the Ministry of Finance in form of a 2% overall cutback in the respective budgetary item groups.[30] The establishment of the "Administrative Organization" steering committee (appointed in 1997), whose function it was to unite the state secretaries of the various ministries and to promote and coordinate the modernization efforts of the federal administration, represented an essential effort to set up a trans-departmental body; however, its consensus-oriented voting mechanisms[31] did not allow that decisions, following the departmental principle (Article 65 of the Basic Law), were made against the wishes of a department. A recommendation of the Federal Audit Office addressed to the Steering Committee contained the advice to promote trans-departmental approaches in investigating the organizational structures and to support a reduction of parallel and double functions in the fulfilment of political tasks. This recommendation, however, cannot be put in effect due to the egotistically motivated priorities in the individual departments.[32] The situation is complicated by political and personnel-related resistance against a reduction of organizational structures and personnel which had to be increased due to the German Unification and the merging of ministries.

The policy of state streamlining primarily manifests itself in a reduction policy as can be seen in the suggested measures of the cabinet decision of 7 February 1996. Since 1992, the total of persons employed with the federal government (381,000) was reduced by 71,000 posts, 85% of which (57,000) affected the Federal Ministry of Defence. So far, it has not been possible to reduce the total of persons employed to 300,000, which was the number of people employed in 1989.[33] According to the 1998 budget, the total of persons employed at the federal ministries amounts to 18,626; compared to the year of reference of 1989, in which the total of persons employed amounted to 19,434, this represents a considerable reduction.[34] Since 1991, the number of federal authorities has been reduced by 148.

With the 1998 change of government in Germany the question arises whether the new federal government will – like the Labour Government in the United Kingdom – adhere to the modernization endeavours made by its predecessors. The formula of a "Lean State", at any rate , has done its duty with the end of the 13th legislative period.[35] What will be the result if it is replaced, let's say, by the vision of an "activating state" is still open.[36]

III. Legacies of National Executive Governments

Between the basic bureaucratic character of public administrations in the west and the various manifestations of the nation state, it is possible to identify certain politico-cultural communities in the Anglo-Saxon area on the one hand and Continental Europe on the other which enable a distinction to be made between civic culture administration and the classic system of administration.[37] Continental European administrations such as that of France and Germany can be termed classic systems because the bureaucratic order created in the modern age has remained in place right up to the present day throughout all the political upheavals and changes. The systems have survived changes in regime from monarchy, republic, dictatorship and democracy, and at times of collapse, have had to shoulder the responsibility for public action. If one can say of classic administrative systems that bureaucracy is older than democracy, the development of public bureaucracies in countries of civic culture administration such as Great Britain and the United States was influenced from the outset by the political regime, the historical continuity of which has been maintained up to the present day.[38] These regimes provided the conditions for the public administrations to exist, set their limits and reinforced the relationship to the democratic and participatory system within the civic culture. This is not to say that the public bureaucracies would not have developed any dynamism of their own. Public servants will always involve bureaucratic values. But there were no historical upheavals which made it necessary for the public administration to go on functioning on is own account. The party political constellations changed, but the political regime maintained control over the public administration of the time, however bureaucratic it was. This permanent dominance of the politicians over the public bureaucracies reflects the system of values of a civic society, while the continental Europeans learned from experience that there are historical situations in which the administration can be expected to provide what politics is not able to - provision of basic services in times of political turmoil.[39]

The continuity in the Anglo-American world has meant that the values of the political regime have become the models of identification for public bureaucracies. The countries of continental Europe, in contrast, had to find a means of giving identity to public administrations which extended beyond the historical situation of monarchies, republics, dictatorships and democracies. They needed a regulative idea which would allow the political system to define itself above and beyond the political regime of the time. This regulative idea was that of the state, and the public servant in consequence became the "servant of the state". At first glance the idea of the state as regulator was one that was perfectly acceptable to public bureaucracies. Yet history proved it to be a risky idea, since abuse on the part of the state was also abuse on the part of its servants. Extra protection was needed and this was provided in the form of the concept of the state governed by the rule of law. Today the concepts of the law-based state and democracy are closely linked in Germany as elsewhere.

As a result of this democratic development and the stabilizing effect it has had, the political and cultural differences between civic culture administration and the classic administrative system are no longer the major distinguishing features between the public bureaucracies on the other side of the Channel and in continental Europe. Today it is more appropriate to distinguish between managerial and legalistic bureaucracies. In the countries of continental Europe, the law, despite all the changing demands of a complex environment, has maintained its importance as the prime control medium for public administration.[40] Apart from anything else, the concept of an administration with its own jurisdiction helps to ensure the real authority of rationally interpreted laws for the state and its citizens. The legalistic bureaucracy is supported in personnel terms by adherence to the principle of a career civil service as a profession in its own right and public officials with knowledge and expertise in the field of public law.

In the U.S. administration there has long been a trend towards managerialism. The historical lines can be traced from Taylorism, through landmarks in science - The Papers on the Science of Administration (Luther Gulick) - and practice - Report on the Brownlow Committee[41]- to the present-day doctrines of entrepreneurial management as expounded in "Reinventing Government"[42] and management policies for "creating a government that works better and costs less".[43] The view that "the study of administration should start from the base of management rather than the foundation of law"[44] sums up current thinking of the opinion-leaders in the higher administrative service looking forward to what they describe as the formation of a "global professional technocracy".[45]

It may be due to traditional cross links with the entrepreneurial economy that U.S. administrative scientists, time and again, emphasize strongly that state and public administration are different. A noteworthy example of this is the aphorism that: "Public and private management are fundamentally alike in all unimportant respects".[46] On the one hand, it is accepted that the general management services to be rendered in both politico-administrative organisations and private business enterprises are similar, namely defining targets and priorities for the organization including the respective operational plans, designing the organisational structures and processes including coordination thereof, staff recruitment, human resources development, manpower management, control under the auspices of coercive budgeting, performances, productivity, etc. Yet in the context of such comparisons the existing differences are revealed all the more distinctly.

This is true for the different authority structures which reflect precisely different environments, namely market and property rights or democracy and the rule of law respectively. The patterns of influence making their respective marks on the politico-administrative management range from voters to the people's representatives, from organized interests to the mass media. There, timelines are brought into harmony with the political timetabling. In top positions there is a specific facticity of office tenure, etc. Generally, the public sector is said to have less autonomy and flexibility, more fragmented competencies, more formalism and so on.

Also legal influences, legislation, and jurisdiction are considered to be more important in public management, even if legalism is seen as a "constraint". Public targets are supposed to be more complex, more indefinite, more intangible and conflicting. The public's expectations as regards fairness, reliability, responsibility, and accountability are rated higher. Emphasis is put on the values of equal treatment, balancing and mediation. One might list further such specific factors of influence, ranging from the monopolist scene of action to an extensive public control. In the United States, too, public service, career system, and problematic incentives are regarded as factors of relevance. In the final analysis, they revert to the statement that public management lacks the clear "bottom line" of private business, namely profitmaking, success in the market, survival in the money economy.

With all this in mind, it was a matter of course that reactions to the economic-managerialist "reinvention" of the state had to be ambivalent in the USA. True, both administrative scientists and practitioners there appreciate keeping pace with innovative private management models. But, to many of them, "reinventing government" then appeared to involve too much market, too much competition, too much customer and too much entrepreneurialism. Even in the officially pursued policy of modernization, it had to be conceded that "government is different". Yet they did not content themselves with a defensive attitude. "Refounding democratic public administration" is being propagated[47]. The discussion about the civil service's professional ethos is reaching another peak. Even the topic of public administration, also in the USA resting on the foundation of public law that has been ignored over many years, has become revitalised.

In Germany, public sector managerial economics used to make it clear, at least, that the transferability of private-economy management concepts to public administration is limited since private enterprises and public administration differ quite fundamentally from one another in various respects. Reference was made to the great complexity of target structures in the public sector, to indefinite efficiency criteria resulting in problems of measurement, to its limited target setting autonomy, to the different modes of legitimation and rationality in its political leadership, to its strong commitment to legal standards, to its obligation to render services to the citizen, to social interdependences, etc. up to and including the rigid organizational, decision-making and staff structures.[48]

The German administration's all-time problem is not a lack of professionality, a lack of competence, or a lack of capabilities, etc. The efficiency and effectiveness of Germany's public administration are, on the contrary, rated highly abroad. So, it may hardly be expected that a new managerialism will bring about more than marginal improvements. This does not mean that public administration in Germany need not be modernized in accordance with efficiency and effectiveness criteria. This is not, however, an issue of general steering modes; democracy and the rule of law are safeguarded in our country. Rather, it is a matter of the legalistic administration's weaknesses with regard to "cost structures". Cost consciousness must be developed. It is not the managerial aspect that has to be strengthened within public administration but calculating and accounting. Reorganization and redevelopment are not feasible without due regard to costs. The secondary efficiencies of workforce, infrastructure, organi- zational dimensions and material equipment outfit are to be included in cost recording. Whether it is possible, beyond this, to integrate elements of quasi-markets and virtual competition into state and administrative action cannot be decided in the abstract. Investigations must be made individually for the various problem areas such as public health, science and research, protection of the environment and so on, to find out to what extent they can be treated as normal products of a merchandise society.

Hence, from the viewpoint of administrative science, the important thing is to point to some fundamental problems inherent in quasi-markets and virtual competition. So due to modern society's functional differentiation, state and market have quite different starting points for steering the supply of goods. This becomes obvious from the formal differentiation between private and public goods. Type, scope and distribution of private goods are decided on by harmonizing individual preferences through the market mechanisms, while decision-making on the production of public goods results from a collective and in fact politico-administrative will formation process. Economic theory has brought forth an abundance of arguments why the division of social functions between state and market cannot be abandoned and the citizens have to be provided with public goods. The characteristic features of state activities include, for example, the non-applicability of the exclusion principle – meaning that enjoyment thereof cannot be made dependent upon respective remuneration – or non-rivalling consumption within the scope of capacities – which means that consumption by one individual does not preclude consumption by others. Other reasons relate to external effects or growing returns-to-scale.

So if one does not want simply to abandon the, inherently, collective, politico-administrative process of will-formation on the production and distribution of public goods, replacing it by privatization, deregulation and so on, but, on the other hand, wishes somehow to win the assumed rationality gains of competitive markets for public matters, then one must integrate elements of quasi-markets and virtual competition into the states's and administration's patterns of steering. This can be done from two directions, namely from either the demand side or from the supply side. Beginning on the demand side, one comes across the widely heard rhetoric of New Public Management which propagates the customer and client orientation.

In modern societies with their differentiation between politico-administrative system and public system, reducing the citizen to a customer falls short of the mark, though. When adequately differentiating the citizen's role as member of a public community, he has rights and obligations, not only including defensive rights but also rights to public services without being dependent on his purchasing power like a customer.

Here, it has become obvious meanwhile that the path towards service enterprises is by no means one-way. This experience had to be made even by the "best run city in the world"[49] as it has been praised under the aspect of New Public Management. Phoenix/Arizona, in its municipal administration, gives preference to market and competition, to "the business model of producer and consumer". Accordingly, its Water Department is producer, supplier and invoicing agency. The city endeavours to offer water efficiently and effectively. Water users are customers. They purchase water in accordance with their individual preferences; and, as prices are low, they do not need to calculate too much. The future of water supplies is not the customer's problem.

But now the communal water sector planners in Phoenix are facing difficulties: the question is how water conservation ethics can be induced, as water supply problems must be expected for the future, while, today, water is pretty well abundant and can be bought cheap. As there is not much to be expected from customers, they have to renounce the city's Customer Service Model and start looking around for a "new model" by-passing the objective of "saving water by saving money". It is the citizenry who is now expected to perceive long-term consequences in the commune, developing both a sense of responsibility and willingness to assume such responsibility. A Citizenship Model, a mutual responsibility partnership, responsible citizens instead of customers, are now seen as the appropriate means of solution.[50]

There is no telling yet what effects the new public managerialism will have on the traditionally legalistic public administration in Germany. This is equally true for the local government area, although there is no lack of favourable self-assessments by the promotors of the New Steering Model. Some continue to plead that public administration implementing legal norms will change into the management of demand-oriented services towards the political sector and the general public. Others advocate that the administrative legalism be assisted by integrating steering instruments of the business-management type thus attaining cost-consciousness. Anyhow, the financial crisis and cost pressures suggest that the current modernization movement will yield better results than the reform discussion of the seventies which dealt with the reception of American management models such as "Management by Objectives". As to European administrative science, this, in any case, means that they, too, will have to tackle the subject of managerialism in the public sector in an absolutely different way.

Notes

*   The present chapter is based on a research project termed "'Schlanker Staat' - eine Agenda der Verwaltungsmodernisierung im Bund" (Lean State, an Agenda for Administrative Modernization at Federal Level), carried out by Prof. Dr. Klaus König together with Natascha Füchtner who has also assisted him in the preparation of this contribution.

1   Klaus König/Joachim Beck, *Modernisierung von Staat und Verwaltung*, Baden-Baden, Nomos, 1997.

2   Frederick Ridley, "Verwaltungsmodernisierung in Großbritannien", in Hermann Hill/ Helmut Klages (eds.), *Qualitäts- und erfolgsorientiertes Verwaltungsmanagement. Aktuelle Tendenzen und Entwürfe*, Berlin , Duncker und Humblot, 1993, 251 ff.

3   Colin Campbell, "Does Reinvention need Reinvention? Lessons from Truncated Managerialism in Britain", *Governance*, vol. 4/1995, 479 ff.

4   Jonathan Boston, "Transforming New Zealand's Public Sector: Labour's Quest for Improved Efficiency and Accountability", *Public Administration*, vol. 65, 1987, 423ff.

5   Helmut Klages, "Möglichkeiten und Grenzen des Modelldenkens in der Soziologischen Theorie", *Soziale Welt*, 1963, 102.

6   Reginald C. Mascarenhas, "Building an Enterprise Culture in the Public Sector: Reform of the Public Sector in Australia, Britain and New Zealand", *Public Administration* Review, 1993, 319ff.

7   Cf. Frederick Ridley, "Die Wiedererfindung des Staates - Reinventing British Government - Das Modell einer Skelettverwaltung", *Die Öffentliche Verwaltung (DÖV)*, 1995, 569ff.

8   Cf. Kommunale Gemeinschaftsstelle für Vewerwaltungsvereinfachung (KGSt) (ed.), *Das neue Steuerungsmodell. Begründung, Konturen, Umsetzung*, Bericht 5/93, Köln 1993; Gerhard Banner, "Konzern Stadt", in Hermann Hill/Helmut Klages (eds.), *Qualitäts- und erfolgsorientiertes Verwaltungsmanagement*, Berlin, Duncker und Humblot, 1993, 57ff.

9   Cf. Graham Scott/Peter Gorringe, "Reform of the Core Public Sector: The New Zealand Experience", *Australian Journal of Public Administration* 1989, 81ff.

10   Cf. Gerhard Banner, "Der (Ober-)Bürgermeister als Verwaltungschef - ein mögliches Modell?", in Dietrich Fischer/Rainer Frey/Peter Paziorek (eds.), *Kommunalverfassung in Nordrhein-Westfalen. Sind unsere Städte noch zu regieren?*, Beckumer Hochschultage 1988, 59 ff.

11   Cf. Contributions in Hermann Hill/Helmut Klages (eds.), *Reform der Landesverwaltung. Tagung der Hochschule für Verwaltungswissenschaften Speyer vom 29. bis 31. März 1995*, Berlin et.al., Raabe, 1995.

12   Götz Konzendorf in cooperation with Tobias Bräunlein, *Verwaltungsmodernisierung in den Ländern. Überblick und Einblicke*, Speyerer Forschungsberichte 198, Speyer 1998.

13   Cf. Federal Ministry of the Interior (BMI) (ed.), "Administrative Organisation" steering committee: *Erster Bericht und Fortschreibung des Aktionsprogramms zur weite-*

ren Steigerung von Effektivität und Wirtschaftlichkeit der Bundesverwaltung. Cabinet decision of 10 February 1998, Bonn 1998.

14 Cf. Federal Ministry of the Interior (BMI) (ed.), *Ergebnisse der Projektgruppe "Privatisierungspotentiale im Bereich der Personalausgaben des Bundes"*, Schriftenreihe der Koordinierungs- und Beratungsstelle des Bundesiminsteriums des Innern (KBSt), Vol. 37, Köln 1997.

15 Cf. "Privatfinanzierung/Privatisierung von Bundesfernstraßen, Sachstand und Perspektiven", in *Sachverständigenrat "Schlanker Staat": Materialband*, Bonn 1998, 247.

16 Cf. *Unterrichtung durch die Bundesregierung: "Schlanker Staat": Die nächsten Schritte*, BT-Drs. 13/10145, 31.01.1996, 7.

17 For more information, see Lucia Eckert, *Beschleunigung von Planungs- und Genehmigungsverfahren*, Speyerer Forschungsbericht 164, Speyer 1997, as well as the Federal Ministry of the Interior (BMI) (ed.), *Zweiter Bericht und Empfehlungen der Unabhängigen Kommission für Rechts- und Verwaltungsvereinfachung des Bundes zur Entlastung der Unternehmen, Bürger und Verwaltungen von administrativen Pflichten*, Bonn n.d., 75.

18 For a survey on modernisation measures in subordinate federal authorities, see the Federal Ministry of the Interior (BMI) (ed.), Lenkungsausschuß Verwaltungsorganisation. "Schlanker Staat", *Bilanz und Ausblick. Zweiter Bericht zum Aktionsprogramm zur weiteren Steigerung von Effektivität und Wirtschaftlichkeit der Bundesverwaltung. Cabinet decision of June 17, 1998*, Bonn 1998, 36.

19 Written Statement of Section Z 14 of the Federal Ministry of Transport of 10 April 1997 and an interview with members of the "Reformstab Bundesverkehrsverwaltung" of 24 June 1998.

20 Cf. Horst Julich, "Neue Steuerungsrationalitäten in der Bundesverwaltung - Obere Bundesbehörden", in Klaus König/Natascha Füchtner (eds.): *"Schlanker Staat" - Verwaltungsmodernisierung im Bund*, Speyerer Forschungsberichte 183, Speyer 1998, 245.

21 Printed in a report by the "Schlanker Staat" expert committee, *Materialband*, ibid., 394.

22 For a survey, see the Federal Ministry of the Interior (BMI) (ed.), *Lenkungsausschuß Verwaltungsorganisation. "Schlanker Staat": Bilanz und Ausblick. Zweiter Bericht zum Aktionsprogramm zur weiteren Steigerung von Effektivität und Wirtschaftlichkeit der Bundesverwaltung*, Cabinet decision of June 17, 1998, Bonn 1998, 85.

23 Press release of the Press and Information Office of the Federal Government of January 14, 1998, No. 9/98.

24 Cf. Udo Bergdoll, "Schlankheitskur für Diplomaten. Kinkel läßt Auswärtigen Dienst auf Kosten und Nutzen durchleuchten", *Süddeutsche Zeitung* of 14./15.2.1998, 1.

25 Cf. Helmut Landes, "Oberste Bundesbehörden - Auswärtiges Amt", in Klaus König/Natascha Füchtner (eds.), *"Schlanker Staat" - Verwaltungsmodernisierung im Bund*, ibid., 235.

26 Cf. Federal Ministry of Family Affairs, Senior Citizens, Women's Affairs and Youth/ Kienbaum Unternehmensberatung (GmbH), *Kurzfassung des Endberichts der Pro-*

jektgruppe "Ziel- und Programmstruktur BMFSFJ mit Organisationsvorschlägen", unpublished document, Bonn, July 31, 1997.

27 For a critical view on the practice of the distribution of tasks and the organisational structure of the federal ministries, see Friedrich-Ebert Foundation (eds.), *"Schlanker Staat" - der Worte sind genug gewechselt. Zur Modernisierung der Bundesverwaltung*; FES analysis conducted by Michael Bürsch, Bonn, June 1998.

28 The same conclusion is drawn by Dorothee Mühl, "Berlin-Ministerium: Das Bundesministerium für Wirtschaft", in Klaus König/Natascha Füchtner (eds.): *Verwaltungsmodernisierung im Bund - Schwerpunkte der 13. Legislaturperiode*, Speyerer Forschungsberichte *196*, Speyer 1999, 85 ff.

29 Law on the Establishment of the Federal Budget for the Financial Year 1998 of December 22, 1997 (*Federal Law Gazette* I p. 3256), § 6 (9).

30 Proposal of the Federal Ministry of Finance No. 69/96 of May 3, 1996.

31 These voting mechanisms were the topic of Cornelia Peters' paper, "Verwaltungspolitik im Bund - Bilanz und Perspektiven", in Klaus König/Natascha Füchtner (eds.), *Verwaltungsmodernisierung im Bund*, ibid., 19.

32 Federal Audit Office: *Statement on the Report of the Federal Government to the Budget Committee of the German Bundestag on the Action Programme Concerning a Further Increase of Effectiveness and Efficiency of the Federal Administration*, 2 October 1997, unpublished document.

33 For more information concerning these numbers, see the Federal Ministry of the Interior (ed.), *Lenkungsausschuß Verwaltungsorganisation. "Schlanker Staat": Bilanz und Ausblick. Zweiter Bericht zum Aktionsprogramm zur weiteren Steigerung von Effektivität und Wirtschaftlichkeit der Bundesverwaltung*. Cabinet decision of June 17, 1998, Bonn 1998, 8-9.

34 These numbers result from adding up the figures listed in the establishment plans of the federal ministries (including the Federal Press Office and the Federal Chancellery) for the 1989 and 1998 budget plans.

35 Werner Jann/Göttrik Wewer, "Helmut Kohl und der "Schlanke Staat". Eine verwaltungspolitische Bilanz", in Göttrik Wewer (ed.), *Bilanz der Ära Kohl*, Opladen, Leske & Budrich,1998, 229.

36 Bernhard Blanke/Stephan Bandemer, "Der "aktivierende" Staat", in: *Gewerkschaftliche Monatshefte*, vol. 6, 1999, 321.

37 Ferrel Heady, *Public Administration - A Comparative Perspective*, 5th ed., New York/Basel/Hong Kong, Dekker, 1996.

38 Richard J. Stillman, *Preface to Public Administration: A Search for Themes and Direction*, New York, St. Martin's Press, 1991,19 ff.

39 Werner Thieme, "Wiederaufbau oder Modernisierung der deutschen Verwaltung", *Die Verwaltung*, 1993, 353ff.; Thomas Ellwein, "History of Public Administration", in Klaus König/Hans-Joachim von Oertzen/Frido Wagener (eds.), Public Administration in the Federal Republic of Germany, Deventer et al., Kluwer, 1997, 21 ff.

40 Sabino Cassese, *Le basi del diritto amministrativo*, secondo edizione, Torino, 1991.

41 Howard E. McCurdy, *Public Administration: A Synthesis*, Menlo Park Cal., Cummings, 1977.

42 David Osborne/Ted Gaebler, *Reinventing Government: How the entrepreneurial spirit is transforming the public sector*, Reading, Mass., Addison Wesley, 1992.

43 Vice President Al Gore, *Report of the National Performance Review*, Washington DC, U.S. Government Printing Office, 1992.

44 Leonard D. White, *Introduction to the Study of Public Administration*, 4th ed., New York, MacMillan, 1955, XVI.

45 Richard Stillman, *Preface to Public Administration*, ibid., 77 ff.

46 Graham T. Allison, "Public and Private Management: Are they fundamentally alike in all unimportant respects?", in Jay M. Shafritz/Albert C. Hyde (eds.), *Classics of Public Administration*, Second Edition, Chicago, Dorsey, 1987, 510 ff.

47 Gary L. Wamsley/James F. Wolf (eds.), *Refounding Democratic Public Administration. Modern Paradoxes, Post-modern Challenges*, Thousand Oaks, Cal. et al., Sage, 1996.

48 Christoph Reichard, *Betriebswirtschaftslehre der öffentlichen Verwaltung*, 2nd. ed., Berlin/New York, de Gruyter, 1987, 148 ff.

49 Alexander Wegener, *Dienstleistungsunternehmen Großstadt. Best run City in the world? Fallstudie Phoenix, Arizona (USA)*, Paper des Wissenschaftszentrum Berlin für Sozialforschung, Berlin,1997.

50 Thomas M. Babcock/Jane H. Ploeser, "From Expert Model to Citizenship Model: Phoenix Revises its Approach to Water Conservation Planning", *PA Times*, Vol. 21, No. 8/1998, 1.

Better Opportunities for Citizens

Klaus-Henning Rosen

Proceeding from the assumption that to better understand one another we must know more about one another. This is useful to discuss perspectives of and possibilities for the modernization of government in a global context, paying particular attention to current transatlantic developments. This is the only way how to learn from the experience made by other countries, to follow successful concepts and at the same time learn from the errors made and wrong paths followed by others. Such a comparison also sharpens our understanding for significant similarities and at the same time for their limits originating from the historically grown differences with regard to the functions we have assigned to our governments and public administrations.

The title of my contribution already points to the limits of similarity. It is more obvious from the German than from the American point of view to focus on "better opportunities for citizens" when discussing the modernization of the state and the administrative system. For in the United States an administrative system that is oriented towards citizens is somewhat more natural - at least to my accord - than it is in Germany. I will return to this later. The similarity is that useful plans and concepts for a reform of the state can only be drawn up if the function of the state, its tasks and the limits of its governance have been clearly understood and defined. For the tasks and responsibilities assigned to the state are put into practise by the administration. Therefore, if fundamental changes are necessary, the reform of the administrative system must become an integral part of the modernization of the state.

Agreement also exists about the motives underlying modern governance at the beginning of the 21st century: protection against internal and external threats; provisions for an emergency and for old age; responsibility for education; professional training, culture, and a modern infrastructure, especially in the field of information technology and transport. The principles of peace, the rule of law, the concept of social welfare, and the state's environmental awareness together form the common objectives of modern constitutional states. How responsibility is shared between the state and society and which tasks thus fall to the administrative system has indeed taken different directions in modern states. Such diversity, of course, originates in the different historical circumstances the effects of which can still be felt today.

Certainly you will have heard of an old story, according to which Benjamin Franklin was confronted by a woman as he left the last session of the Constitutional Convention in Philadelphia in September 1787. "What kind of government have you given us, Dr. Franklin?" she asked. "A Republic or a Monarchy?" "A Republic, Madam", he answered, "if you can keep it."

This illustrates that under the Constitution of the United States of America state matters are, by definition, public matters. In Germany, a thorough transformation of the state into a republic was not realised before the end of the First World War and the drafting of the Constitution of the Weimar Republic in 1919. Whereas in France the French Republic had been established after an armed revolution, Germany experienced a "top-down" modernisation of the state. The transformation of the absolutist state of the 18th century, the authoritarian state of the 19th century into the administrative state of the 20th century was not the result of a revolutionary process but of an evolutionary one which allowed the state as an institution to preserve and maintain its unbroken prestige. From this the conclusion can be drawn that administration in Germany is traditionally based on the authoritarian principles.

After the German state had been thoroughly discredited as the autocratic authoritarian state during the time of the national socialist's regime and the Second World War, it took on full responsibility for the reconstruction and the establishment of a social market-economy in the Federal Republic of Germany after 1945. The fact that scholars who had specialized in constitutional and administrative law and who had started their academic career in the Third Reich still had the say may have shaped the state's conception of itself with regard to "securing its own existence". Indeed, since the sixties public institutions have taken on more and more responsibilities so that the demands of the society on the state, or the desires conveyed by politics in society, were constantly growing. The state felt responsible and was held responsible - not only for basic individual risks but practically for every social, economic, or ecological problem. This was above all mounted by an attitude which was inspired by France and its so called *"Planification"* - namely the belief that the evolution of a society can be fully planned. Thus, the expanding welfare state raised expectations which it was unable to live up to.

This has significant consequences: The legal and administrative instruments for government action have reached the limits of their capacity, not least because life in society is getting more and more complex, until it finally eludes regulation by obsolete instruments. Today almost everything that can be regulated has been regulated: the number and arrangement of washing basins in a kindergarten with the same passion as the number of toilets in a restaurant. Such over-regulation not only hampers government action but also prevents the individual as well as society as a whole from taking on responsibility.

As a consequence of such expansion, the ability of the state to act has also reached its financial limits. Higher public expenditure can neither be justified economically nor politically. Though, since the end of the Second World War the budgets of all Western states have suffered from the shortness of funding - apart from exceptions in West Germany at the beginning of the fifties. If the circumstances so required this was counteracted by an increase in public debt. Other countries, such as the United States of America or in Europe the United Kingdom and the Netherlands had early become aware of this problem, even before the discussion about the introduction of the Euro, the new European currency, led to rigid standards with regard to budgetary policies.

Germany took the necessary political steps in September 1999. The future program adopted by the Cabinet will help to cut public expenditure by DM 150 billion (until 2003) over the next three years. This is urgently needed since currently one fourth of the total tax revenues is spent on interest payments. Germany is facing a gigantic mountain of debt which by now has reached the height of DM 1.5 trillion. This leaves us with DM 82 billion of interest payment for this year alone, which equals DM 150,000 per minute, or every three minutes the value of a single-family home. There is no alternative to this consolidation course. But it is important that we understand the necessary cutting of expenses as a chance for modernisation which we must take.

This has inspired the federal government to make the concept of the "state as enabler" the guiding model for government reform. This model contains important maxims to solve the conflict of an overload of tasks on the one hand and a lack of resources on the other.

On December 1, 1999 the federal government adopted the program "Moderner Staat - Moderne Verwaltung" (Modern state - Modern administration; document in the annex page 64). The four main principles of the program are: new distribution of responsibilities; more orientation towards the citizens; public diversity; efficient administration. Based on these principles, the program defines detailed objectives for modernization and reform projects.

The program proceeds from a different conception of the state, based on a new way of sharing responsibility between the state and society. Or, to say it in a nutshell: What society is able to do or to do better than the state, should be done by society. This only reflects our experience that the people are actually willing and prepared to take on social responsibility. Now it is left to us to encourage the people to make their contribution. Which does not relieve the state of the full responsibility for its key tasks - which include, *inter alia*, legislation, the police, and financial administration. Beyond that, there are many public tasks which are equally important but need not be fulfilled by the state itself. Of course, the state remains responsible, but secondarily. It is this new distribution of tasks which the state must trigger off and steer. It must support the citizens, but not patronise them. The "state as enabler" should keep a low profile so as to leave enough space for creativity and willingness to perform to unfold.

To make the administrative system more efficient requires the renewal of the internal structures of the federal administration in order to better use the limited financial resources. From the guiding model of the "enabling state" follows that the people may demand a responsible use of the resources which they make available to the state through their tax payments. Our aim is to create a powerful, cost-efficient, and transparent administrative system. Through a comprehensive quality management and best-practice management instruments, such as controlling and cost-to-performance accounting, the administration will render a better performance for fewer costs, as Al

Gore put it to the point with regard to the program "Reinventing Government".

To this end, we should also rely on modern information and communication technologies. In this context, the idea was born that the citizens would only need one stop if the public administration was fully networked. This means that the *information* must "go" from place to place and *not the citizens*. No matter which authority is in charge of a particular matter, the relevant inquiry should reach this competent authority via the Internet. Moreover, different tasks should be inter-linked. Public administration must primarily be designed for the people and geared to their needs, and not to the distribution of competencies between authorities.

At the federal level we have begun to develop an adequate concept based on the idea of the "one-stop government" and to put it under scrutiny in a pilot project. At the same time we will be closely following the developments elsewhere. For example, the European Commission has made three million Euro available to support a pilot project for the introduction of a smart card as Identity Card. This would provide the possibility to change address and vehicle registration as well as the social insurance system in one single procedure. We observe both, with interest and envy, that in Finland more than 80% of the households are connected with the Internet, and that a new law obliges public authorities to offer the full range of their services via the Internet by 2001. This far Germany will not have come by then.

However, electronic government will only have a chance if the use of the Internet becomes daily routine for a far greater number of people. To achieve this is one of the objectives of the "Initiative Germany 21 - Emergence into the Information Age". More than 100 companies, together with the federal government, help to ensure Germany's smooth transition to the information society. As regards the use of the new media, Germany is not yet one of the leading countries. For example, in the USA the number of homes connected with the Internet is three times that in Germany, measured against the total population. Accordingly, the economic importance of the information and communications branch is significantly higher in the United States: While in the USA it accounted for a 7.6% share in the gross domestic product in 1998, in Germany this share amounted to a mere 4.5%. And let me give you another example in a European context: In the Netherlands, in Sweden, Denmark, and Norway 9% of the workforce are employed in the information and communications branch, whereas in Germany it is 5%. We want to change this in co-operation with the private sector. The program has already borne fruit. Many individual initiatives and projects have begun, for example, to promote the early use of the new media technologies by children and young people. The announcement of Deutsche Telekom that it will provide free Internet access for every school in Germany can be seen as an outstanding achievement. So we will be able to make the new media accessible for a greater public, to promote innovative jobs, and to strengthen co-operation on both, the European and the international level.

With the modernization of government and administration we pursue an overall political objective. It is not only the internal structures that need to be changed but also the relationship between the state and its citizens. The state has to care for his citizens. According to the concept of the "enabling state", they are equal partners in fulfilling tasks for the public benefit. Or, as a German author put it in more illustrative words: the times are gone when two classes of people existed in Germany, those who sit behind a counter and those who cue at the counter. This requires that the interests and motives behind government decisions are transparent and players in society have better information at hand. Only then will those concerned be able to identify the changing tasks and achieve a new distribution of responsibilities. Therefore, the federal government wants to enhance the transparency of public administration and boost participation of the people. As I see it, the empowerment of the citizen also has the function of strengthening democracy and of encouraging the people to get more involved.

Usually, at the federal level, administrators do not have direct contact with the citizens. Therefore, the state must act on another level. In his capacity as legislator, the state has to create the legal framework for more orientation and closeness to the people as well as for a partnership between the state and society. To this end, the Federal Ministry of the Interior will present a draft act on the freedom of information by 2001. In our work we will profit of the experience made in the USA and in many European countries. People will then have easier access to information from public authorities, of course subject to compliance with the Data Protection Act. This is a prerequisite to create a state which shares tasks and responsibility.

Since modernization on the federal level is, in many areas, a legislative task, the federal government will improve the effectiveness and acceptance of our legislation. It is not indispensable that the number of laws and regulations grows steadily. Reversing this trend would mark a great success. Also, there is a need to reduce the number of regulations. This is probably the most difficult task we will have to face during our modernization programme. At the moment we are selecting the best strategic means to achieve these ambitious aims.

Proceeding from these considerations, it seems a good approach to adopt new laws for a limited period of time, that is to determine an "expiry date" for legal provisions. If a law stands the test and is to stay in force, a new decision must be taken.

In order to enhance the quality of laws already at the stage of their preparation and to improve their effectiveness, the Federal Ministry of the Interior will set up a manual for assessing the consequences of legal provisions. This manual shall help to evaluate the need for and the effect of a legal provision, and to systematically compare alternative means of regulation.

Another project is intended to look into legal obstacles for new service areas, based on actual cases, with the focus on the software branch, mobility services, and the energy sector. The project is designed as a research co-operation project which will be implemented in three stages: review of the best-practice statutory regulations for the said areas, e.g. in the field of competition law, protection of industrial property rights, provisions regarding liability, consumer protection law, or licence provisions; examination whether, and if so, to what extent the current legal provisions constitute an obstacle to innovation. This can only be achieved in co-operation with those concerned. Finally, the project will lead to recommendations regarding the abolition or amendment of these regulations.

In this context, the project "Reduction of Bureaucracy" launched by the Federal Ministry of Economics and Technology should also be mentioned. The project aims at reducing the bureaucracy companies have to deal with in order to comply with legal provisions regarding tax law, construction law, or social law. To achieve this, first it is the laws themselves as well as law enforcement where bureaucracy must be reduced. Therefore, the Federal Ministry of Economics and Technology has established a point of contact for business companies where inquiries are recorded to find out what is bothering these companies. By the end of the year detailed recommendations for action should be prepared and subsequently implemented through a change in the respective legislation or administrative practice. Our aim is to facilitate the communication between companies and administration. This regards, for example, all matters related to printed forms, the obligation to furnish specific information to health insurance companies, local authorities or to labor authorities.

Germany has seen a significant rise in the number of laws and legal provisions. From 1989 through 1999 the lower house of the German parliament has adopted as many laws as over the proceeding forty years. This effect is also reflected in the Federal Law Gazette the total volume of which was temporarily five times that of the year 1950. Though this year's edition, as of mid-May, contains a mere 650 pages. I am aware of the fact - to which worried staff has drawn my attention - that the quantity of adopted laws and the number of articles contained therein is no scientifically accurate proof of over-regulation. However, it indicates that legislation has suffered a loss in quality in as much as laws have become less stringent and lost some of their appeal. We have to get rid of the idea that we can and must regulate any given matter. Such attempt is doomed to failure, not least because the reality of life is getting more and more complex and is changing so rapidly. Instead we should remember that laws must be abstract universal rules which are responsive to individual cases only in the way they are interpreted. This requires a new way of thinking of those who prepare the laws, of the administrative authorities, which enforce them, of the courts and, last but not least, of the citizens themselves.

The guiding model of the "enabling state" not only affects the relationship of the federal government to the citizens but also that to the *Länder* and to local government. Also vis-à-vis the other government levels, a new way of thinking is needed. Only then will a sustained modernization of the state and the administrative system be possible in a federal state like Germany, mainly because the various administrative levels are much more intertwined with each other than in the United States, for example. It is true that the German Constitution guarantees the independence of the *Länder* and of local government. Nevertheless, the federal government is responsible for legislation in crucial sectors of society and has the sovereign power of administrative enforcement. The *Länder* and the local governments demand from the federal government to give them greater discretion fulfilling their public duties. The current federal government supports their demand; not least to bring public administration closer to the people and enhance its orientation towards citizens. Here we have made first sustainable achievements and brought about a cultural change within the federal administrative system: The *Länder* and local governments are no longer considered as mere recipients of orders given by the federal government.

The main idea behind this endeavour was to promote the reform efforts of the *Länder*. What has guided the federal government in its work is the following assumption: If enforcement of federal law is devolved to the *Länder*, their power of discretion should not be limited by federal government provisions. So in many cases, the federal government should abstain from determining which local authority is responsible for a particular matter and rather leave this to the *Länder* to decide, not least because the importance of a task is subject to constant change. The constitution allows the federal government to exercise influence on the organization of the administration of the *Länder*. Though it does not *have* to.

What is needed is constitutional self-restraint. Admittedly, it has been a huge effort to trigger off a new way of thinking in the Ministries. To examine the almost two hundred appeals of the *Länder* asking the federal government to retransfer such responsibilities, cost us an immense amount of work. But the importance of the far more than 100 cases in which the federal government could meet the wishes of the *Länder* shows how much painstaking detailed work has to be done. To put it in a somewhat exaggerated way: In order to make deregulation a broad success we must make it the conviction of all ministerial departments that their existence does not correlate to the quantity of regulations produced every year.

In a next step the federal government wants to become active itself and abolish further statutory provisions which bind the *Länder* and local governments. From this we expect public administration to become more transparent and more citizen oriented.

This is an ambitious but realistic program for the modernization of government and administration. Its implementation is not an easy task. Huge efforts will be needed to make a progress. Our aim is to help build Germany's way to become a state of the 21st century by creating a future-oriented administrative system. Only then will we be successful when we encourage every employee to disassociate from old traditions and routines in order to develop a new understanding of their own position and realise that administration does not exist for its own stake but instead is under an obligation to benefit the citizens. Our success also depends on whether the reform of the administrative system will be given utmost priority. Chancellor Gerhard Schröder has reaffirmed that this is definitely the case. This will

help to overcome occasional obstacles which may result from the departmental sovereignty provided for in the Basic Law.

Annex

Modern state - Modern administration
The programme launched by the federal government
Cabinet decision of 1 December 1999

Contents

Preface by Otto Schily, Federal Minister of the Interior

Modern State - Modern Administration
- programme of the federal government for renewal and reform

I. Aims of the enabling state
    1. A new distribution of responsibility
    2.   Responsive public service
    3. Diversity of public bodies
    4. Efficient administration

II. The programme
    1. Improvement of the efficiency and acceptance of the law
    2. The federal government as a partner
        a)   Co-operation between the different tiers of administration
        b)   Co-operation with the private sector
    3. A competitive, cost-efficient and transparent administrative system
    4. Highly motivated employees

III. Implementing structures
        1.   Committee of State Secretaries on "Modern State - Modern
                Administration"
        2.   Secretariat on "Modern State   Modern Administration"

The state and the administrative system must redefine their tasks and competences taking into account the changed conditions within society. Therefore, the transformation into a modern state with a modern administrative system is an important task of domestic policy. With the launching of the programme "Modern state - Modern administration" on 1 December 1999 the federal government laid the foundation for a comprehensive reform of the state and its administrative system.

The aim of the programme is the creation of the enabling state. It stands for a new conception of the state, and its maximes will have a lasting effect on the structures of the state and public administration.

It is implemented through 15 guiding projects and involves the entire federal administration. These guiding projects demonstrate that modernisation on a federal level not only means modernisation of federal administration but also covers the relationship between the state and its citizens, groups of social players, the *Länder* and local authorities (*Gemeinden*). Of the great number of reform projects launched by the federal government, 23 additional projects were selected, representing the multiple facets of the modernisation programme.

This brochure, drawn up by the federal government, documents the start of the programme "Modern state - Modern administration". We want to inform citizens, the *Länder* and local authorities, the scientific community, associations and, last but not least, the staff in the federal administration, to make our objectives and ideas transparent, and to start a dialogue about the future of the state and its administration. In addition, you may contact the federal government via the Internet at *www.staat-modern.de* and tell us your views about the process of modernising government.

Otto Schily, Federal Minister of the Interior

Modern State - Modern Administration
Guiding model and programme of the federal government

I. The aim of the enabling state

It is the aim of the federal government to adapt the state and its administrative system to the changed conception of the state's role and the changing tasks of government and administration. To this end in its Coalition Agreement entitled "Mobilisation of resources, and renewal - Germany's way into the 21st century" (Coalition Agreement of 20 October 1998, chapter IX, n°11, paragraph 2) the federal government the federal government has embarked on making the concept of the enabling state its guiding model. This model determines a new political direction for the modernisation of the state and administration.

Methods of modernising the state and the administrative system have been known for some time now; yet, the final plunge has not been taken - to launch a concerted overall reform on the federal level. The concept of the "lean state" which was pursued in the past was too much limited to reducing public tasks, i.e. it only set negative goals.

In contrast, the federal government will go beyond the isolated approaches of internal modernisation which were made in the past. The enabling state opens a future-oriented perspective taking into account the different understanding of the roles of the state and administration. Together with an actively participating society we will be able to successfully steer a middle course between, on the one hand, merely making the state leaner and, on the other, too much intervention by the state and excessive regulation. This requires a high degree of flexibility and the preparedness for reform on the part of all parties concerned - the public administration and its staff, the citizens and the other players of society.

1. A new distribution of responsibility

The state and the administrative system must redefine their tasks and competencies taking into account the changed conditions within society. The enabling state will promote the devolution of social responsibility where it is feasible. This means that there will be a new distribution and grading of responsibilities between the state and society:

On the one hand the state continues to have the duty to protect the freedom and security of its citizens as its core task for which it remains solely responsible (e.g. internal security, legal protection, and tax collection). Beyond that, there are many tasks which so far have been deemed to be public tasks, which are equally important but need not be fulfilled by the state itself. Here, however, the state must ensure that they will be fulfilled.

The guiding model of the enabling state is responsive to this new distribution of responsibilities between the state and society. A reform of the state and its administrative system which is based on such a model must create a new balance between state duties, individual initiative and social commitment. This will shift the focus in such a way that the state becomes less of a decision taker and producer and more of a mediator and catalyst of social developments which it cannot and must not control on its own. The enabling state means strengthening society's potential for self-regulation and guaranteeing the necessary freedom of action. Above all, this requires the concerted action of public, semi-public and private players to achieve common goals. This interaction needs to be developed and enhanced. In this context, it is the special responsibility of the federal government to create the legal framework for a state geared to the needs of its citizens, acting like a partner for them and endowed with an efficient administrative system.

2. Responsive public service

The state is there for its citizens. According to the concept of the enabling state, they are equal partners in fulfilling tasks for the public benefit. This requires the interests and motives behind government decisions to be transparent, and players in society to have better information at hand. Only then will those concerned be able to see how tasks are changing and to achieve a new distribution of responsibilities. Therefore, the federal government wishes to enhance the transparency of public administration and boost participation by the people. To this end, the state and the administrative system will have to prepare themselves for the transition from a society based on industrial production to a knowledge-based service society, and use the possibilities offered by information technologies as a basis for keeping citizens informed and for communicating with them.

3.   Diversity of public bodies

The guiding model of the enabling state has not only an impact on the relationship between the federal government and the citizens but also that between the federal government and the *Länder* and local authorities. A sustained modernisation of the state and the administrative system will only be possible if the different tiers of public administration work closely together and respect each other. Hence, the distribution of competencies and the sharing of responsibility will play a greater role as elements of the principle of federalism. The federal structure of the Federal Republic of Germany and of its administrative system, which allows "diversity within unity", makes this indispensable. That is also why complaints about the federal level "lagging behind" the *Länder* and local authorities with regard to the modernisation process have to be taken very seriously. After all, the *Länder* only have a chance to make headway with their efforts for a reform of their administrative systems which in part are already well-advanced if the federal government provides them with more room for manoeuvre. In this context, Germany's integration into the European Union and its role in the international community has to be taken into account.

Therefore, the federal government strives for closer co-operation between the different tiers of administration and, where possible, greater freedom of decision. Its aim is to strengthen the preparedness of people to assume responsibility for themselves, to give more weight to the principle of subsidiarity and to foster diversity within the federation by reducing the number of federal government provisions.

4. Efficient administration

It is indispensable to renew the internal structures of the federal administration, not least to allow a better use of limited financial resources. One of the consequences of the guiding model of the enabling state is that the citizens demand a responsible use of the resources which they make available to the state through their tax payments. Hence, more performance-oriented and cost-efficient procedures are an essential contribution of the administration to the enabling state. State action must meet the requirements of efficiency and effectiveness. Administrative processes must be reviewed in order to avoid superfluous red tape. This can be achieved through competition and benchmarking. Competing approaches and orientation towards "best-practice solutions" help those concerned to optimise administrative processes and create viable structures

This can only be achieved, if a much more efficient use is made of human and financial resources. Similar experience from other countries, the *Länder* and local authorities has shown that an efficient administration is only possible if employees understand modernisation as their own concern and are prepared to take on responsibility. They must be able to actively participate in this process. This requires better legal framework conditions for employees to get involved and reliable career prospects. To this end, the federal government will include more performance –related elements into the remuneration and career schemes of the public service and elaborate concepts for human resources development in the federal administration.

II. The programme

It is a joint political programme of the federal government to modernise the state and administration on the basis of the guiding model of the enabling state. To put it into practice, 15 guiding projects were selected to serve as a standard by which the implementation of the model of the enabling state will be measured. It is a dynamic process which allows the updating of the guiding projects. They are complemented by 23 additional projects which define more specifically the modernisation programme of the federal government. All these modernisation projects, which affect all levels of federal administration but are implemented individually by each authority, add up to the overall project "Modern State - Modern Government".

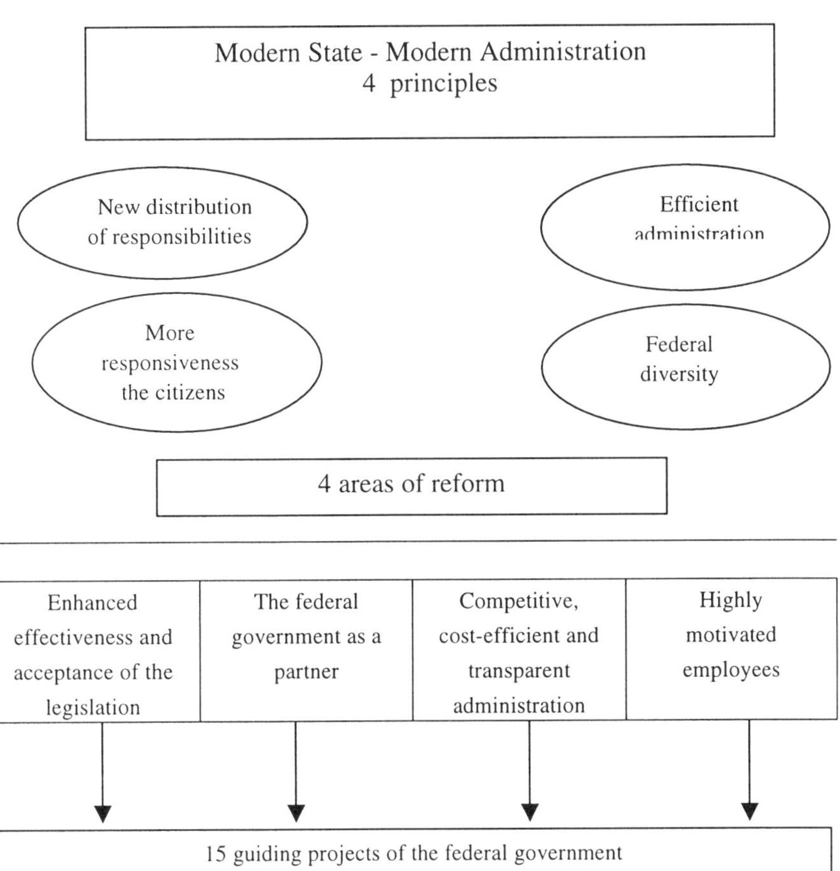

1. Enhanced effectiveness and acceptance of legislation

The federal government wishes to improve the effectiveness and acceptance of legislation in general. Where the federal government itself introduces a bill or adopts a law it will make use of all possibilities to improve both, the legal regulations and the process of legislation, and if appropriate, to reduce the number of regulations.

Guiding projects:

a)   *Manual for assessing the consequences of legal provisions* (Federal Ministry of the Interior; to be finalised by June 2000): The manual shall provide instruments to assess the monetary and non-monetary effects of laws. Based on selected examples of legislation, it shall help to further develop, systematise and generalise the experience gained so far. The manual will be structured in a way as to meet both, theoretical and practical requirements. To facilitate its practical use, an empirical guide will be developed.

b)   *Identification and dismantling of obstacles for new services* (Federal Ministry of the Interior, Federal Ministry of Education and Research; to be finalised by 2001): On the basis of existing cases, this project is intended to look into problems for new service areas that result from legal provisions. The regards mainly the software industry, mobility services and the energy sector. This project will result in the drawing up of guidelines and recommendations on how to overcome legal restrictions for innovation.

2.   The federal government as a partner

a)   Co-operation between the different tiers of administration

The federal government will remove barriers which hamper independent action by the *Länder* and local authorities. The aim is to extend the scope of action of the *Länder* and to strengthen local self-government.

Guiding projects:

aa)   *More competences for the Länder* (federal government; to be finalised by May 2000): The federal government has taken up the proposal made by the *Länder* and is subjecting the provisions under Federal law relating to responsibilities to a thorough review aimed at relaxing competences as far as possible to give the *Länder* more scope for their administrative reforms and the discharge of their administrative tasks.

bb)   *Commitment to improving the involvement of the Länder and local authorities* (Federal Ministry of the Interior; to be finalised by spring 2000): In areas where the federal government sees a need to initiate legislation which will affect different tiers of administration it undertakes to consult the *Länder* and local authorities before the drafting of the respective regulations in order to assess their regulatory requirements. This is the only way to ensure that draft legislation takes equal account of and integrates the needs of the federal government, the *Länder*, and the local authorities. In its work the federal government must provide for more room for the concerns and interests of the *Länder* and local authorities than in the past. The Amendment to the Joint Rules of Procedure of the Federal Ministries has created the necessary conditions.

cc)   *Restructuring of federal construction tasks* (Federal Ministry of Finance; to be finalised by 2002): The federal government will review the procedures in infrastructure building so as to make the carrying out of public building tasks more efficient and cost-saving. In addition, administration shall be streamlined by facilitating examination and permit procedures.

b)   Co-operation with the private sector

In fulfilling its task of meeting public needs and ensuring a better life for people and businesses, the federal government will create scope for the development of self-initiative and self-regulation and will promote voluntary work. It will remove restrictions and create new forms of co-operation between the state, the private sector, the welfare organisations and other non-profit-making institutions.

Guiding projects:

aa)   *Legal provisions on Public Private Partnership* (Federal Ministry of the Interior; to be finalised by 2001): The federal government will create the legal framework for cooperative contractual relationships. At the moment, the contract under public law, in its obsolete form, is the only means available to the public and private sectors to regulate their co-operation. This is insufficient for an enhanced co-operation in line with the concept of the enabling state and for a new distribution of responsibilities. Therefore, new types of contracts and contractual clauses which will be appropriate for the shaping of such co-operations will be incorporated in the law of administrative procedure.

bb)   *"Germany 21 – New departure into the Information Age"* (federal government; to be finalised by 2002): With the aim to jointly smooth the path for Germany's transition into the information society, the federal government and the IT industry have established five working groups under the aegis of the Federal Chancellor (Regulating framework and access to the Internet; The state as the trailblazer in applying modern technologies; Education and qualification; Boosting business start-ups; Promotion of women in IT jobs). In this context, actions and projects will be carried out within the framework of the programme of action entitled "Innovation and jobs in the information society of the 21st century".

cc)   *The promotion of the audit approach – e.g. the Federal Data Protection Act* (Federal Ministry of the Interior; completion of the projects scheduled for mid 2001): Within the framework of the forthcoming amendment to the Federal Data Protection Act (BDSG), the data protection audit will be embodied as a general cross-sectional provision which in a next stage, i.e. during the subsequent substantial redrafting of the Data Protection Act (second stage), will be given a more concrete form with the creation of a Federal Data Protection Audit Act. Private businesses who offer customer-specific solutions for data protection and security may then have their products and technical equipment examined and certified by independent experts and publish the results of such audits. This is to encourage the private sector to take on responsibility for data protection, help to establish data security as a criterion for competitiveness, and to contribute to a continuous improvement of data protection and data security through the participating businesses.

3. A competitive, cost-efficient and transparent administrative system

The administration will take on the challenge to achieve higher performance targets while cutting expenses. To this end, it will adapt more and more to competitive conditions, making the use of instruments of business administration, such as accrual accounting and controlling, common practice in the federal administration. However, an administration can become more efficient only if it improves the way in which the citizens are involved in administrative decision making and if it makes its administrative actions more transparent. The intention behind this opening-up is to make it possible to enter into a concrete dialogue with the citizens and to reveal red tape. To this end, the federal government will make use of modern information and communication technologies on a broad basis, thus accomplishing the transition towards the "electronic government".

Guiding projects:

a)   *Introduction of modern management techniques in the federal administration and in the armed forces* (Federal Ministry of the Interior; Federal Foreign Office; Federal Ministry of Finance; Federal Ministry of Economics and Technology; Federal Ministry of Defence; anticipated end of project 2002): By implementing a comprehensive quality management, controlling will be introduced in appropriate areas to improve effectiveness and efficiency of government action. Visions, agreed targets, accrual accounting, procedures for continuous improvement and budgeting/product oriented financial planning will result in a change of administrative culture in the federal administration.

b) *Testing and further development of standards for accrual accounting* (Federal Ministry of Finance; permanent project): The Federal Ministry of Finance has developed an accrual accounting system to be used in the federal administration. This method allows an output-oriented performance assessment and the control of required resources. Accrual accounting is to become the integrated part of controlling systems of which agreements on operational targets are an essential component. Operating figures can be derived and tested on the basis of this procedure which can then be used for overall steering purposes and for the comparison of the performance of authorities.

c) *Benchmarking/best practices* (federal government; scheduled end of project 2001): Benchmarking and best practices have been put on trial by numerous departments to optimise administrative processes. The experience gathered from these test runs will be pooled to extend the possibilities for the application of benchmarking.

d) *Freedom of Information Act* (Federal Ministry of the Interior; scheduled end of project 2001): With a view to making state action more transparent for citizens, the federal government intends to introduce a bill to regulate access by the citizens to information from administrative authorities. This is to strengthen the participation of citizens with, of course, due regard to data protection.

e) *IT strategy* (Federal Ministry of Transport, Building and Housing, Federal Ministry of the Interior; to be finalised by 2002): The federal government will improve the efficiency of administrative processes through the use of modern information technologies. So far, the federal administration has seen IT as a technical tool and as a substitute for "pencil and paper". Substantial improvements, however, will only be made, if IT is understood as a means to manage information and knowledge. Real improvements will be achieved if we make innovative use of information and become learning organisations. This works out in areas where structured knowledge is used to carry out routine work. The integration of new technologies, such as semi-automated Internet searches, allows employees better access to unstructured knowledge directly from their desktops. Such technologies are put on trial in pilot projects launched by the Federal Ministry of the Interior together with the Federal Ministry of Transport, Building and Housing. Following the example of industrial production, the aim is to use systematic logistics in order to make knowledge and information available "just in time".

4. Highly-motivated employees

High performance and commitment depend on a competitive personnel structure and highly motivated employees. Personal responsibility, better career opportunities and flexible, self-determined working structures (collaborative working) ensure that the existing potential for modernisation is actually used.

Guiding projects:

a) Amendment to the Public Service Law (Federal Ministry of the Interior; to be finalised by mid-2001): An up-to-date public service law is a crucial element of a competitive public administration. With its reform of the public service law, the federal government wishes to open up new perspectives for public employees, strengthen their willingness to perform, support their creativity, and remove unnecessary bureaucracy to enable public employers to gear personnel management to their individual needs. To this end it is intended to optimise management structures, establish flexible payment margins and (*introduce*) performance-related pay, particularly in education and science, as well as to attach greater importance to performance with regard to career regulations. Also, opportunities for part-time work will be improved to make it easier for people to combine family life with their jobs.

b) *Personnel development in the federal administration* (federal government; to be finalised by 2001): In view of the requirements of efficient and effective administrative action the federal government intends to develop meaningful ways for the promotion of its personnel.

during the life of this parliament all Ministries are requested to come up with concepts for the development of their personnel which will open up possibilities for agreements on specific targets, for further training measures and individual career planning for staff members. Great importance will be attached to equal opportunities for men and women in the public service. Attention will also be focussed on making the staff "fit for Europe". A working group consisting of members of the personnel departments of the different ministries will be established in order to ensure the exchange of information and experience between government departments. At the same time, the Federal Ministry of the Interior is drawing up a concept which shall help tailor the further training courses offered by the Federal Academy for Public Administration, especially those targeted at senior officials, to meet the needs and agreed targets.

III.   Implementing structures

1. Committee of Permanent Secretaries
   Modern State - Modern Administration

A Committee of State Secretaries on the modernisation of the state and administration under the aegis of the Federal Ministry of the Interior (State Secretary Ms. Zypries) will be responsible for the implementation of the programme and the steering of the modernisation process within the federal government. It will determine targets and strategies and solve conflicts resulting from target agreements with the departments concerned.

2. Task force on Modern State - Modern Administration

The committee will be supported by a task force located at the office of State Secretary Zypries at the Federal Ministry of the Interior. Its task is to co-ordinate and promote the modernisation process. This includes, *inter alia*:

- inter-ministerial co-ordination and promotion of the guiding projects
- informing public authorities and the public about the progress of the project as a whole
- informing the Cabinet about progress of the modernisation process
- co-operation with respective task forces in the *Länder*.

II. Federalism and Devolution

Introduction

Arthur B. Gunlicks

The United States and Germany have dramatically different political systems (presidential vs. parliamentary), party systems (two broadly based nonmembership catch-all parties supported almost wholly by private contributions vs. a member-based multiparty system with two dominant parties supported in large part by public funds), and electoral systems (single-member district plurality system vs. a proportional party list system combined with a single-member district plurality system). On the other hand, unlike most other European states, Germany shares with the United States a federal system of territorial organization; however, these two federal systems differ from each other just as parliamentary systems differ from one another in a variety of ways. The difference between American and German federalism is captured in the different concept of dual federalism. In the United States dual federalism refers to separate powers or "competencies" assigned by the constitution to the national and state levels. That is, each level has certain responsibilities for certain areas and deals with these responsibilities autonomously by passing its own laws, administering them with its own bureaucracy, and raising its own taxes. In Germany the concept of dual sovereignty refers to the responsibility of the national parliament to pass almost all legislation and for the regional governments, i.e., the *Länder* (singular form=*Land*), to administer most of it on their own responsibility. The *Länder* are autonomous, however, not only in administration but also in the areas of culture (education; music, arts, museums), local government, and a few other less important fields. In the United States dual federalism has been severely undermined by the growing tendency, especially since the New Deal, for the federal government to enter new areas of responsibility never imagined by the Founding Fathers for either level or to pass concurrent national legislation in areas some states were regulating in order to promote more uniformity among the states or to provide matching funds to help finance minimum standards. This system of "cooperative federalism", now called more often "intergovernmental relations", has led to a highly complex federal system in which most government policy on most issues is shared to some degree by federal, state, and/or local governments.

In Germany also there has been a tendency since the founding of the Federal Republic in 1949 toward more "cooperative federalism" or what Germans call *Politikverflechtung*. This term refers to an "interlocking" of federal and *Land* government policy-making which involves especially executive authorities in consultations and negotiations between levels or, in the case of the *Länder*, within the level at conferences of *Land* Minister-Presidents ministers and cabinet ministers. These developments along with others, such as the sharing of tax revenues among the *Länder* rather than their having autonomous taxation powers, have also made the German federal system more complicated and less transparent. As in the United States, this had led to much criticism of the current federal system and to many proposals for reforms.

A major issue in both political systems, then, is the distribution of autonomous powers or competencies at the national and regional level in each federal system and the efforts to sort these out in some rational and politically acceptable and practical manner. Whether these efforts should be called devolution, decentralization, delegation, deregulation, or something else - a matter discussed below by John Kincaid - is an important practical question, the "correct" answer to which would surely help promote a better understanding and discussion of the basic issues involved. The major point, however, is that in the United States and Germany there is a discussion, which is not new, of the "proper" relationship between the national and regional levels of government and the degree of autonomous decision-making each should or even can realistically have.

William Pound notes that there is much talk today in the United States about devolution from the federal level to the states. The question he raises is whether this is really devolution or just another in a long series of adjustments. The evidence from the Clinton Administration is mixed, and serious attempts to define the actual relationship between the two levels are inconclusive.

He suggests that we have moved toward a more balanced federalism in recent years. Whether this can be maintained in the future, given numerous challenges such as globalization, remains to be seen. It is encouraging that there is stronger public support for subnational governments, while there is considerable distrust of the federal government. On the other hand, it is not clear that the public understands the intergovernmental nature of most public policies.

Changes that he points to include the increased flexibility for the states and at the same time the greater federal involvement in traditional areas of state authority such as law enforcement and criminal justice. One could also point to education. A major example of devolution is the welfare reform law of 1996. Another example concerns an education act in 1999 and a law regarding unfunded mandates passed in 1995. Nevertheless, Congress still tends to preempt states in certain areas by, for example, federalizing a variety of crimes. Somewhat pessimistically, he suggests that "[n]o area, no matter how large or small, seems immune from Congressional reach at the present time", and he argues that "[l]ittle attention is paid to federalism as a governing principle."

Some of the significant adjustments that have occurred recently have come through Supreme Court decisions. In contrast to the previous fifty years, the Supreme Court in the past decade has adopted a more restrictive view of federal powers. This can be seen especially in the rediscovery of the Tenth Amendment as a limitation on congressional action. At the same time the states seem to be asserting more authority over their local governments. Thus, states have received more authority via devolution and Supreme Court decisions and have also assumed more authority vis-à-vis their local governments.

Pound notes that the states increasingly are becoming a source of innovation in a variety of policy areas. On the other hand, the future of federalism depends on the revenue situation. State and local spending is growing faster than federal spending. At the moment the states are in a healthy financial condition, but this could change. Revenues of states and local governments are growing at a lower rate than at the federal level. A major source of revenue for the states is the sales tax, but internet commerce threatens these revenues, as does federal preemption of the state tax base.

John Kincaid takes issue with the whole notion that there has been a "devolution revolution" in the United States. He suggests it is an assertion promoted by liberal (left) academics, not a fact. He reviews the literature on devolution, notes the liberal antipathy to Ronald Reagan's efforts to devolve powers to the states, and argues that Reagan did not succeed in his efforts. The literature on the "devolution revolution" is based primarily on the welfare reform law of 1996, but in fact, even with a Republican Congress after 1995, "the centralization rabbit is still outrunning the devolution turtle . . . ."

Kincaid argues that the literature on the "devolution revolution" is incorrect on four important issues, i.e., it is weak on evidence, propagandistic, often misleading, and purely speculative. Yet it does raise some legitimate concerns, such as the proper roles of federal and state governments and the possible consequences, negative or positive, of a greater role for either level. He also discusses the constitutional arguments regarding devolution and dual sovereignty and notes the importance of defining terms often used carelessly in the debate about the "devolution revolution".

Kincaid points to developments favoring "restorations of state powers", including actions taken by federal authorities. In his view "flexibility for state and local administration of federal programs, not devolution of federal programs, has been the hallmark of the Clinton Administration." He sees the Supreme Court as having "returned to the field to umpire the constitutional game of federal-state power-balancing with rulings surprisingly favorable to the states." He says, however, that there has been "no wholesale restoration of state powers or denigration of federal powers." His overall conclusion is that "no substantial shift of power to the states has yet been executed." Rather, there have been only "turtle steps toward devolution" within the framework of a major debate over federalism and the nature of the American society now and in the future.

He then points to numerous forces favoring federal powers, including public opinion, the Republican tendency to favor individualism over the principle of federalism, conflicts over funding, the popularity of many federal programs, the benefits Congressmen receive from the status quo, and the federal temptation to preempt the states or mandate functions. In short, there has been a shift in federal policy-making from places to persons that began in the 1960s which has focused attention more on individuals than on the states.

Turning to Germany, Ursula Männle points to the discussion Germany today about a redistribution of legislative competencies between the federation and the *Länder*. The focus of this discussion has been on the growth of federal legislative power at the expense of *the Länder* and the resulting deformity in the German federal system. She notes that concrete efforts to regain competencies for the *Land* parliaments were initiated by Bavaria in the Bundesrat, but she also describes how these efforts were at first rejected and then weakened by a majority of the *Land* government representatives, namely bureaucrats in the working committees in the *Bundesrat*. But she also argues that even the *Land* politicians are more comfortable with participation rights in the Bundesrat than in accepting real political responsibility for the *Land* parliament. She notes that commissions have been formed in Hesse and Bavaria that have been charged with proposing ways and means of strengthening *Land* parliaments. This is a challenging task, and whether concrete reform will emerge remains to be seen. Professor Männle is a strong advocate of more autonomy for the *Länder*, but she does not deal with the objections raised by Arthur Benz, who takes a very different approach in his chapter.

Arthur Benz notes that today federalism is blamed for causing political immobility and inefficiency in Germany. The call is for "modernization", which means decentralizing many responsibilities in order to allow more regional diversity; reducing the cooperation and coordination among *Länder* executives which has a negative effect on the competencies of the *Land* parliaments in particular and in general blurs the transparency of the political process; and promoting competition among the *Länder* in a variety of policy areas. He notes, though, that skeptics doubt the system can be reformed, given the institutional restraints, or even that it should be reformed.

Benz suggests that the German federal system has functioned better than many critics contend. The system of cooperative federalism and the party system have combined to promote uniform policies that met popular expectations regarding the German welfare state. Whether these popular expectations are being met today or can continue to be met in the face of numerous challenges is the question which Benz addresses in his chapter.

84

He notes that the reform proposals that have been offered are either unrealistic or undesirable. "Competitive federalism" is unrealistic because the poor *Länder* will not accept the model, and it is undesirable because of the regional disparities it would most likely create. The real issue is *fair competition*. This involves continuing the transfers of funds to the new *Länder* based on need rather than on the principle of equivalent living conditions. Rather than devolution of legislative powers, there should be more deregulation of federal policies to ensure only that certain standards are maintained within a more flexible framework. And, finally, the *Länder* need to become more assertive in the area of decentralized policies.

It is clear from the above summaries of the chapters in this section that there is a lively and controversial discussion of the distribution of powers in the American and German federal systems. This discussion is not new in principle, but new issues are being raised in the current debates that require those on the different sides to rethink some of their positions and draw the lines of argument in somewhat different places. The chapters which follow help not only to illuminate the discussion but also to clarify some of the alternatives.

The American Devolution Derby:
The Devolution Turtle vs. The Centralization Rabbit

John Kincaid

In recent years, some observers of American federalism have proclaimed the onset of a "devolution revolution"[1]. The Century Foundation, for example, is even publishing a series of reports entitled "The Devolution Revolution". The series purports to analyze "the impact of the widespread shift of government responsibilities from the national to the state and local level".[2] Yet, when one looks for such widespread devolution, one finds a molehill of evidence overshadowed by a mountain of rhetoric. At times, even the evidence offered by proclaimants of devolution is either wrong or fantastic. A recent nationwide survey of municipal officials, moreover, found that most city officials perceived little evidence of devolution.[3]

The notion of a devolution revolution, therefore, is more interesting as a study of liberal (i.e., the left side of politics in the United States) academics, the poverty of social science, and interest-group tactics than as a study of change in American federalism. However, given that federalism is one focus of this book, I will address the politics of the matter, the issues and evidence for devolution, and the forces operating for and against shifts of power from the federal government to the states in the United States.

The Politics of the Devolution Literature

The core political divide on this matter is between liberals who support federal power, especially over redistributive social-welfare policies, and conservatives who wish to limit federal power, especially over social-welfare policies. The notion of a devolution revolution has been put forth, not by conservatives, but by liberal academics and interest groups in opposition to what conservatives call "the Reagan Revolution". Most liberals were horrified by the Reagan presidency (1981-1989) and by Reagan's New Federalism rhetoric of shifting power back to the states. They predicted dire consequences from such policies, and they invented new metaphors to describe those consequences, such as "shift-and-shaft federalism" and "fend-for-yourself federalism". In reality, however, the Reagan administration did not shift power back to the states; instead, it vastly increased federal power vis-à-vis the states, and it allowed a novel federal-aid program, General Revenue Sharing (GRS), which is now cited as a precursor of devolution, to expire in 1986. Moreover, the phrase "fend-for-yourself federalism" was promoted in 1988, the last full year of Reagan's presidency and the very year in which federal aid to state and local governments halted a decade-long decline and began to skyrocket.

The new devolution-revolution metaphor is a successor to fend-for-yourself federalism. The new metaphor was put forth in 1996[4], the year that Congress enacted a major welfare-reform law. The metaphor reflects the new liberal horror at the Republican victory in the 1994 congressional elections, a victory that raised the specter of a Republican Congress completing the Reagan Revolution. Yet, after six years of holding majority power, the Republican Congress has been unable, and often unwilling, to shift significant power from the federal government to the states. The centralization rabbit is still outrunning the devolution turtle, as was also the case during the Reagan years.

Consequently, the literature proclaiming a devolution revolution has four disturbing characteristics. First, it is short on evidence. Most common are assertions like the following: "Republicans began a wholesale transfer of federal programs to the states. Most prominently, they replaced most federal welfare entitlements with block grants".[5] The author gives no other examples of, or evidence for, devolution. Another author proclaims the existence of a devolution revolution[6] and quotes a newspaper report claiming this to be "the greatest transfer of power since the New Deal".[7] The author then details ways in which devolution is a barrier to reinventing government and concludes, among other things, that: "Because devolution has failed in many instances to bring government any closer to the people whom it serves, it does not improve the public accountability of agencies".[8] The author presents his bold claims and confident conclusions without analyzing a single case of devolution.

Second, the literature is often incorrect, in fact so wrong for observers who should know better that it can only be regarded as propagandistic misinformation. For example, in one of the statements quoted above, the author asserts that Republicans "replaced most welfare entitlements with block grants".[9] This is not true; only one entitlement - Aid to Families with Dependent Children (AFDC) - was replaced with a block grant. Indeed, the single largest welfare entitlement for poor people who are not senior citizens, namely, Medicaid (i.e., health care for the poor), never had significant support, even among most Republicans, for conversion to a block grant. Medicaid, therefore, remains a categorical grant. It is also the single largest federal-aid program, accounting for about 42 percent of all federal aid to state and local governments. Another example of misinformation is the preface to each of the Century Foundation's reports, which states that: "Under Reagan, more than five hundred categorical programs were consolidated into nine block grants".[10] This is nonsense. Only 77 categoricals were merged into nine block grants, and 62 categorical grants were eliminated.[11] The total number of grants dropped from 539 to 404 by 1984, but then proliferated again, to 492 by 1988, 593 by 1992, and about 660 today.

Third, the literature on the devolution revolution is often misleading. It frequently criticizes Republicans for this supposed revolution while ignoring or downplaying the Democratic role. The 1996 welfare-reform law, which is the most cited example of devolution, is regularly blamed on the Republicans. Little attention, if any, is given to President Clinton's 1992 campaign pledge to "end welfare as we know it," to Clinton's support of the welfare-reform bill, and to congressional Democratic votes for this reform. This misleading rhetoric is similar to that of the 1980s, which attributed the decade-long decline of federal aid to President Reagan when, in fact, aid had begun to decline in 1978 during Carter's Presidency. Similarly, liberals blamed the 1986 expiration of GRS on Reagan, even though Carter and a Democratic Congress had ended GRS payments to the states in 1980, and, in 1986, the U.S. House of Representatives, which was Democratic, declined to rescue GRS.

Fourth, the literature on the devolution revolution is, consequently, purely speculative. Given its political motivations, this literature almost uniformly predicts dire consequences resulting from devolution. This, too, is similar to the fend-for-yourself literature of the 1980s which predicted dire consequences ensuing from the Reagan Revolution. Had these predictions come true, most major U.S. cities would have been bankrupt and swamped with homeless people during the 1990s, and most states would have been fiscally decimated and overrun by armies of poor and unemployed people. None of the predictions were borne out by subsequent history, and even the brief recession during George Bush's presidency produced nothing more than the levels of fiscal stress and unemployment that one would expect from such a recession.

The literature on the devolution revolution, therefore, is an example of what might be called preemptive social science. Its intention is to prevent a devolution revolution by claiming that the revolution is already under way and that it is having, and will have, devastating consequences, especially for the poor. The devolution-revolution metaphor has been remarkably successful, moreover. Since its invention four years ago, it has embedded itself in mainstream academic literature on American federalism as well as in textbooks on American government. The diffusion of this metaphor is probably due to several factors: (1) most academics in political science and public administration are liberal and, therefore, receptive to the message delivered by the devolution-revolution literature; (2) ever since Morton Grodzins popularized the marble-cake metaphor 40 years ago, much academic and journalistic writing about American federalism has been metaphor-driven rather than data- and theory-driven; and (3) most writers of American government textbooks do not specialize in the study of federalism.

This is not to say that the concerns addressed by the devolution-revolution literature are illegitimate. Reagan's 1980 presidential victory and the Republicans' 1994 congressional victory made conservatives electorally competitive for the first time since 1932, thus creating an embattled divide between liberals and conservatives about the nature and operation of government. This divide necessarily separates liberal supporters of New Deal and Great Society conceptions of expansive and benign federal power from conservatives who, since Dwight D. Eisenhower's presidency, have advocated limits on federal power and some restorations of powers to the states.

Proponents of real devolution argue that it will produce a more efficient and effective federal government and more robust and responsive states. The generally recognized objectives of devolution include (1) more efficient provision and production of public services; (2) better alignment of the costs and benefits of government for a diverse citizenry; (3) better fits between public goods and their spatial characteristics; (4) increased competition, experimentation, and innovation in the public sector; (5) greater responsiveness to citizen preferences; and (6) more transparent accountability in policymaking.

Opponents argue that devolution will cripple the federal government and allow the states to be more unresponsive to issues of concern to liberals. Opponents argue that devolution will (1) elevate efficiency over equity without even necessarily producing more efficiency; (2) dismantle redistributive social-welfare programs that should be financed and operated by the federal government; (3) produce competitive "races to the bottom" in which states and localities will reduce welfare spending, environmental regulation, consumer protection, and the like; (4) reduce accountability to citizens; (5) parochialize responsiveness to citizens, especially for middle and upper income citizens; and (6) reduce transparency in public policymaking by dividing it up among 50 states and thousands of localities.

Thus, ambitious claims are put forth by both sides; however, it is extremely difficult to evaluate these claims because, to date, there is no political consensus on devolution, no plan of execution, and few examples of devolution. Indeed, there are only two commonly cited examples of devolution: congressional repeal of the national 55-mph speed-limit and welfare reform. The prospects for significant devolution during the foreseeable future are not bright, largely because federal officials are reluctant to relinquish powers they have acquired in the twentieth century to advance national policy objectives. Hence, the only claim that can be evaluated is whether devolution is plodding along at a turtle's pace or racing ahead at a rabbit's pace.

Devolution and Dual Sovereignty

Strictly speaking, there can be no congressional devolution in the American federal system. Unlike British parliamentary supremacy, whereby Parliament can unilaterally devolve powers to regional and local authorities that possess no sovereignty, the U.S. Congress possesses only limited, delegated powers, and the U.S. Constitution establishes dual sovereignty characterized by the U.S. Supreme Court in 1869 as "an indestructible Union of indestructible States"[12]. The Congress possesses limited, enumerated powers delegated to it by the sovereign peoples of the several states; all other powers are reserved to the states or to the people as stipulated by the Tenth Amendment. The U.S. Constitution, therefore, does not contemplate devolution of powers from the federal capitol to the state capitols.

Furthermore, while the Constitution implicitly allows the states to exercise some powers that have been delegated to the Federal government but not exercised by the Congress (e.g., regulation of economic activities not regulated by the Congress under the interstate commerce clause), the Constitution does not authorize the Congress to exercise reserved powers of the states that are not exercised by some or all of the states. In other words, states have historically served as backstops for the federal government, reserving authority to act in the face of federal inaction so long as state action does not violate the U.S. Constitution or run afoul of what the U.S. Supreme Court calls the "dormant commerce clause" by enacting laws that interfere with interstate or foreign commerce even though the Congress has not occupied a policy field or preempted state action.

Dual sovereignty is further entrenched in the constitutional amendment processes (Art. V), which guarantee that no transfers of constitutional powers can be effected between the federal government and the states without the concurrent consent of the Congress and three-fourths of the state legislatures (or the people of the states, in the never-used constitutional-convention method of amendment). Changes in the allocation of constitutional powers require the joint consent of both the "indestructible Union" and the "indestructible States". If this were not the case, the United States would be a decentralized unitary polity rather than a noncentralized federal polity.

Defining Terms

Identifying "devolution", moreover, is not easy because the term is used loosely, and often interchangeably, with many other terms, such as "decentralization". For biologists, devolution means de-evolution, namely, evolutionary degeneration toward greater simplicity and, often, disappearance.

This is not the commonly understood political definition of devolution, although the biological definition might resonate with some advocates of devolution who envision a steadily shrinking federal government, as well as with some opponents of devolution who fear an enfeebling degeneration of federal power.

Ordinarily, devolution has been defined as a transfer of specific powers or functions from a superior government to a subordinate government. The transfer is of constitutional magnitude, even if not effected through a written constitution; it is ordinarily intended to be permanent; it surrenders all the powers associated with the devolved functions (namely, political, legislative, administrative, and fiscal); and it leaves the functional field vacant for occupancy by subordinate governments. Devolution occurs in the context of a vertical intergovernmental relations. Hence, devolution can occur within the British parliamentary system and can also be said to occur within the fifty American states where, constitutionally, local governments are creatures of their state, but it cannot occur between the U.S. government and the states without constitutional change.

Delegation can be defined as one government authorizing another government to carry out functions on its behalf, much like a representative. The implementing government remains accountable to the delegating government and may or may not enjoy freedom to design methods of implementation. Delegation can occur in the context of vertical or horizontal relationships between governments. Delegation is common in the American federal system and is, in reality, what is often labeled "devolution". The 1996 "welfare reform" act (The Personal Responsibility and Work Opportunity Reconciliation Act), for example, fits a delegation model much better than a devolution model because, even though delegation gives states greater discretion to design, implement, and finance certain welfare programs, the states remain accountable to the federal government and reliant on federal funds, and they are subject to penalties from federal authorities for failures to achieve federal performance objectives. The federal government can also prohibit certain modes of implementation, examples being President Bill Clinton's 1997 decisions (1) to prohibit the outsourcing of certain welfare functions to private firms and (2) to extend federal labor-law mandates to welfare recipients in state workfare programs.

Delegation, therefore, more accurately describes what has been mistakenly labeled "devolution". One suspects that the word "devolution" was selected to describe such policy delegation only because it rhymes better with "revolution" and has a better sound-bite ring than "delegation revolution" or "administrative flexibility revolution".

Deregulation (in the public sector) can be defined as the loosening or removal of regulations enacted or promulgated by one government to control or direct the behavior of another government or set of governments. The states, in principle, have plenary regulatory authority over their local governments, except where prohibited by the U.S. Constitution. The federal government has a limited range of direct regulatory authority over the states under the supremacy clause of the U.S. Constitution (Art. VI), although this clause has been broadened by twentieth-century interpretations of the Fourteenth Amendment (1868). The federal government has an even broader range of indirect regulatory authority over the states through grants-in-aid enacted pursuant to the Congress's spending and general welfare powers (Art. I, Sec. 8). The rise of "regulatory"[13] or "coercive" federalism[14] since the mid-1960s has become a matter of concern to most state and local officials; consequently, calls for intergovernmental deregulation are often intermixed and confused with calls for devolution.

Decentralization has been subject to a host of definitions, plus distinctions between legislative, administrative, political, fiscal, and spatial decentralization. Decentralization can be defined as the transfer of responsibilities of various kinds to subordinate administrative units or subordinate units of government, much like most states decentralize functions through counties. This was, for example, Alexis de Tocqueville's preferred model of federalism. Rather than "an incomplete national government" like that created by the U.S. Constitution, a strong federal union, according to de Tocqueville, needs a complete national government in which political power is centralized while administrative authority is decentralized through subordinate units of government like counties.[15] Given that the U.S. states are not county-like administrative arms of the federal government and given that the federal government is, in effect, an incomplete national government, the concept of decentralization, like devolution, does not fit the American federal polity, even though the net results of devolution, delegation, and deregulation may look like decentralization.[16]

If devolution and decentralization do not, strictly speaking, fit the American situation, then what is occurring, or being advocated, under the rubric of devolution? The answer would appear to be restoration, deaccession, and rebalancing: that is, limited restorations of powers to the states and their local governments as well as some deaccessions of functions no longer wanted by the federal government, which, together, could produce some rebalancing of power between the federal government and the states. Few of the powers and functions nominated as candidates for devolution were even exercised or performed by the federal government a generation or two ago. These powers and functions were exercised by the states or, in some cases, could have been, and perhaps should have been, exercised by the states under their general police power. Hence, when the U.S. Advisory Commission on Intergovernmental Relations advocated a shift of most federal highway functions and revenue sources to the states, the commission used the term "turnback", not devolution.[17] Similarly, the "devolution" language used most often by elected officials is that of restoring or reviving state powers or states' rights and rebalancing the federal system.[18]

Although we may be stuck with the term "devolution" because the media and some academics have embraced it, many different things are occurring in the federal system, some of which point, for the first time since the 1930s, to the possibility of restorations of some state powers and of limits on certain further expansions of federal power while, at the same time, centralization or "counter-devolution" continues apace.

Forces Favoring Restorations of State Powers

The most immediate force propelling discussions of shifting powers back to the states was the 1994 midterm elections, which brought a Republican majority into both houses of Congress. The 1994 elections ended more than 60 years of nearly continuous Democratic control of the Congress (with Democratic control of the U.S. House of Representatives having been the longest period of one-party rule in U.S. history) and also unseated an incumbent House Speaker for the only time in the twentieth century.

The Republicans' "Contract with America" contained several provisions aimed at curbing federal power and restoring state powers, beginning with mandate reform, which was enacted in 1995 with bipartisan support as the Unfunded Mandates Reform Act (UMRA). The state-friendly provisions of the "Contract with America" reflected Republican concerns dating back to

President Eisenhower, who had likened the centralization of power and the rise of the "military industrial complex" in the United States during the New Deal and World War II to the "extreme and dictatorial concentration of power" then occurring in communist Eastern Europe.[19]

Eisenhower was not, however, able to tilt power back toward the states. On the contrary, Eisenhower's nomination of Earl Warren to be chief justice of the U.S. Supreme Court, his support for the National Defense Highway Act of 1956 and for the National Defense Education Act of 1957, his dispatch of federal troops to Little Rock, Arkansas, in 1957 to enforce desegregation pursuant to the U.S. Supreme Court's ruling in *Brown vs. Board of Education* (1954), and other policy actions, all enhanced federal power. Thus, federal policymaking during the supposedly conservative 1950s reinforced Alpheus T. Mason's observation that: "For two generations American political and economic life has been moving swiftly toward 'bigness', toward monolithic organization".[20]

President Richard M. Nixon's New Federalism, which echoed Eisenhower's federalism sentiments, was, despite General Revenue Sharing (1972-1986), no more successful in stemming the growth of federal power. President Reagan began his administration in 1981 with strong support for a New Federalism aimed at shifting substantial power back to the states. Reagan's success was modest at best, and the federal government continued to expand its power through mandates, preemptions, and conditions attached to federal aid.[21]

This brief history suggests two hypotheses. First, many of the Republicans elected to the Congress in 1994 arrived with strong commitments to long-frustrated desires to limit federal power which for some, though not all, also meant restoring state powers. This was reinforced by the new Republicans elected from the increasingly Republican South and from the Mountain West - both growing regions historically suspicious of, and often hostile to, the federal government. Second, it is the Congress more often than the White House that alters the balance of power in the federal system. If these conclusions are correct, then some significant restorations of state powers are likely to occur if the Republicans maintain control of the Congress, if the Republicans capture the presidency in 2000, and if the federalism-friendly majority on the U.S. Supreme Court is maintained or increased after 2000.

These prospects are further strengthened by support for rebalancing federal-state power among more members of the Democratic party than was true in the past. In a 1997 statement, for example, the Democratic Leadership Council, with which President Clinton was affiliated, said:

> "The New Democrat movement has consistently rejected the old-fashioned liberal prejudice against state governments and state elected officials. . . .Now more than ever, state elected officials represent the future of our party and our country. State capitals are the battlegrounds where the big challenges of American domestic policy on the eve of the 21st century are being met."[22]

The 1996 Democratic party platform even claimed that "Republicans talked about shifting power back to the states and communities - Democrats are doing it."

This is a far cry from Governor George Wallace standing in the doorway of the University of Alabama in 1963 defying federal authority over racial desegregation, but the states have since experienced a remarkable rehabilitation, which has placed them in a more favorable light. Well into the 1970s, most Americans expressed more trust and confidence in the federal government than in the states. Since then, however, public trust and confidence - to the extent the public has any trust and confidence in any governments - has shifted gradually and substantially from the federal government to the states. For example, a 1995 poll conducted by Princeton Survey Research Associates found that 61 percent of Americans trusted their state government to "do a better job of running things" than the federal government. Nearly every subgroup except black Americans and Jews expressed similar support for the states. Adults under age thirty favored the states by 72 to 21 percent, Democrats, by 48 to 35 percent, and self-described liberals, by 49 to 36 percent[23]. These findings are consistent with trends in most polls asking similar questions for the past decade. Likewise, the trend toward increased public trust and confidence in state and local governments was sustained in a December 1999 poll.[24]

This opinion change is due partly to the "modernization" of state and local governments and political systems that has occurred since the 1950s, with much assistance and pressure from the federal government. The structural changes highlighted by most observers - such as constitutional revision, legislative reapportionment, professionalized legislatures, four-year tenure for 48 governors, and strengthened judiciaries[25] - have been important, but the most significant change has been the altered relationship between citizens and their state and local governments. State and local political systems are more electorally inclusive and representative of diversity than in the past, and they are no less inclusive than the federal arena. Previously excluded groups have more opportunities to win office and to gain employment in state and local governments than in the federal government. On average, state and local governments are also more accessible to citizen reform, not simply because they are smaller arenas but also because state constitutions and amendments require popular ratification in 49 states; because state constitutions compel recourse to the people and to supermajority consent on many important matters; and because a number of state constitutions give citizens initiative, referendum, and/or recall powers. The federal government is constitutionally impervious to direct citizen participation. State and local governments are also better equipped today than in the past to provide more and better services for citizens, and with the appearance of less corruption. Furthermore, state and local tax systems are more diversified than in the past and often less regressive than the federal tax system, where Social Security and Medicare taxes - the largest tax bites for most Americans - are regressive. In addition, most state and local governments have been more fiscally disciplined than the federal government.

The case for devolution has been bolstered as well by a recovering economy. As a result, most states had year-end budget surpluses during the 1990s; state and local government spending has increased by more than 14 percent in real terms since 1990; most states have reduced taxes; and state and local government employment has increased by about 1.8 million persons since 1990 while federal government employment has declined by more than 345,000 since 1990.

Adding force to rebalancing efforts has been migration to the suburbs and to the Sunbelt. The United States has been, and continues to be, a nation of small and medium-size communities. Never in the history of the United States have more than 30 percent of Americans lived in urban places having 100,000 or more residents. The high points of big-city life in America occurred between 1920 and 1970. By the late 1980s, the United States had become a suburban nation. In addition, population continues to migrate southward and westward as most Sunbelt states experience tremendous growth.

A major political characteristic of suburban life is local self-government, jealously guarded and combined with stout resistance to metropolitan consolidation or other arrangements perceived as hostile to local autonomy, as well as a proclivity for service-efficient council-manager governance free of "politics".[26] Hence, the suburban mentality is receptive to "devolution", and the federal government and most state governments have been deferential to this mentality. This deference is reflected, for instance, in the U.S. Supreme Court's unwillingness to extend court-ordered school busing beyond central-city boundaries, in the Congress's and the states' overwhelmingly preferential funding for highways rather than mass transit, in the unwillingness of both the federal government and the states to enforce fair housing laws with vigor, in the reduced federal funding since the Reagan era for metropolitan regional structures (e.g., councils of governments), and in the unwillingness of state legislatures to mandate consolidations of local governments.

Migration to the Sunbelt is having at least two devolutionary effects. For one, given that most Sunbelt states have, historically, been states' rights states, migration into those states has strengthened the states' rights voice in Washington, D.C. At the same time, migration has helped to "modernize" those states, to make many of them more progressive and innovative and to soften the hard surfaces, such as racism, historically characteristic of politics in many of those states. Migration has helped to pull the Sunbelt states toward the center of the national political spectrum while simultaneously pulling the national political center slightly rightward.

Stemming in part from this suburban and Sunbelt migration has been the emergence of Republican control of a majority of the governorships (32). On average, Republican governors have been more supportive of restoring state powers than Democratic governors, and Republican governors, for example, played a major role in shaping "welfare reform" in 1996. The governors, however, including Republican governors, do not champion state prerogatives across the board. Most governors continue to advocate federal preemptions of state powers in many areas affecting interstate commerce, and most governors supported the preemption-laden North American Free Trade Agreement (NAFTA) in 1993 and the Uruguay Round of the General Agreement on Tariffs and Trade (GATT) in 1994.

Both Democratic and Republican state and local officials have given strong support to deregulatory measures and other efforts to reduce federal "micromanagement" of state and local affairs. Here, elected state and local officials have been nearly unanimous, as reflected in their concerted lobbying for the Unfunded Mandates Reform Act. The state-local coalition constructed to support UMRA was unusual because state and local officials rarely speak with one voice in Washington, D.C.

Certain historical imperatives, especially the perceived fiscal crisis of the federal government, added force to rationales for shifting power toward the states. This was the reality facing President Clinton when he declared the end of the era of "big government". The weight of public opinion perceived these to be serious problems, even though the public did not endorse draconian remedies. The federal government lacks the fiscal resources, and perhaps the political will as well, to sustain, let alone augment, the kinds of expansive and state-intrusive policies associated with the New Deal of the 1930s and the Great Society of the 1960s. By a combination of default, deaccession, and disinvestment, therefore, certain powers and responsibilities must necessarily flow back to the states, and the Congress will likely dump certain fiscally onerous and politically volatile functions onto states and localities.

The growth of entitlement spending, which now dominates the federal budget, adds more pressure on Congress to off-load "discretionary" programs that carry real budget costs. Although the 1996 "welfare reform" ended a long-standing entitlement, its costs pale in comparison to the costs of Social Security, Medicare, and Medicaid. These entitlements are likely to remain entrenched federal responsibilities not only because they are advocated by influential reformers[27] but also because they are predominantly middle-class entitlements. Even Medicaid has become a middle-class entitlement because of the high costs of long-term health and nursing-home care for the elderly. Entitlement pressures on the federal budget will, moreover, begin to skyrocket in 2010 when the post-World War II baby boomers commence retirement.

Public disaffection from the federal government has also contributed to support for restoring state powers. The federal government has experienced an erosion of legitimacy in recent decades, coupled with disillusionment and skepticism about the efficacy of many federal programs - an attitude reinforced by a generally critical media. Although many federal programs are more successful than is generally believed by voters, reality is what citizens perceive it to be, and this perceived reality underwrote President Clinton's pledge to "reinvent" government and, among other things, "to end welfare as we know it". Whatever its past successes, welfare as Americans knew it became widely viewed as a failure.

Undoubtedly, some advocates of restored state powers desire little more than to shrink, even cripple, the federal government, while still others wish to abolish or reduce certain federal policies and programs by using the subterfuge of federalism to turn them over to the states where, they hope, the policies and programs will be dismantled or cut back. Such opportunistic forum shopping has long been common in the federal system, and one can expect the debate over restorations of state powers to continue to be clouded by opportunism.

Federal Actions Restoring State Powers and Limiting Federal Powers

Despite predictions of a "devolution revolution"[28] and prognostications of doom that "wholesale devolution invites the balkanization . . . of America"[29], there are few examples of "devolution", although a discernible crawl toward some rebalancing of the federal system is under way in the Congress, the Presidency, and the Supreme Court.

Congressional Federalism

Early steps toward rebalancing were General Revenue Sharing, enacted as the State and Local Fiscal Assistance Act of 1972, and enactment of two of six block grants proposed by President Nixon. GRS was created when it was still credible to argue that the federal government was positioned to generate surplus revenue that could be disbursed to fiscally handicapped state and local governments. GRS funds were delivered to state and local governments by formula and with few regulatory strings. The basic idea was that state and local governments, with citizen input, were best positioned to set priorities for spending GRS monies in ways most appropriate for their jurisdictions. The Congress expected GRS funds to be expended primarily for capital investments; however, many states and localities used GRS to support current operations and/or to reduce taxes. Such "misuses" of GRS confirmed the belief of skeptics that state and local governments cannot be trusted to behave responsibly without congressional direction and that restoring powers to state and local governments will not enhance policy efficiency, effectiveness, or equity. GRS was terminated for the states in 1980 and then allowed to expire for local governments in 1986.

Another step toward providing states with greater flexibility in using federal funds occurred when 77 categorical grants were consolidated into nine new or amended block grants in the Omnibus Budget Reconciliation Act of 1981. Although President Reagan had sought to consolidate about 85 categoricals into only seven block grants, the Congress refused to go that far. It also declined to remove as many grant reporting and oversight rules as had been proposed by Reagan. Nevertheless, the number of block grants leaped from four to twelve, and additional block grants were enacted up through the 1996 Temporary Assistance for Needy Families (TANF) block grant and the 1997 State Children's Health Insurance Plan block grant. Block grants, however, are not sterling examples of devolution for three reasons: (1) the Congress tends to re-categorize block grants over time, not only for political reasons but also for accountability reasons; (2) block grants have proven to be more vulnerable to funding reductions than categorical grants-in-aid; and (3) only about 15 percent of federal aid to state and local governments flows through block grants. The Congress has a distinct preference for more controlled categorical grants, and 618 such grants were funded in fiscal year 1995 compared to only 15 block grants.[30]

A de facto fiscal dumping of certain functions can be said to have occurred from 1978 to 1989 when federal aid to state and local governments declined from 17.0 percent of federal outlays to 10.7 percent, and federal aid as a proportion of state and local outlays declined from 26.5 percent to 17.3 percent. Although federal aid has since increased to about 22 percent of state and local outlays, functional dumping has continued because nearly two-thirds (63 percent) of federal aid is now dedicated for payments to individuals (mostly social welfare), whereas in 1978 more than two thirds (68 percent) of federal aid was dedicated for state and local government policy functions and operations.

Discussions of devolution, however, have been stimulated by more recent enactments. The Intermodal Surface Transportation Efficiency Act of 1991 (ISTEA), along with President George Bush's 1992 Executive Order 12803 on infrastructure privatization and President Clinton's similar 1994 Executive Order 12893, are cited by some observers as harbingers of devolution. ISTEA created a multimodal surface-transportation block grant, gave states more discretion over certain aspects of surface transportation while also requiring statewide transportation plans, placed more emphasis than previously on "performance" standards for states and localities, permitted funds transfers between transportation programs when requested by state officials or metropolitan planning organizations (MPOs), authorized the same state-local funding match for most programs so as not to disadvantage certain transportation choices, and provided the country's 339 MPOs with more authority over transportation planning and federal funds allocations. Although the outcomes of ISTEA appear to be generally satisfactory, there is also evidence that "regulatory and workload burdens have grown significantly"[31], particularly for MPOs.

Federal highway-aid, moreover, remains a prime target for congressional "crossover sanctions"[32]. These are reductions of aid to states that fail to comply with aid conditions that are arguably not germane to the aid's central objectives and original intentions. One of the first crossover sanctions was the Highway Beautification Act of 1965, which was prompted by Lady Bird Johnson's dislike of highway billboards. A recent prominent example is the 21-year-old drinking age requirement that was attached to federal highway-aid in 1984 and upheld by the U.S. Supreme Court in 1987.[33] However, the Congress did repeal a crossover sanction in 1996, namely, the 55-mph speed-limit enacted under the Emergency Highway Energy Act of 1976, thus giving states freedom to set highway speed-limits, but it also enacted a new condition requiring states to prohibit persons under age 21 from driving with a blood alcohol level of 0.02 percent or higher. Any state failing to enact a law to enforce this prohibition within three years of 1996 would have lost 5 percent of its federal highway-aid in the first year and 20 percent each year thereafter.

Amendments enacted in 1996 to the Safe Drinking Water Act of 1974 altered the regulatory regime within this field by giving states more funding to comply with environmental standards as well as more flexibility to exercise authority over drinking water standards and their enforcement. The act also responded favorably to complaints from local governments, especially small localities, about out-of-reach costs of bringing water systems into compliance with regulations and about time limits promulgated by the U.S. Environmental Protection Agency (EPA). Small jurisdictions can now choose to comply with alternative treatment and monitoring standards. Environmental remediation is likely to be a continuing intergovernmental issue because EPA has estimated that local governments will bear about 88 percent of the cost of public sector compliance.

Other recent measures viewed as restoring some state and local powers include food-safety legislation that withdrew an earlier standard of "zero cancer risk" for pesticide residue on processed food and provided instead for a uniform health-oriented standard for chemical residues on agricultural produce and processed food. The Selected Housing Program Extensions Act of 1996 delegated more powers to local public housing authorities to evict residents who abuse drugs or alcohol and to set aside housing exclusively for senior citizens and persons with disabilities. The commuter policies included in the 1990 Clean Air Act made voluntary previous mandates that had required states with carbon monoxide and ozone non-attainment areas to reduce employee commuting trips through car-pooling and other measures.

The Case of Welfare Reform.

The premier specimen of "devolution", however, is "welfare reform", which one observer terms "the most vivid example of authority cascading to lower levels of government".[34]

The devolutionary centerpiece of "welfare reform" is the Temporary Assistance for Needy Families (TANF) block grant. This reform eliminated the open-ended, matching-grant Aid to Families with Dependent Children (AFDC) entitlement, along with JOBS and Emergency Assistance. TANF will provide $16.38 billion per year to states during fiscal years 1997 to 2003 to operate time-limited cash-assistance for needy families, coupled with work requirements for most recipients. States can use their federal money in any way "reasonably calculated to accomplish the purposes of TANF" (Section 404(a)). States have broad discretion to determine eligibility, methods of assistance, and benefit levels; to operate new Food Stamp and employment and training programs; and to decentralize welfare functions to local governments. Many state officials, especially Republican governors, helped to shape TANF and supported its enactment. The legislation also made substantial though not always state-friendly changes in child care, the Child Support Enforcement program, Food Stamps, SSI for children, and benefits for legal immigrants. It also set funding for the Social Services Block Grant (SSBG) at $2.38 billion in fiscal years 1996-2002 and at $2.8 billion in fiscal year 2003 and thereafter. A number of technical changes have been made since 1996, most of which have been favorable to the states.

Three other elements of TANF are interesting for their implications of future restorations of state powers.

One is Section 417, which reads: "No officer or employee of the Federal Government may regulate the conduct of the States under this part or enforce any provision of this part, except to the extent expressly provided in this part." This signals the executive branch not to interpret the law liberally so as to extend regulations beyond the boundaries expressly set out by the Congress.

Second, TANF overturned *Shapiro vs. Thompson*[35] by allowing states to treat newly arrived welfare claimants differently than residential recipients by applying for up to 12 months the welfare rules of the migrant's former state of residence. This provision was intended to reduce rent-seeking migration that might drive states into "a race to the bottom", though more significant was the willingness of the Congress to overturn a 27-year-old state-restrictive and rights-protective ruling of the U.S. Supreme Court. In 1999, however, the Supreme Court struck back by striking down this provision as a violation of the right to travel.[36] What is also interesting about this case is that 41 social scientists submitted a brief disputing the idea that high-benefit states are "welfare magnets", thus contradicting one of the key arguments of opponents of devolution, namely, that devolution will produce a "race to the bottom" in state welfare-benefits. The "welfare magnet" notion was another metaphor that gained considerable acceptance by academics and journalists in the late 1980s and early 1990s, and continued to be influential despite repeated studies disproving the notion.[37]

Third, the Brown Amendment added to the Personal Responsibility and Work Opportunity Act of 1996 enhances the authority of state legislatures over budgetary and nonbudgetary aspects of devolution. The amendment affirms the authority of the legislatures to appropriate block grant monies for Temporary Assistance for Needy Families and for child-care development rather than leaving these matters in the hands of the governors who, in the past, had served essentially as administrative agents for the federal government. The amendment, therefore, also increases legislative leverage over the governor, places state legislatures on a more equal policymaking footing with governors and the Congress, and exposes welfare policymaking to greater voter input through legislative elections and popular initiatives.

While the above provisions constitute the major "devolutionary" elements of "welfare reform", other provisions suggest a continuing and enhanced federal regulatory role. For example:

- States cannot use federal funds to aid families that have received TANF-related assistance for a cumulative total of five years, although states can set time limits under five years, and they can exempt up to 20 percent of their caseload in any one year from the five-year limit.

- States must meet maintenance-of-effort rules requiring them to spend on TANF-related activities 80 percent of what they spent with state and local funds on AFDC and related programs in fiscal year 1994.

- States can lose up to 25 percent of their TANF allotment for failure to meet work participation requirements, which increase annually so that by 2002, 50 percent of all recipients from all welfare families should be working at least 30 hours per week, and 90 percent of all recipients from two-parent welfare families should be working at least 35 hours per week. (Although most states are rhetorically emphasizing "work first", most have used a waiver in the law that allows them to opt out of the workfare mandate. For example, Massachusetts "has excused 82 percent of the 72,500 families on the rolls from the 60-day workfare deadline".[38] Many states are also diverting families from multi-year cash assistance to part-time work and to short-term service provision, such as job-search programs and education.)

- States can be penalized for failure to participate in the Income and Eligibility Verification System and for failures to submit required reports to federal officials.

- States must comply with paternity establishment and child-support enforcement rules set by the federal government, and states can be penalized up to 5 percent of their TANF grant for failure to deduct a minimum of 25 percent from a family's cash assistance when the recipient does not cooperate with child-support rules without good cause.

- States must enact laws to suspend driver's, professional, occupational, and recreational licenses of individuals whose child-support payments are in arrears.

- Pursuant to welfare reform as well as immigration reform, Social Security numbers must be recorded on a variety of official documents, including driver's licenses and birth certificates.

- States must maintain assistance when parents cannot locate child care for a child under age 6.

- States must use at least 4 percent of their combined grant funds under TANF and the newly consolidated Child Care and Development Block Grant to increase the availability and improve the quality of child care.

- States must implement Electronic Benefit Transfer programs by October 1, 2002, unless waived by the U.S. Department of Agriculture.

- Beginning in fiscal year 1998, a mandatory formula grant was added to the Maternal and Child Health Block Grant to provide $50 million annually to states to operate abstinence sex-education programs.

- No more than 15 percent of a state's TANF grant can be used for administration.

If "welfare reform" is a vivid illustration of "devolution", then the states may find themselves in the proverbial predicament of the dog who finally catches the speeding car. The states won new discretion and flexibility to design, fund, and operate welfare programs, but they also inherited onerous and prescriptive requirements, especially in work participation and child support (although the 43 states that had already received waivers to reform welfare do not have to comply with every aspect of the new act for five years).

In effect, the federal government is requiring the states to accomplish what the federal government could not accomplish during its 60-some years of co-funding, overseeing, and tinkering with welfare. When states fail to meet the work-participation requirements, or to meet them adequately with upwardly mobile jobs that do not displace currently working low-income persons, they will likely be criticized as being unfit for devolution.

Several other aspects of "welfare reform" are problematic too. The anticipated reduction of $54 billion in federal welfare spending during the six years following reform and the caps on federal funding for TANF and the SSBG could prove costly for states during recessions. Local governments will be the most fiscally vulnerable because persons who fall through the safety net will land on their doorsteps. In addition, the restriction requiring state use of federal funds for abstinence-only sex education is an extraordinary dismissal of state prerogatives, although it is consistent with the "family values" advocated by many Republicans in Congress. It is also consistent, for example, with the Defense of Marriage Act of 1996, which, while relieving the states of a constitutional obligation to recognize same-sex marriages solemnized out of state, also establishes a national definition of marriage as a heterosexual union for purposes of federal benefits. The power to define marriage, including marriage for federal-benefit purposes, had belonged exclusively to the states since 1776.

In 1997, President Clinton and congressional Republicans concluded a budget agreement that includes a new program to provide $24 billion to the states over five years to cover uninsured children for health care. The law gives states implementation choices, such as bringing uninsured children into Medicaid, into a state's largest health-maintenance organization, into a state's health insurance program for public employees, or into programs comparable to health insurance for federal employees. Forty-eight states submitted plans fairly quickly to participate in this program,[39] however, it is too early to assess this program's success, although one news reporter called it the devolution dilemma. The good news is that the five-year budget deal the president signed in May 2000 gives states a free hand and $24 billion in new money to extend medical coverage to millions of uninsured children.

The bad news: State officials may be unprepared to assume control of the largest expansion in health care services in 30 years.[40]

One can point to other hints of delegation-like elements in congressional policymaking, but, in the final analysis, there have been few substantive turnbacks of functions from the federal government to the states.

Presidential Federalism

President Clinton came into office two years before the congressional Republicans. He also promised to restore state powers: "I intend to do my very best", he told the governors, "to be faithful to the lessons that I learned as a governor - that most of what you do ought to be done by you and not by us".[41] Yet, conclusions similar to those for the Congress pertain to Clinton's initiatives, beginning with his "reinventing government" campaign headed by Vice President Al Gore under the name National Performance Review (NPR). Although NPR addressed a wide range of management issues primarily within the federal government, the NPR report, issued in September 1993, contained the following intergovernmental recommendations.

1. Create flexibility and encourage innovation by designing a bottom-up solution to the problem of grant proliferation and its accompanying red tape. Also, support the pending proposal for Federal-State Flexibility Grants that has been developed by the National Governors' Association and the National Conference of State Legislatures. Establish a Cabinet-level Enterprise Board to oversee new initiatives in community improvement.

2. Issue an Executive Order addressing the problems of unfunded federal mandates and regulatory relief and authorize Cabinet Secretaries and agency heads to obtain selective relief from regulation or mandates in programs they oversee.

3. Modify OMB Circular A-87, "Cost Principles for State and Local Governments", to provide a fixed fee-for-service option in lieu of costly reimbursement procedures covering actual administrative costs of grant disbursements.

4. Simplify OMB's requirements to prepare multiple grant compliance certifications by allowing state and local governments to submit a single certification to a single point of contact in the federal government.

5. Modify OMB Circular A-102, "Grants and Cooperative Agreements to State and Local Governments", to increase the dollar threshold for small purchases by local governments from $25,000 to $100,000.

6. Reinvent the Advisory Commission on Intergovernmental Affairs (ACIR) and charge it with the responsibility for continuous improvement in federal, state and local partnership and intergovernmental service delivery. Direct the ACIR to identify opportunities to improve intergovernmental service delivery and develop a set of benchmarks.[42]

Many other recommendations affecting intergovernmental relations were embedded elsewhere in the NPR report.

NPR's recommendations were modest. The first recommendation, similar to the block grant proposals of Reagan's New Federalism, called for consolidating 55 categorical grants worth $12.5 billion into broader "flexibility grants". This recommendation has not been enacted by the Congress, but President Clinton did endorse "bottom-up" consolidation plans submitted by Indiana and West Virginia in 1994 to coordinate 199 federal grants affecting children and families, thus setting precedent for other states to follow suit. When the new Republican Congress floated proposals for larger block grants that would have included major entitlement programs, Clinton opposed most of the proposals, arguing that these programs need a significant, continuing federal role. The Republicans' major block grant proposals covered cash welfare-benefits (consolidating seven programs), child welfare and abuse (consolidating 38 programs), child care (45 program consolidations), food and nutrition (10 consolidations), housing (27 consolidations), health (22 consolidations), Medicaid, employment and training (154 consolidations), social services (33 consolidations), and law enforcement (12 consolidations). The first result was a mouse: a small block grant, approved in 1995, which authorized $503 million for local law-enforcement.

Federal categorical grants continued to proliferate during the Clinton Presidency, reaching more than 640 by 1996. Categoricals procreate not only because the Congress is reluctant to channel funds to states through more discretionary block grants, but also because small grants provide a means to satisfy various interest groups with small federal expenditures.

Pursuant to NPR's first recommendation, the administration established a Community Enterprise Board in 1993, chaired by the vice president. Among other things, the board coordinates the administration's implementation of the Local Empowerment and Flexibility Act of 1994 through 31 empowerment zones, two supplemental empowerment zones, and 95 enterprise communities, four of which are enhanced enterprise zones. This act is one of the economic development benefits the administration was able to obtain for local governments, and it does provide significant flexibility for local governments.[43]

"Designated zones and communities receive tax benefits and flexible grants and are entitled to apply for waivers of certain federal regulations; the underlying principle of the program is that communities know best how to solve their own problems but may lack the necessary resources."[44]

Progress has been made on the second through fifth recommendations[45], in part because implementation of these primarily administrative recommendations requires little if any congressional consent. In the process, the administration has also given the regional offices of many federal agencies more decision-making authority. This has especially been the case for the U.S. Department of Housing and Urban Development, which is important to the president's relations with the country's mayors and other local officials.

Regarding NPR's last recommendation, the administration initially tried to reinvigorate ACIR, but the commission was de-funded in 1996. The president did not defend it, primarily because ACIR's staff had produced a preliminary report (required by the Unfunded Mandates Reform Act) that recommended reductions and terminations of a number of federal mandates. The report sparked a political firestorm; more than 300 interest groups, many representing constituencies important to President Clinton, lined up against the report; and the commission killed the report in a partisan vote.[46]

The Clinton administration has also sought to create more flexibility in federal-state relations by establishing "performance partnerships", whereby states develop performance measures for implementing federal programs and rules; in return, they are given more flexibility by federal agencies to meet their performance objectives. The most developed performance partnership was forged with Oregon, which conducted a six-year statewide initiative to identify benchmarks against which to measure its policy progress. The benchmarks also apply to performance-based contracts between state and federal agencies under conditions that eliminate or relax the requirements attached to multiple categorical grants.[47]

EPA has sought to build a "National Environmental Performance Partnership System" to give states more voice in program decision-making and, in the case of states meeting performance objectives, reduce EPA's regulatory oversight. EPA has also asked the Congress to enact performance partnership grants that would enable states to consolidate multiple EPA grants and use them more flexibly.[48] The General Accounting Office noted in early 1996 that:

> "The historically poor EPA-state relationship has improved, but it continues to be strained, and program implementation suffers as a result. . . .EPA has taken positive, though tentative, steps toward improving its relationship with the states, in particular trying to provide the states with the flexibility to achieve cost efficiencies and to address the states' priorities. However, one of the root causes of the agency's past problems - a prescriptive, media-based legislative framework - remains firmly in place."[49]

Under the Government Performance and Results Act of 1993, the administration also launched pilot projects to develop performance measures in selected units in all Cabinet departments and a number of independent agencies. Each unit began to develop a strategic plan, define its mission, set goals, and establish performance standards for measuring results. These pilot projects were then extended to a number of federal grant programs, particularly Goals 2000 for education.

The second phase of reinventing government was initiated in President Clinton's fiscal year 1996 budget proposals, which contained sweeping intergovernmental reforms involving greater scope for program devolution to the states, program terminations, grant consolidations, privatization, and more performance partnerships. The administration proposed, for example, to consolidate many U.S. Department of Transportation grants into three block-like programs: a discretionary grant, a more unified allocation of transportation funds to state and local governments, and the establishment of state infrastructure banks. Clinton also proposed to consolidate 60 programs managed by the U.S. Department of Housing and Urban Development into three, more flexible and performance-based programs for community economic opportunity, affordable housing, and modernization of public housing. Altogether, the administration proposed to consolidate 271 grant programs. These more sweeping proposals of the second wave of "reinventing government" appear to have been motivated in part by a belief that the Republican Congress would be more receptive to such consolidations than previous Democratic Congresses and in part as a counterplay to Republican block grant proposals.

The most significant block grant signed by Clinton, of course, was Temporary Assistance for Needy Families. After his own welfare-reform initiative failed to gain steam, Clinton pledged to the governors to expedite administrative waivers for welfare experimentation and to make changes in Food Stamp rules. From the states' perspective, however, the waiver process moved too slowly. The average wait for approval was 210 days.[50] Initially, Clinton vetoed a Republican welfare-reform measure in December 1995, which included sizable reductions in Medicaid spending, as well as a follow-up measure in January 1996. After gaining some concessions from the Congress, especially the removal of Medicaid from the proposal, Clinton signed the Personal Responsibility and Work Opportunity Reconciliation Act of 1996.

Aside from the "devolutionary" elements of TANF, very little in the president's rhetoric and that of members of the Congress suggests that devolution or even delegation was a fundamental principle or primary objective of welfare reform. Instead, reform seemed far more motivated by election-year political advantage. The stigma attached to welfare and the weakened political clout of interest-group advocates for welfare made AFDC a much easier candidate for conversion to a block grant than any of the other block grants proposed by the Republicans. Indeed, opposing the other block grant proposals contributed to President Clinton's increasingly successful reelection strategy of portraying the Republicans as radical opponents of benign government and as insensitive to the needs of children, women, senior citizens, minorities, and the poor. As a Democrat, moreover, Clinton believes in most of the programs targeted for reform by the Republicans; consequently, his Democratic principles took precedence over his federalism principles. While being tough on welfare, Clinton could not appear to participate in what columnist Carl Rowan saw as the consequences of the Republican revolution: "'States rights' is about to reign again in America, and millions of Americans are going to be hurt by it."[51]

Clinton has also supported regulatory and mandate relief for state and local governments, and initially responded administratively to state and local concerns. On September 30, 1993, he issued Executive Order 12866, "Regulatory Planning and Review". A major purpose of this executive order is to ease the federal regulatory burden on state, local, and tribal governments by planning the issuance of regulations more carefully; coordinating and streamlining regulations; consulting closely and regularly with state, local, and tribal officials; and limiting the promulgation of regulations only to those "required by law, or [that] are made necessary by compelling public need, such as material failures of private markets to protect or improve the health and safety of the public, the environment, or the well-being of the American people." Although this clause leaves open a wide field of action for federal regulators, the basic intent of the executive order is to limit the impacts of federal mandates on states and localities to what is required by law or to what is reasonably necessary.

On October 26, 1993, Clinton issued another executive order (E.O. 12875) entitled "Enhancing the Intergovernmental Partnership". This order was a preemptive response to "National Unfunded Mandates Day", a protest held by state and local officials on October 27. The executive order requires federal agencies to expedite and streamline their waiver-application processes for state, local, and tribal governments. "Furthermore, E.O. 12875 declares that no agency shall promulgate any regulation not required by statute or impose a mandate on a state, local, or tribal government, unless: (1) funds necessary to pay the direct costs incurred by the state, local, or tribal government for complying with the mandate are provided by the federal government, and (2) the agency provides, before the formal promulgation of regulations, a description of consultations with state, local, and tribal representatives, the nature of their concerns, and the agency's position supporting the need to issue the regulation containing the mandate."[52] Subsequently, Clinton supported and signed the Unfunded Mandates Reform Act of 1995.

Nevertheless, despite Clinton's sympathy for state and local concerns about mandates, he has signed many bills containing mandates, such as the Handgun Violence Prevention Act of 1993 (the Brady Bill), the Family and Medical Leave Act of 1993, the Full Faith and Credit for Child Support Order Act of 1994, the Multiethnic Placement Act of 1994, the Safe Drinking

Water Act of 1996, the Health Insurance Portability and Accountability Act of 1996, and the federal Megan's Law of 1997.

In examples in other fields, the Student Loan Reform Act of 1993 requires states where institutions of higher education have a student-loan default rate of more than 20 percent to assume partial responsibility for the cost of the defaults. The 1993 Reform Amendments to the Hatch Act prohibit any elected state official from making or transmitting to any officer or employee of a federal agency, any verbal or written recommendation or statement about an employee or applicant, except for recommendations based solely on job performance. The Comprehensive Child Health Immunization Act of 1993 requires state Medicaid programs to cover some recommended childhood vaccines and to reimburse providers for administering vaccines. The National Child Protection Act of 1994 requires authorized state criminal justice agencies to report child-abuse crime information to the national criminal background-check system.

The Special Case of Crime

President Clinton has also contributed to the extraordinary federalization of criminal law that has occurred since the late 1960s. Thomas Jefferson, in drafting the Kentucky Resolutions of 1798 in response to the Federalists' Alien and Sedition Acts, noted

> "that the Constitution of the United States... delegated to Congress a power to punish treason, counterfeiting the securities and current coin of the United States, piracies and felonies committed on the high seas, and offenses against the laws of nations, and no other crimes whatever."

In short, the U.S. Constitution specifies only four criminal offenses punishable by the federal government. Today, the federal government can punish individuals for more than 3,000 criminal offenses and invoke the death penalty for more than 50 offenses, including federal criminal offenses committed in the 13 states that prohibit capital punishment. This federalization of criminal law is a matter of growing alarm to civil libertarians.

Although even the administration's 1992 policy blueprint "Mandate for Change" identified crime as a policy area in which "no federal role is justified", Clinton strongly advocated The Violent Crime Control and Law Enforcement Act of 1994. This act provides $39.3 billion to state and local governments over a six-year period for prisons, 100,000 "cops on the beat", drug treatment in prisons, youth-crime prevention, and other programs. The law requires, as a condition of full funding, that states, among other things, enact a truth-in-sentencing statute, assure that violent offenders serve a substantial portion of their sentences, recognize victims' rights, and register violent sexual offenders upon their release from prison and being placed on parole or on supervised release. A current address for the offender must be provided to a designated law-enforcement agency. The statute also requires clerks of state courts to report to the Internal Revenue Service information on persons who post cash bail-bonds in excess of $10,000.

Clinton pressed for this legislation, in part, because being "tough on crime" has become politically popular for presidents and members of Congress from both political parties. Republicans are no less eager than Democrats to intrude upon traditional state and local prerogatives when it comes to "fighting crime". Clinton also advocated this legislation because it was a backdoor mechanism for channeling more federal money to local governments, especially big cities - a prime Democratic constituency. Congressional Republicans attacked this strategy and succeeded in reducing the final flow of money to local governments.

In summary, flexibility for state and local administration of federal programs, not devolution of federal programs, has been the hallmark of the Clinton administration. Although President Clinton has supported and implemented devolution-like measures that have provided greater administrative flexibility and regulatory relief for state and local governments, the president, like the Congress, has not sent "authority cascading to lower levels of government", nor has he acted to constrain significantly his ability to support or implement virtually any politically desirable mandate. Even Clinton's first use of the line-item veto in 1997 was anti-devolutionary because one of the three items struck from the budget was a waiver that had been granted by the U.S. Department of Health and Human Services (HHS) to New York State to tax health-care providers to help cover Medicaid costs. One of the ironies, then, of Clinton's presidency is that when the Congress was in Democratic hands, he could not push his intergovernmental reform agenda far enough because of old-guard opposition. Now that the Congress is in Republican hands, he cannot go far enough to support the Republicans' more ambitious devolution proposals.

Judicial Federalism

In contrast to the Congress and the presidency, the United States Supreme Court is playing a major role in restoring state powers and rebalancing the federal system because the accession of power by the federal government during the twentieth century required judicial deference to broad interpretations of the Congress's constitutionally enumerated powers as well as activist judicial interpretations of the U.S. Constitution, especially the Fourteenth Amendment and the Bill of Rights.

This is one reason why issues of fidelity to constitutional federalism and of constitutional amendments to rebalance federal-state power have surfaced in the Congress and in the states. A proposed Enumerated Powers Act, for example, would require the "Congress to specify the source of authority under the United States Constitution for the enactment of laws." A proposed Tenth Amendment Enforcement Act is intended to have a similar effect. Neither of these bills is likely to be enacted, although the U.S. House of Representatives did adopt a rule in early 1997 requiring committee reports on bills to cite each bill's constitutional authority. State legislators and governors have also debated four statutory and constitutional proposals developed at their 1995 Federalism Summit:

- A federalism act to enhance political safeguards of federalism and give states a more effective voice in congressional deliberations.

- A mechanism to provide the people of the states, through their legislatures, the power to require Congress to reconsider laws, specific provisions of laws, or regulations that interfere with state authority.

- A mechanism that would allow the states to propose specific amendments to the U.S. Constitution subject to ratification by the United States Congress.

- Statutory remedies and/or constitutional reforms to address the problems of conditions attached to [federal] spending grants, regulations, and mandates.[53]

Portions of these statutory proposals might be enacted by the Congress, but the proposed constitutional amendments are unlikely to pass muster in the Congress and the state legislatures. Indeed, in August 1997, the National Conference of State Legislatures failed to achieve a three-fourths vote to endorse the above constitutional proposals. Many legislators believe that the Congress and the U.S. Supreme Court are moving in a state-friendly direction and that constitutional change is not now necessary.

Consequently, in late 1997, state legislators and governors adopted an 11-point plan for statutory federalism reform: (1) declare and justify the constitutionality of legislation enacted by the Congress; (2) limit and clarify federal preemption of state law; (3) prohibit federal conscription and coercion of state governments; (4) use points of order on the floors of the U.S. House and U.S. Senate to help protect states against excessive mandates and preemptions; (5) consolidate many more categorical grants-in-aid into block grants; (6) protect state laws and procedures in expending federal funds; (7) prohibit conditions of federal aid not germane to aid purposes; (8) clarify the intent of the Unfunded Mandates Reform Act; (9) require congressional and executive federalism-impact statements for proposed bills and regulations; (10) streamline federal regulatory procedures; and (11) simply federal financial reporting requirements.

Given the reluctance of state leaders to redress state powers through constitutional change, questions of constitutional federalism and the parameters of congressional power are being decided principally by the U.S. Supreme Court. In the 1990s, the Court turned away from its 1985 ruling in *Garcia vs. San Antonio Metropolitan Transit Authority*[54] in which the Court sought to abandon its role as umpire of the federal system by holding that states could not seek Tenth Amendment redress from the Court for federal encroachments upon state powers. Instead, the states, like interest groups, would have to rely on the political safeguards of federalism to defend their powers in the national political arena.

Although the Court has not overturned *Garcia*, it has increasingly ignored it by seeking to limit federal authority and to protect or restore state authority in seven basic ways.[55]

State Autonomy

First, Justice Sandra Day O'Connor has advanced a "state autonomy" defense of federalism[56] based on the Tenth Amendment and the U.S. Constitution's republican guarantee clause (Article IV, Section 4). In this view, the federal government cannot deprive citizens of a state of their essential democratic right to make fundamental decisions about their state polity. O'Connor advanced this argument in *Gregory vs. Ashcroft* (1991), which upheld a provision of the Missouri Constitution requiring state judges to retire at age 70 despite the federal Age Discrimination in Employment Act (ADEA). What is especially interesting in this era of individual rights is O'Connor's reconceptualization of the Tenth Amendment as not protecting traditional states' rights but, rather, as protecting the dual citizenship rights of state residents. As O'Connor has argued repeatedly:

> "The Constitution divides authority between federal and state governments for the protection of individuals. State sovereignty is not just an end in itself: Rather federalism secures to citizens the liberties that derive from the diffusion of sovereign power. . ."[57]

Nevertheless, this doctrine is still narrow, lacks majority support, and is weakened by O'Connor's concession that the Congress could have extended the reach of the ADEA to cover state judges if it had "expressly" declared its intent to restrict state governments.

Plain Statements

A second judicial strategy is to require "express" or "plain statements" in legislation of the Congress's intent to preempt state authority (e.g., *Gregory vs. Ashcroft* 1991); to abrogate states' Eleventh Amendment immunity[58]; to permit civil-rights suits against states under 42 U.S.C. Section 1983[59]; and to attach conditions to grants-in-aid.[60] These rules are also limited, however, because this strategy allows the Congress to expand its power simply by "expressly" stating its intent to do so.

Federal Conscription.

A third strategy is to prohibit the Congress from "conscripting" or "commandeering" state officials to carry out federal laws. This doctrine was best articulated in *New York vs. United States*[61]. Here, the Court declared unconstitutional the "take title" provision of the federal Low-Level Radioactive Waste Disposal Act. This statute requires states to provide for the proper disposal of low-level radioactive waste within their own borders or in other states through interstate compacts. Failure to do so by 1996 would have required state governments to take title to such waste and be liable for harms caused by them. The Court held that the Congress violated the Tenth Amendment by compelling states to enact such laws and regulations.

Justice O'Connor's state autonomy argument also figured in this decision, but with a new twist. The "take title" provision had been enacted as part of a set of compromises negotiated between the governors and the Congress. Hence, the National Governors' Association vetoed a proposal for the State and Local Legal Center to file a state-supportive *amicus brief* in *New York*. The Council of State Governments, therefore, filed, for the first time, an *amicus brief* before the Court. The majority opinion held that even though the "take title" provision was an example of cooperative federalism, the governors lacked authority under the Tenth Amendment to surrender state sovereignty to the Congress and thereby sell out the citizenship rights of state taxpayers.

This anti-conscription doctrine was in 1997 reaffirmed in *Printz vs. United States* [62] wherein the Court struck down the provision in the Brady Handgun Control Act that required local law-enforcement officers to conduct background checks of handgun buyers. Justice Antonin Scalia delivered an impassioned opinion upholding "dual sovereignty" in the federal system and protecting the sovereignty of the states against congressional encroachments through liberal interpretations of the "necessary and proper" clause of Art. 1, Sec. 8 of the federal Constitution.

Limits on the Commerce Power.

A new strategy not seen since 1936 emerged in *United States vs. Lopez*[63], in which the Court struck down the Gun-Free School Zones Act of 1990 as an unconstitutional exercise of the Congress's interstate commerce power. During oral argument, the solicitor general was asked to identify a human activity that could not be brought under congressional regulation through broad interpretation of the commerce clause. The solicitor general could not identify a single activity. Reversing 60 years of precedent, the majority opined: "To uphold the Government's contentions here, we would have to pile inference upon inference in a manner that would bid fair to convert congressional authority under the Commerce Clause to a general police power of the sort retained by the States."

Indeed, in May 2000, the Court issued its second decision in line with *Lopez*. In *U.S. vs. Morrison*, the Court struck down a key provision of the 1994 Violence Against Women Act (VAWA) as an unconstitutional overextension of Congress's commerce power as well as its power under the Fourteenth Amendment. Although it is unlikely that the Court will roll back congressional economic regulation in significant ways, *Lopez* and *Morrison* signal the Congress that the Court is prepared in limited but sometimes politically explosive ways to prohibit regulation that unduly restricts state powers in areas not substantially related to interstate commerce.

State Immunity

In a fifth strategy, the Court has resurrected the Eleventh Amendment to the U.S. Constitution. This amendment affirms the immunity of states against lawsuits in federal courts filed by "Citizens of another State, or by Citizens or Subjects of any Foreign State." As with the Tenth Amendment, the Court had been willing since the New Deal to allow the Congress to abrogate states' Eleventh Amendment immunity for various reasons, especially federal needs to protect individual rights. Beginning in 1996, however, the Court began to strike down some congressional abrogations of states' immunity.[64] The Court has continued this trend in subsequent decisions, especially *Alden vs. Maine*[65], *College Savings Bank vs. Florida Prepaid Postsecondary Education Expense Board*[66], *Florida Prepaid Postsecondary Education Expense Board vs. College Savings Bank*[67], and *U.S. vs. Morrison*[68]. The net effect of these decisions is to cripple the enforcement of certain federal laws by declaring that states are immune from suits brought by citizens against them under these federal laws in federal or state courts. For example, under VAWA, a woman could file suit under VAWA in a federal or state court against a man who had raped or otherwise assaulted her. Congress enacted the VAWA on (1) Fourteenth Amendment grounds that state courts are biased against crimes committed against women and, thus, do not afford women sufficient justice under state laws and on (2) commerce-clause grounds that violence against women has adverse effects on interstate commerce. In *U.S. vs. Morrison*, the Court invalidated both of these grounds as being unconstitutional.

Laboratories of Democracy

A sixth strategy is a "laboratories of democracy" view of state powers, derived from Justice Louis D. Brandeis' famous opinion that "a single courageous state may, if its citizens choose, serve as a laboratory, and try social and economic experiments without risk to the rest of the country".[69] This view was expressed in a quite different context than today when many states were enacting innovative and progressive rights and social welfare laws while the Congress and especially the Supreme Court were often hostile to such initiatives.

This strategy was reflected in *Vacco vs. Quill*[70] and *Washington vs. Glucksberg*[71], wherein the Court declined to recognize physician-assisted suicide as a fundamental right under the Fourteenth Amendment to the U.S. Constitution, thus upholding state prohibitions of physician-assisted suicide. The Court did not deny that such a right might exist; it held instead that hitherto unrecognized Fourteenth Amendment rights must be deeply rooted in the nation's history, legal traditions, and moral practices, not in "the policy preferences of the members of this Court." Hence, the Court reserved to the democratic processes of the 50 states the task of deciding, over the long term, whether physician-assisted suicide is to be recognized as a fundamental right. There is "no reason to think the democratic process will not strike the proper balance", wrote the majority.

A corollary to this strategy is the Court's endorsement of "the new judicial federalism"[72] in *Michigan vs. Long*[73], which immunizes from federal judicial review state judicial and legislative expansions of individual rights protections based on "independent and adequate" state constitutional grounds that go beyond rights protections recognized by the U.S. Supreme

Court under the U.S. Constitution. For example, the federal Court has ruled that the right of household privacy and protection against warrantless searches and seizures does not cover trash placed outside one's home for public collection. The New Jersey Supreme Court, however, has ruled that state and local police in the Garden State do need, pursuant to the state constitution, a warrant to search someone's curbside trash. State high courts have issued about 800 such rights - expansive rulings since the mid-1970s. Similarly, even though the U.S. Supreme Court struck down the federal Religious Freedom Restoration Act of 1993 (RFRA) in June 1997, the New York State Assembly passed a state RFRA in early August 1997 in direct reaction to the Court's rights-restrictive ruling.

Final Arbiter of the Constitution

A seventh, related strategy was reflected in *City of Boerne vs. Flores*[74], which struck down the Religious Freedom Restoration Act. "The power to interpret the Constitution in a case or controversy remains in the judiciary", opined the majority, and the Congress has no authority to expand the scope of the Fourteenth Amendment beyond the "proportionality and congruence" of the problem being addressed by legislation. Many state and local officials contested RFRA because it required them to demonstrate a "compelling interest" justification for restricting religious freedom. Justice Anthony Kennedy wrote that RFRA was a "considerable intrusion into the states' traditional prerogatives and general authority to regulate for the health and welfare of their citizens." More generally, since the Court's ruling on abortion in *Roe vs. Wade*[75], the Court has often curbed, reduced, or declined to expand individual rights, especially in criminal proceedings, that excessively intrude or impose upon state and local governments.

The Court has acted in other ways to protect the states by showing greater deference to state-court proceedings under the abstention doctrine, by restricting the authority of federal judges to entertain habeas corpus claims from state prisoners, by upholding various types of state economic regulation, and by loosening the constraints of some federal court orders.

In summary, the U.S. Supreme Court has returned to the field to umpire the constitutional game of federal-state power-balancing with rulings surprisingly favorable to the states; however, there has been no wholesale restoration of state powers or denigration of federal powers, nor is the Court in a political position today to make the kind of swift "switch in time that saved nine" that it made in 1937. Instead, the Court has breathed new life into constitutional federalism through emerging doctrines pregnant with implications for future umpiring more supportive of state sovereignty. The cases conveying these doctrines, however, are of limited scope, uncertain precedent, and mixed motives, and are supported only by 5-to-4 and 6-to-3 majorities. If only one justice in the majority in most of these federalism cases - especially William Rehnquist, Sandra Day O'Connor, or Clarence Thomas - were to be replaced by a justice with the minority views expressed in these cases, the umpire might retire from the field again or, at best, oversee the game from the bleachers. This is why appointments to the Court have become an issue in the 2000 presidential election. As one Democratic pollster declared: "The American people are hanging on the 5-4 majority and the federalism issue! In focus groups they talk about it all the time!"[76]

In summary, then, no substantial shift of power to the states has yet been executed, and the most oft-cited example of devolution, namely, "welfare reform", was driven as much or more by the political advantages of ending welfare as Americans knew it as by principled arguments for restoring federalism as Americans once knew it. These turtle steps toward devolution are potentially significant but currently limited because the debate over federalism is part of a larger debate over the nature and future of American society. The United States is perhaps on the threshold of a paradigm shift comparable to those of the Civil War, Progressive, and New Deal-Great Society eras. Consequently, emerging forces favoring rebalancing necessarily collide with obstacles to restoring state powers.

Forces Favoring Preservation of Federal Powers

One obstacle to "devolution" is public opinion. Even though there is a generalized public preference for local and state performance of public functions, just as there is a generalized preference for a balanced federal budget, each particular "devolution" proposal like each particular item slated for a budget cut encounters opposition from beneficiaries anxious to maintain the status quo while being willing to devolve someone else's programs. Even in welfare reform, for example, despite negative public attitudes toward welfare, half of the respondents to a survey by the Kaiser/Harvard Program[77] supported granting more flexibility to states to experiment with welfare programs, but also agreed that the "Federal government has to set guidelines when it gives money to states…. in order to assure that the states will treat everyone fairly and do the right thing for poor people."

The devolution of any function or shift of any power to the states poses risks and uncertainties for the interests that benefit from the maintenance of federal control. Opposition is likely to stiffen, moreover, when proposals to shift powers to the states are linked to calls for policy reform, budget cuts, deficit reduction, and downsizing.[78]

Devolution is also frustrated because even though the Republican majority in the Congress has tended to express the most support for devolution, Republicans are often more committed to principles of individualism than of federalism. As U.S. House Speaker Newt Gingrich has expressed it:

> "The last sixty years has seen so much centralization in Washington that at this point the best we can do is start by shifting power back to the state capitals. Power in fifty different cities is better than power centralized in one city.
>
> Yet our ultimate goal is to move power even beyond the state capitals. Many governors and county commissioners are deeply suspicious of state governments and would prefer bloc [sic] grants and programs that come straight to them. . . .
>
> However, much as I sympathize with both state and local governments, what we really want to do is to devolve power all the way out of government and back to working American families. . . . Republicans envision a decentralized America in which responsibility is returned to the individual."[79]

Principles of individualism and federalism frequently collide because the promotion of individualism often requires constraints on state and local governments as well as on the federal government. As a result, for example, on grounds of individual liberty, many Republicans as well as some Democrats support federal preemption of state authority to re-regulate sectors of the economy deregulated by the Congress.

Unconditional devolution has not been on the Republicans' agenda. Regarding block-grants, for example, most Republicans support only block grants "with moral principles"[80],namely, rules and regulations that limit or prohibit states from using block-grant funds for liberal rather than conservative purposes. Republicans are also sharply divided over some issues.

In 1998, for instance, the Republican Congress enacted the Internet Tax Freedom Act. This law placed a three-year moratorium on new state taxes on the internet and established a commission to study and make recommendations about state taxation of the internet. The commission reported its findings in April 2000 but failed to achieve the two-thirds vote needed to make official recommendations because the commission was split over internet taxation. The two Republican governors on the commission vigorously opposed each other, with one supporting state taxation of the internet and the other opposing state taxation. A simple majority of the commission recommended that the Congress extend the tax moratorium for five more years.

Politically, the limited devolution agenda that was set forth by the Republicans encountered numerous other obstacles that blocked enactment of nearly the entire agenda. Proposals to devolve various health and social welfare programs, for example, jeopardize the entitlement status of programs for both states and individuals. Many state officials have sought to maintain state entitlements to federal support in order to guarantee adequate and predictable federal aid while many congressional Republicans have sought to reduce expenditures. In turn, numerous advocacy and clientele groups have sought to maintain individual entitlements in order to prevent states from denying or reducing benefits to currently eligible citizens. Entitlement advocates have also expressed concern, for example, "that removing individual entitlement in the Medicaid program would lead states to concentrate resources on popular and powerful clienteles, such as the frail elderly in nursing homes."[81]

Conflicts over funding formulas also frustrate devolution. "Formula fights" are among the most vigorous in Congress because they pit states and regions against each other. In essence, no state or region wants to be a net loser in devolution. States, however, have generally been united in seeking federal guarantees of increased funding during recessions, while many congressional Republicans have opposed such guarantees. Some devolution proposals have also pitted states against their local governments, as local officials sought to defend their prerogatives and shield their jurisdictions from negative fallouts. Devolution proposals have sparked vigorous debates as well, over maintenance-of-effort requirements, maintenance of federal standards, mandates, and accountability. In the end, many Republicans as well as Democrats are unwilling to let go of policy objectives that might be defeated by devolution to states having different policy objectives.

Additionally, many policy functions that enhance federal power and reduce state powers, such as civil rights, environmental protection, middle-class entitlements, and crime control, enjoy broad and deep public support. Issues are often framed in ways that make it politically impossible to refuse federal action. How many members of Congress, for instance, can oppose a widely publicized federal crime bill? However strongly President Reagan wished to shrink federal power, he could hardly refuse to sign the bill supported by Mothers Against Drunk Drivers that made it a condition of federal highway-aid that states increase the minimum drinking age to 21 in order to reduce teenage highway fatalities and clean up "blood borders". This political dynamic was again reflected in President Clinton's proposal, which was approved by the U.S. Senate but narrowly defeated by the U.S. House, to establish - as a condition of federal highway-aid - a national blood-alcohol standard of 0.08 percent for drunk driving in contrast to the 0.10 standard in force in 33 states. Proponents of the proposed standard regard it as good public policy; many opponents argue that it intrudes upon the historic constitutional prerogatives of the states. Hence, the most viable candidates for devolution are powers and functions that do not enjoy strong public support as well as functions of a more administrative nature that are invisible to the general public.

Similarly, a number of federal policy functions are highly beneficial for members of Congress and serve to benefit the constituency interests of the federal government generally. Thus, for example, "in contrast to the bipartisan embrace of welfare-reform block grants, there has been deafening bipartisan disinterest in major devolution of infrastructure activities, such as highways, to the states, despite the existence of a strong performance rationale and incentives for state leadership of these activities."[82]

In addition, there continue to be strong incentives to use three key tools of coercive federalism: mandates, conditions of aid, and preemption.[83] Unfunded and underfunded mandates are especially tempting because they allow the Congress and the White House to claim credit for "feel good" policies and to respond to interest groups while "devolving" the costs of those policies to state and local governments. Although the Unfunded Mandates Reform Act appears to be limiting the enactment of new unfunded mandates[84], the act has many exemptions, its point of order can be overridden by a simple majority vote in either house of Congress, and it is no barrier to politically popular or compelling mandates such as the bipartisan support for increasing the federal minimum wage in 1996, which would cost state and local taxpayers about $1.3 billion during the ensuing five years, according to the Congressional Budget Office. Furthermore, Republicans have proved to be no less eager than Democrats to mandate their policy preferences nationwide now that they are in power on Capitol Hill.

Conditions of aid remain one of the most open flanks for federal encroachments upon state powers and for federal accessions of powers wholly outside of the Congress's constitutionally enumerated powers. The U.S. Supreme Court has upheld such conditions on the ground that federal aid is voluntarily accepted by the states[85], even though, as a practical political and fiscal matter, states cannot opt out of the large grant-in-aid programs, such as Medicaid and highways. In the case of highways, moreover, if a state were to decline federal highway-aid in order to avoid compliance with objectionable conditions, the state's residents would, presumably, still be required to pay the federal motor-fuels tax while deriving no benefit from it. Consequently, the large federal-aid programs like highways and Medicaid become vehicles for expanding federal power.

The single greatest devourer of state-local powers, however, is preemption, namely, federal displacement of state law under the supremacy clause of the U.S. Constitution (Art. VI). More than 53 percent of all explicit preemption statutes enacted by the Congress since 1789 have been enacted only since 1969.[86] The new Republican majority in Congress, like previous Democratic majorities, has a healthy appetite for preemption (e.g., Shenk 1997[87]). Indeed, Republican efforts to preempt state product liability, food and drug labeling, internet taxation, and medical malpractice laws, among others, have made a number of congressional Democrats ardent states' rights advocates. Pressure in the federal system for preemption is enormous, primarily for economic reasons. For one, many businesses engaged in interstate commerce would rather be regulated by one 500-pound gorilla in Washington than by 50 monkeys on steroids. Second, deregulation of the economy has increased preemption so as to prohibit state regulators from rushing into regulatory vacuums created by federal withdrawal. Third, rising concern about international economic competition has spurred preemptions of state and local barriers to business competitiveness. For example, as Secretary of the Treasury Nicholas Brady said on introducing President George

Bush's proposals to preempt certain state powers over interstate banking, something is seriously amiss when a bank in California can open a branch in Birmingham, England, but not in Birmingham, Alabama.[88] Fourth, foreign-trade agreements eliminating not only tariffs but also non-tariff barriers to free trade pose substantial, long-term preemption threats to a broad range of state and local tax, regulatory, and policy powers.[89]

All of these mechanisms for expanding federal power also reflect a major structural change in the federal system that first occurred during the 1960s, namely, a shift in federal policymaking from places to persons and a reconceptualization of the federal union as one constituted by individuals, not sovereign states.[90] This shift reflects a long-standing debate in American history that reached a flashpoint during the 1980s when President Reagan declared that "the Federal Government did not create the States; the States created the Federal Government." President Reagan's opponents countered along the lines of William H. Seward in 1850: "The States are not parties to the Constitution as States; it is the Constitution of the people of the United States." As Justice Harry A. Blackmun later put it: "Ours . . . is a federal republic, conceived on the principle of a supreme federal power and constituted first and foremost of citizens, not sovereign states."[91] This individualist view of the union is one reason why Justice O'Connor has sought to transform the Tenth Amendment from a guarantor of states' rights to a guarantor of individual rights. Neither the Congress nor the president are interested in protecting states' rights; they are interested in legislating for individual rights and individual benefits in response to interest-group pressures.

Still another barrier to devolution, therefore, is the set of fears often expressed about the possible consequences of devolution, especially destructive interstate competition, limited state capacities to assume responsibility for devolved functions, accountability for policy and expenditure outcomes of devolved programs, and greater disparities of service provision and quality among jurisdictions.

Conclusion

To date, therefore, there is no evidence of wholesale devolution, although there is a discernible and, until recently, unanticipated nudging toward restoring some state powers and rebalancing federal-state relations in the federal system, especially by the U.S. Supreme Court. It is difficult to predict the outcome if this nudge should become a surge because such rebalancing will occur within historical circumstances quite different from those that prevailed at the outset of the Federal government's twentieth-century power expansion. There is no a priori reason, therefore, to expect that substantial devolution, should it ever occur, would be more malignant than benign.

Notes

1   Richard P. Nathan, "The Devolution Revolution: An Overview", *Rockefeller Institute Bulletin 1996*, Albany, Nelson A. Rockefeller Institute of Government, State University of New York, 1996, 5-13; Lenny Goldberg, "Come the Devolution", *The American Prospect*, vol. 24 (Winter 1996), 66-71.

2   John D. Donahue, *Hazardous Crosscurrents: Confronting Inequality in an Era of Devolution*, New York, The Century Foundation Press, 1999; Harold A. Hovey, *Can States Afford Devolution? The Fiscal Implications of Shifting Federal Responsibilities to State and Local Governments*, New York, The Century Foundation Press, 1999; Paul Offner, *Medicaid and the States*, New York, The Century Foundation Press, 1999.

3   Richard L. Cole, Rodney V. Hissong, and Enid Arvidson, "Devolution: Where's the Revolution?", *Publius: The Journal of Federalism,* vol. 29 (Fall 1999), 99-112.

4   Richard P. Nathan, "The Devolution Revolution: An Overview", *Rockefeller Institute Bulletin*, Albany, Nelson A. Rockefeller Institute of Government, State University of New York, 1996, 5-13.

5   Peter Levine, *The New Progressive Era: Toward a Fair and Deliberative Democracy*, Lanham, MD, Rowman & Littlefield, 2000, 63.

6   Michael E. Norris, *Reinventing the Administrative State*, Lanham, MD, University Press of America, 2000.

7   Sam Verhovek, "With Power Shift, State Lawmakers See New Demands", *The New York Times* (September 24): A-1, 1995.

8   Michael E. Norris, *Reinventing the Administrative State*. Lanham, MD, University Press of America, 2000, 82.

9   Peter Levine, *The New Progressive Era: Toward a Fair and Deliberative Democracy*, Lanham, MD, Rowman & Littlefield, 2000, 63.

10   Harold A. Hovey, *Can States Afford Devolution? The Fiscal Implications of Shifting Federal Responsibilities to State and Local Governments*, New York, The Century Foundation Press, 1999, viii.

11   David B. Walker, *The Rebirth of Federalism*, New York, Chatham House, 2000, 8.

12   *Texas vs. White*, 74 U.S. 700 (1869), 725.

13   U.S. Advisory Commission on Intergovernmental Relations, *Regulatory Federalism: Policy, Process, Impact, and Reform*. Washington, DC, 1984.

14   John Kincaid, "From Cooperation to Coercion in American Federalism: Housing, Fragmentation, and Preemption, 1780-1992", *Journal of Law and Politics*, vol. 9 (Winter 1993), 333-433.

15   Alexis de Tocqueville, *Democracy in America*, ed. J. P. Mayer; Trans. George Lawrence, New York, HarperPerennial, 1969.

16   Jeffrey L Mayer (ed.), "Dialogues on Decentralization", *Publius: The Journal of Federalism*, vol. 6 (Fall 1976).

17 U.S. Advisory Commission on Intergovernmental Relations, *Devolving Selected Federal-Aid Highway Programs and Revenue Bases: A Critical Appraisal*, Washington, DC, 1987.

18 Council of State Governments, *Restoring Balance to the American Federal System.* Lexington, KY, 1996.

19 William G. Coleman and Delphis C. Goldberg, "The Eisenhower Years and the Creation of ACIR", *Intergovernmental Perspective*,vol.16 (Summer 1990), 19-23.

20 Alpheus T. Mason, "American Individualism: Fact and Fiction", *The American Political Science Review*, vol. XLVI (March 1952), 1-18.

21 Timothy Conlan, *New Federalism: Intergovernmental Reform from Nixon to Reagan*, Washington, DC, The Brookings Institution, 1988; John Kincaid, "From Cooperation to Coercion in American Federalism: Housing, Fragmentation, and Preemption, 1780-1992", *Journal of Law and Politics*, vol. 9 (Winter 1993), 333-433.

22 Democratic Leadership Council, "DLC and the States", State Focus: Supplement to *The New Democrat*,vol. 9, (July/August 1997), 1.

23 John D. Donahue, "Disunited States", Basic Books, New York, 1997, 13.

24 Richard L. Cole and John Kincaid, "Public Attitudes on Intergovernmental Issues and Related Tax Matters", *Publius: The Journal of Federalism*, vol. 30 (Winter/Spring 2000), 189-201.

25 U.S. Advisory Commission on Intergovernmental Relations, *The Question of State Government Capability*, Washington, DC, 1985; Mavis Mann Reeves, "The States as Polities: Reformed, Reinvigorated, Resourceful", *Annals of the American Academy of Political and Social Science*,vol. 509 (May 1990) 83-93.

26 Earl M. Baker (ed.) "The Suburban Reshaping of American Politics", *Publius: The Journal of Federalism*, vol. 5 (Winter 1975).

27 Alice Rivlin, *Reviving the American Dream: The Economy, the States, and the Federal Government*, Washington. DC, The Brookings Institution, 1992; Paul E. Peterson, *The Price of Federalism*, Washington, DC, The Brookings Institution, 1995.

28 Richard P. Nathan, "The Devolution Revolution: An Overview", *Rockefeller Institute Bulletin 1996*, Albany, Nelson A. Rockefeller Institute of Government, State University of New York, 1996, 5-13.

29 John D. Donahue, *Hazardous Crosscurrents: Confronting Inequality in an Era of Devolution*, New York, The Century Foundation Press, 1999, 14.

30 U.S. Advisory Commission on Intergovernmental Relations, *Characteristics of Federal Grant-in-Aid Programs for State and Local Governments.* Washington, DC, 1995.

31 Robert W. Gage and Bruce D. McDowell, "ISTEA and the Role of MPOs in the New Transportation Environment: A Midterm Assessment", *Publius: The Journal of Federalism*, vol. 25 (Summer 1995), 148.

32 U.S. Advisory Commission on Intergovernmental Relations, *Regulatory Federalism: Policy, Process, Impact, and Reform*, Washington, DC, 1984, 43.

33 *South Dakota vs. Dole*, 483 U.S. 203, 1987.

34 John D. Donahue, *Disunited States*, New York, Basic Books, 1997.

35 *Shapiro vs. Thompson*, 394 U.S. 618, 1969.

36 *Saenz vs. Roe*, 119 S.Ct. 1518, 1999; Davis, Martha F., "The Evolving Right to Travel: Saenz vs. Roe", *Publius: The Journal of Federalism*, vol. 29 (Spring 1999), 95-110.

37 Scott W Allard,. and Sheldon Danziger, "Welfare Magnets: Myth or Reality?", *Journal of Politics,* vol. 62 (May 2000), 350-368.

38 David Whitman,. "Despite Tough Talk, States Avoid Workfare", *U.S. News & World Report*, vol. 124 (January 12, 1998), 26-27.

39 Malcolm Goggin, "The Use of Administrative Discretion in Implementing the State Children's Health Insurance Program", *Publius: The Journal of Federalism*, vol. 29 (Spring 1999), 35-51.

40 Jon Jeter, "The 'Ultimate Test' of Devolution", *Washington Post National Weekly Edition*, (August 11, 1997), 29-30.

41 David S Broder, "Clinton Vows Not to Forget States," *Washington Post*, February 2, 1993, A10.

42 National Performance Review, *Creating a Government that Works Better and Costs Less: Report of the National Performance Review*, Washington, DC, U.S. Government Printing Office, 1993.

43 Sarah F. Liebschutz, "Empowerment Zones and Enterprise Communities: Reinventing Federalism for Distressed Communities", *Publius: The Journal of Federalism*, vol. 25 (Summer 1995), 117-132.

44 *Economic Report of the President*, Washington, DC, U.S. Government Printing Office, (February 1998), 34-35.

45 William A. Galston and Geoffrey L. Tibbetts, "Reinventing Federalism: The Clinton/Gore Program for a New Partnership Among the Federal, State, Local, and Tribal Governments", *Publius: The Journal of Federalism*, vol. 24 (Summer1994), 23-48.

46 Bruce D. McDowell, "Advisory Commission on Intergovernmental Relations in 1996: The End of an Era", *Publius: The Journal of Federalism*, vol. 27 (Spring 1997), 111-127.

47 John M. Goshko, "As Oregon Goes, So Could the Rest of the Nation", *Washington Post National Weekly Edition*, (August 1995), 14-20, 31.

48 U.S. General Accounting Office. *Environmental Protection: Status of EPA's Initiatives to Create a New Partnership with State,* Washington, DC; (February 1996).

49 U.S. General Accounting Office, *Environmental Protection: Status of EPA's Initiatives to Create a New Partnership with States,*Washington, DC, (February 1996), 3-4.

50 Dana Milbank, and Laurie McGinley,. "While Washington Fiddles, Many States Devise Solutions to Problems with Welfare and Health Care", *Wall Street Journal*, May 31, 1996, A12.

51 Alan Ehrenhalt, "Out in the States, It's Not the 1930s Anymore", *Governing*, (December 1995), 7.

52 William A Galston and Geoffrey L. Tibbetts, "Reinventing Federalism: The Clinton/Gore Program for a New Partnership Among the Federal, State, Local, and Tribal Governments", *Publius: The Journal of Federalism*, vol. 24 (Summer 1994), 28.

53 Council of State Governments, *Restoring Balance to the American Federal System*, Lexington, KY, 1996, 75.

54 *Garcia vs. San Antonio Metropolitan Transit Authority*, 469 U.S. 528, 1985.

55 Michael C. Tolley and Bruce A. Wallin, "Coercive Federalism and the Search for Constitutional Limits", *Publius: The Journal of Federalism*, vol. 25 (Fall 1995), 73-90.

56 Deborah Jones Merritt, "The Guarantee Clause and State Autonomy: Federalism for a Third Century", *Columbia Law Review*, vol. 88, 1988, 1-97.

57 *Gregory vs. Ashcroft*, 501 U.S. 452, 1991.

58 *Atascadero State Hospital vs. Scanlon*, 473 U.S. 234, 1985.

59 *Will vs. Michigan Department of State Police*, 491 U.S. 58, 1989.

60 *Suter vs. Artist*, 112 S.Ct. 1360, 1992.

61 *New York vs. United States*, 505 U.S. 144, 1992.

62 *Printz vs. United States*, 117 S.Ct. 2365, 1997.

63 *United States vs. Alfonso Lopez, Jr.*, 115 S. Ct. 1625, 1995.

64 *Seminole Tribe of Florida vs. Florida*, 517 U.S. 441, 1996.

65 *Alden vs. Maine*, 119 S.Ct. 2240, 1999.

66 *College Savings Bank vs. Florida Prepaid Postsecondary Education Expense Board*, 119 S.Ct. 2219, 1999.

67 *Florida Prepaid Postsecondary Education Expense Board vs. College Savings Bank*, 119 S.Ct. 2199, 1999.

68 *U.S. vs. Morrison*, 146 L Ed 2d 658, 2000.

69 *New York Ice Co. vs. Liebman*, 285 U.S. 262, 1932.

70 *Vacco vs. Quill*, 117 S.Ct. 2293, 1997.

71 *Washington vs. Glucksberg*, 117 S.Ct. 2258, 1997.

72 John Kincaid, "State Court Protections of Individual Rights Under State Constitutions: The New Judicial Federalism", *The Journal of State Government*, vol. 61 (September/October 1988), 163-169.

73 *Michigan vs. Long*, 459 U.S. 904, 1983.

74 *City of Boerne vs. Flores*, 117 S.Ct. 2157, 1997.

75 *Roe vs. Wade*, 410 U.S. 113, 1973.

76 Richard L. Berke,. "Who Will Name the Next Supreme Court Justice?", *New York Times*, (May 21, 2000), Sec. 4, 3.

77 Kaiser/Harvard Program on the Public and Health/Social Policy, *Survey on Welfare Reform: Basic Values and Beliefs; Support for Policy Approaches; Knowledge About Key Programs*. The Henry J. Kaiser Family Foundation, January 1995, Table 25.

78 R. Kent Weaver, "Deficits and Devolution in the 104th Congress", *Publius: The Journal of Federalism*, vol. 26 (Summer 1996), 45-85.

79 Newt Gingrich, *To Renew America*, New York, Harper Collins, 1995.

80 Robert Rector, "The case for 'strings-attached' welfare reform", *Madison Review*, vol. 1(2), 1996, 13-16.

81 R. Kent Weaver, "Deficits and Devolution in the 104th Congress", *Publius: The Journal of Federalism*, vol. 26 (Summer 1996), 49.

82 Paul L. Posner and Margaret T. Wrightson,. "Block Grants: A Perennial, But Unstable, Tool of Government", *Publius: The Journal of Federalism*, vol. 26 (Summer 1996), 87-108.

83 John Kincaid, "From Cooperation to Coercion in American Federalism: Housing, Fragmentation, and Preemption, 1780-1992", *Journal of Law and Politics*, vol. 9 (Winter 1993), 333-433.

84 National Governors' Association, "States Feel Relief from Unfunded Mandates", *Governors' Bulletin*, vol. 30 (June 17, 1996), 1-2.

85 *South Dakota vs. Dole*, 483 U.S. 203, 1987.

86 U.S. Advisory Commission on Intergovernmental Relations, *Federal Statutory Preemption of State and Local Authority: History, Inventory, and Issues*, Washington, DC, 1992.

87 Joshua Wolf Shenk, "Washington's counter-devolutionaries", *U.S. News & World Report*, vol. 123 (November 24, 1997), 34

88 U.S. Advisory Commission on Intergovernmental Relations, *Federal Statutory Preemption of State and Local Authority: History, Inventory, and Issues*, Washington, DC, 1992, 38.

89 Conrad Weiler, "Foreign-Trade Agreements: A New Federal Partner?", *Publius: The Journal of Federalism*, vol. 24 (Summer 1994) 113-133.

90 John Kincaid, "Constitutional Federalism: Labor's Role in Displacing Places to benefit Persons", *PS: Political Science & Politics*, vol.26 (June 1993), 127-177.

91 *Coleman vs. Thompson*, 111 S.Ct. 2546, 1991.

From Cooperation to Competition?
The Modernization of the German Federal System

Arthur Benz

1. The quest for modernization

Cooperative federalism in Germany is currently subject to intensive debate. While about ten years ago it seemed desirable and necessary to incorporate the former German Democratic Republic into a united federal Germany, today this very federalism is blamed for causing political immobility and inefficiencies. Many experts and politicians call for modernization. The co-operation among executives is said to weaken elected parliaments and to undermine the democratic legitimacy of the political system.[1] Reform proposals are more or less radical. But their common denominator is requests for more decentralization, more diversity among *Länder* and regions, less intergovernmental cooperation and more competition among *Länder* governments.[2]

On the other hand, political scientists have raised doubts as to whether the German federal system can be reformed at all. Fritz W. Scharpf has argued that cooperative federalism is caught in the "joint-decision trap".[3] For an institutional reform to be executed the constitution has to be amended. This requires a two-thirds majority of votes in both chambers, the *Bundestag* and the *Bundesrat*. Since any institutional reform of the federal system will bring about disadvantages varying from *Land* to *Land*, it is a thorny problem to attain such a qualified majority. Due to their veto power in the *Bundesrat*, a minority of *Länder* governments can stop reforms. Therefore, Scharpf concludes, despite a low performance of the existing federal system, modernization is doomed to fail. To put it more precisely, German federalism went through several important reforms. However, all of them contributed to stabilizing patterns of interlocking politics and unitarization in policy-making.[4] Proposals for more decentralization, more diversity and more competition among *Länder* and regions put forward since the 1970s regularly failed. "Interlocking without end"[5] seems to be the fate of German federalism.

These theoretical and public debates often ignore the fact that during the 50 years of its existence, the German federal system has proved better than it is often said to be.[6] The reason for this is that co-operative federalism merged with politics in the party system. This combination promoted unitary policies conforming to the accepted model of the German welfare state which implied equivalent living conditions in all parts of the country. Without a differentiated analysis of the interplay between federal institutions, politics and policies, we cannot understand why in the past German federalism worked fairly well. Neither are we able to clearly appreciate the problems of cooperative federalism arising during the last decade.

Since about 1990, there have been indications that the "fit" between institutions, politics and policies of cooperative federalism no longer exists. Particularly relevant are the developments in party politics and the erosion of consensus concerning the welfare state in the face of economic stagnation and growing disparities among regions. These changes are responsible for malfunctions of cooperative federalism. But at the same time, they may open a window of opportunity for a new federalism. However, it is questionable whether a purely competitive federalism can and should be implemented under these conditions. I suggest that policies aiming at a modernized federalism might only be successful in so far as they implement a system of *fair competition* among *Länder* and regions and that these compete for the quality of policies rather than for resources. Cooperative federalism and competitive federalism are not contradictory.

2. The West German federal system: Institutions of cooperative federalism, interlocking politics and welfare state

The unique type of federalism that developed in Germany was created as a compromise between centralization and decentralization, as a result of state building with the consent of powerful *Länder* governments. From the very beginning, this institutional framework significantly limited the autonomy of both the federal and the *Länder* governments. It was neither centralized nor decentralized. Yet, it emerged as an adequate structure of government to harmonize a federal polity with the requirements of a modern welfare state. This is a rather untypical combination, since federalism usually curbs the expansion of welfare spending of governments. In clear contrast, e.g., to the U.S. political system, federalism and the welfare state in Germany merged to form a non-centralized unitary system.

- This permitted a considerable degree of decentralization despite the centralist trends that characterize all welfare states. *Länder* governments participate in redistributive policies. And despite a continuous expansion of federal legislation, we find many cases of external effects of decentralized policy-making being dealt with by intergovernmental cooperation, not by central regulation.

- Cooperative federalism allowed the implementation of redistributive policies designed to make living conditions in all regions equivalent. These policies contributed to an integration of German society.

- Finally, the institutions of co-operative federalism helped to realize a unitary legal order while accounting for regional variations in social realities, either by transmitting specific regional concerns into federal legislation or by decentralized implementation.

The variety of intergovernmental cooperation evolving in the German federal system can be categorized into two types. On the one hand, "vertical" cooperation between federal and *Länder* governments intensified as a consequence of the sharing of powers. The federal government fully exploited its jurisdiction in legislation granted to it by the Basic Law and extended it even further through a series of constitutional changes. The *Länder* governments agreed to this centralization in legislation, in return for veto rights in the *Bundesrat*. Moreover, the reforms of the financial constitution in 1955 and 1967 supplemented the original system of fiscal autonomy of governments (which was hardly realized) with elements of revenue sharing. Consequently, financial policies became increasingly a matter of cooperation between federal and *Länder* governments.

On the other hand, *Länder* executives coordinated their policies without interference to the federal government. This "horizontal" cooperation was designed to impede centralization of policies by coordination among the

Länder. Already in the early fifties, the most important bodies of cooperation among the *Länder* were established, such as the *Ministerpräsidentenkonferenz* (Conference of Minister-Presidents) and the conferences of *Länder* Ministers. Many more conferences and networks of special administrations followed.

This structure has often been labeled "executive federalism". It has been argued that intergovernmental cooperation occurred in isolated negotiations of members of governments or in administrative policy networks. However, this interpretation is not convincing, since it ignores both the embeddedness of federalism in the German parliamentary system and the role of substantive conflicts. That cooperative federalism worked fairly well during the existance of the West German federal republic can be explained mainly by two factors: One is the integrative effect of the party system, the other is the low degree of distributive conflicts.

The German Constitution combines cooperative federalism and parliamentary democracy with a competitive party system. Such a mixed constitution is susceptible to tensions, because competition in the parliamentary arena may reflect negatively on the cooperation among governments. On the other hand, cooperating executives may dominate their respective parliaments instead of being controlled by them. These tensions do exist in the German political system. However, their impact is alleviated by the party system. The structure of the party system contributed to unitarization of policy-making, and it created favorable conditions for intergovernmental cooperation.

- The large parties Christian Democratic Union (CDU) and Social Democratic Party (SPD), are organized in a federal structure. Until about 1982, regional party organizations followed the ideologies and programs formulated on a nation-wide basis. Like the big associations, parties did not significantly reflect diversities between regions. On the contrary, by linking federal and regional organizations, they promoted a unitary policy in all territories.

- Moreover, the parties, through their hierarchical organization, enhanced significantly the effectiveness of the federal-*Länder*-cooperation. This was especially important during the periods of opposed majorities in the *Bundestag* and in the *Bundesrat* and intense party conflict. As Gerhard Lehmbruch showed in his study on party competition in cooperative federalism[7], the federal organizations of the CDU and the SPD incorporated conflicts on policies between the federal and the *Länder* governments as well as among the *Länder* in their respective bodies and thus reduced the structures of conflict to a bilateral confrontation of party coalitions (so-called A- and B-*Länder*). In case of ideological conflicts, such a confrontation could hardly be overcome and negotiations often ended up in a deadlock. However, in many policies the definition of interests in terms of party politics made the behavior of individual governments reliable for their partners in intergovernmental bargaining.

- Through the important role of the political parties the democratic deficit of cooperative federalism, namely the weakening of *Länder* parliaments, was compensated to a certain degree. Of course, this meant that policy-making proceeded to a considerable degree outside the institutions of parliamentary democracy. Yet not only executives, but democratic political parties as well, became central players in German politics. As Lehmbruch put it, "parties moved into the center of 'overarching' networks linking the federal and *Land* governments as well as issue networks".[8]

Another important reason for the functioning of cooperative federalism was a relatively low degree of distributive conflicts. Until the 1970s, this condition was due to three developments:

- First, the former territorial structures disappeared after World War II. In the West German republic, the historical and cultural differences between the *Länder* were significantly smaller than in the past. When the Allied Powers reestablished *Länder* in artificially drawn territories, in many cases historically grown areas were split up. Moreover, migration after the war and the favorable economic development in all parts of West Germany reduced the existing cultural differences between regions. Thus, the territorial structures of West Germany were more balanced than those of the first German *Reich* or the *Weimar* republic.

- Second, although the *Länder* did, of course, differ in terms of economic strength, these disparities did not create serious distributive conflicts. This was prevented by a consensus that the tradition of the welfare state ought to be continued. Not only should specific social disadvantages of individuals or groups be reduced, but furthermore equivalent living conditions in all regions were to be be created. This consensus can be traced back to a long tradition in German history. After World War II, German social policy developed as the result of party competition and neo-corporatist cooperation between government and major interest groups. The federal government and the leading associations of industry and unions negotiated and agreed on a welfare system which was financed mainly by contributions and not by taxes. Therefore, the expansion of welfare policies had no immediate repercussion on the *Länder* governments' budgets. On the contrary, it freed the *Länder* budgets from welfare aid for people without income. Therefore, federalism and the welfare state merged to form a unique unitary system.[9]

- Finally, economic growth during the first two decades allowed the federal government, which benefited from unexpectedly high tax revenues in the early 1950s, to support economically weak *Länder* with financial aid. This vertical redistribution was much more important for them than the initially modest horizontal transfer of money from more to less affluent *Länder*. Redistributive policies designed to reduce regional disparities were feasible in the institutional setting of cooperative federalism as long as the effects of these policies did not harm the regions not profiting from aid.

In sum, cooperative federalism worked because of the "fit" between institutions, politics, and policies of the welfare state. Institutions require intergovernmental cooperation in many policies. The integrative function of the party system helps to manage conflicts and find agreements. And the notion of the welfare state provided for a realistic and accepted norm of distributive justice.

3. The federal system after unification and European integration: cooperative federalism, regionalization of party politics and distributive conflicts

During the 1970s, the centripetal forces in the German federal system attenuated, but there was no turn in the trend towards intergovernmental cooperation. One reason was the failure of territorial reorganization. Moreover, the political confrontation of the Social-Liberal (SPD-FDP) coalition with a CDU-CSU majority in the *Bundesrat* made reform policies impossible. Incremental policy changes based on compromises on the "smallest common denominator" prevailed. The *Länder* governments reinvented their autonomy in some policies, in particular in regional development policy, and they took initiatives in other policies, e.g. in environmental protection.[10]

The patterns of "interlocking politics", introduced by the "Joint Tasks" in 1969, were attacked by political scientists[11] and some *Länder* governments. When in the 1980s the *Länder* governments felt the fiscal consequences of economic stagnation, they increasingly expressed disapproval of the aim of equivalent living conditions.[12] Nevertheless, neither institutional reforms nor significant policy changes altered the overall architecture of the unitary federalism, which was still supported by a vertically integrated party system.

Since the end of the 1980s, cooperative federalism has shifted out of balance. The dual challenge of European integration and German unification accelerated changes that had begun already in the second half of the 1970s. These developments did not effectuate the greater institutional changes that most observers had expected after German unification.[13] Quite the contrary, they contributed to institutional stability. However, these institutions now have to operate under the condition of a changed party system and of a different policy framework.

a) Institutional stability

The enlargement of the federal territory as a result of German unification modified the framework for intergovernmental relations. Nevertheless, it did not open a "window to reform". The constitutional reform prescribed in the unification treaty did not meet expectations. Neither the *Länder* governments gained more legislative power, nor was a decisive step taken toward more autonomy for the *Länder*. The procedure for territorial reorganization was improved, but the reform issue as such is no longer on the agenda since the fusion of Berlin and Brandenburg failed. A revision of fiscal federalism was postponed and is still an unaccomplished task.[14] In the face of the rapid developments after the fall of the "iron curtain" and the uncertainties of the unification process, a transfer of the institutions of the West German federal system seemed – at least in the short run – the best solution.[15] However, what scholars praised as a surprising degree of continuity and adaptability after unification[16] in the end petrified an institutional framework which makes further adjustments to changing problems more and more complicated. Experts have raised doubts as to whether the challanges in the wake of German unification and European integration as well as the pressure for reforms in economic policy, environmental policy, health care, education and other policies can be met by merely incrementalist reactions.[17]

European integration contributed to this situation. It brought about some institutional changes. This led, however, to an extension of joint decision-making and its consolidation by institutionalization. The more the *Länder* governments realized they are in a weak position at the European level of policy-making, the more they tried to strengthen their power vis-a-vis the federal government. The revised version of Article 23 of the Basic Law embodied the participation of the *Bundesrat* in the federal government's European Union decision making and thus raised what had been up to then a matter of statutory law to the constitutional level. Thus, European policies became a new joint task of federal and *Länder* governments. The *Länder* governments' position is further improved when guidelines of the European Union have to be transformed into national law. In cases which require the consent of the *Bundesrat* for legislation, they can exercise considerable pressure on the federal government. The fact that the federal parliament is forced to take a decision because it is bound by the results of European politics strengthens the bargaining power of the *Länder* governments. Thus the development triggered by Europeanization stabilizes the cooperative federal system and does not deviate from historically marked developments.[18]

b) Pluralization and regionalization of the party system

While the institutional framework of cooperative federalism remained nearly invariable, the party system changed. During the 1980s tendencies of a moderate pluralization and regionalization gained ground. They developed further momentum after German unification.[19]

- During the 1980s, the *Greens* (Grünen) grew into an additional party with the potential to enter into a governing coalition. The integration of the East German *Bündnis 90* with the Greens supported this development, since it strengthened the pragmatic forces in the party. Thus the former duality of the party competition turned into a moderate pluralism.

- More important are the processes of regionalization in the party system. In both parts of united Germany different party political structures emerged.[20] The PDS gained weight as an East German regional party[21], whereas in West Germany the Greens (which failed to gain ground in the East) became the third political force on the *Länder* level.

- In the *Länder* we now find a variety of government coalitions so that a simple distinction of SPD-led and CDU/CSU-led *Länder* is no longer correct. In the *Bundesrat* there is no clear majority of one party. Majorities have to be negotiated from case to case.

- Moreover, the large parties have lost their ability to integrate federal and *Länder* politics.[22] Inside the CDU and the SPD, regional organizations restored independence from the central party leaders. During periods of opposition, the leaders of *Länder* governments gain decisive weight in the federal party organization. This could be observed in the CDU between 1969 and 1982. The SPD experienced the same development between 1982 and 1998 and is now a much more decentralized party than in the 1970s. German unification reinforced this trend. Despite the parties' institutional framework having been transferred, the social basis of the East German regional party organizations and their ideologies differ from their Western counterparts. This is true for the CDU as well as for the SPD.[23]

c) Regional disparities and conflicts on distributive justice in the welfare state

The diversification of the former party system has been triggered by the changes in the territorial framework of the post-unification German federal system. The regional disparities between East and West Germany and the new challenges for regions caused by globalization and Europeanization have led to distributive conflicts. The erosion of the consensus on welfare policies has contributed to this development.

- The decline of the East German economy led to economic imbalances between regions that were unknown in the Western federal republic. Even ten years after unification, disparities have been only slightly reduced. Massive transfers to Eastern *Länder* did not stimulate sufficient growth. One reason is that among the 140 billion DM per year going to the East, about 75 per cent have been used to finance social security payments. Investments in the renovation of infrastructure are currently decreasing.

- Regional disparities are exacerbated by globalization and European integration. In the global economy and in particular in the European Common Market it is no longer nations that compete to attract firms and corporations, but regional locations. Economic development depends increasingly on the infrastructure offered by *Länder* and local governments in competition with other regions. The capability of individual *Länder* governments to invest in improving their regional infrastructure depends on their present financial strength. Thus, regions with structural economic problems suffer from a double drawback. Their revenues are not sufficient and their infrastructure is of significantly inferior quality compared to that of the West German *Länder*. European Union programs within the framework of its cohesion and structural policies aim at reducing these imbalances. However, it is questionable whether they will produce significant effects. All things considered, it is likely that existing imbalances in the structure of the German state will be reinforced in the wake of globalization and European integration.

- Increasing territorial imbalances go along with increasing problems with the welfare state. Structural changes in economy and society accelerated by globalization and Europeanization have caused rising demands for payments to unemployed, retirement funds, health care etc. At the same time, governments' tax revenues and contributions to social insurance funds are no longer keeping up with expenditures. Reforms of the welfare state are pressing. However, in contrast to the period of an expanding welfare state, structural reforms of the welfare system immediately affect the interests of *Länder* governments. If a bigger share of the social security payments is financed by taxes, the revenue sharing between federal and *Länder* governments may get out of balance and have to be revised. If entitlements are curtailed, *Länder* and local governments would be burdened with additional payments for people in need. If incomes in industry and commerce are more differentiated according to the productivity of individual firms, this would impinge on regions in quite different ways and would increase inequalities. Even if the large parties agree on a reform of the welfare system (which is all but certain)[24], the problem remains that disputes among federal and *Länder* governments will persist.

- Redistributive conflicts are intensified due to different policy preferences of *Länder* governments. West German *Länder* increasingly feel the burden of transfer payments to East Germany, necessary for keeping up the system of fiscal equalization and social insurance payments. Behind these disputes on fiscal matters stands a fundamental conflict on the welfare state. Governments of Western *Länder* – independent of party political orientation – pursue a policy of privatization, deregulation and subsidiarity. In East Germany, public services, redistribution and control of the market are still predominating values. As a consequence, the principle of solidarity among the *Länder* and the objective of equivalent living conditions are now openly challenged. However, without an accepted norm of distributive justice an agreement on a welfare reform is difficult to achieve. In the existing institutional framework, important elements of a reform require the approval of a majority of votes in the *Bundesrat*. Under these conditions reforms are likely to be blocked.

In the changed framework of politics in cooperative federalism, the success or failure of intergovernmental cooperation becomes dependent on random factors in negotiations. Decisions reached by coalition governments in individual *Länder* – which not seldomly include parties that support as well as parties that oppose the federal government – may be turned into key decisions in legislation.[25] Cooperation deadlock is just as possible as innovative policies. Yet the latter are the less probable the more the relationship between East and West German *Länder* is affected. Divergent interests of *Länder* governments and distributive conflicts resulting from the economic disparities between the two parts of Germany are thus reinforced by diverging party political orientations. More often than in the past intergovernmental policy-making threatens to end up in the joint-decision trap: Cooperation between federal and *Länder* governments is still necessary due to the persistence of the institutional structures; however, the diverging interests among the *Länder* and between federal and *Länder* governments render cooperation more difficult.

4.   Inadequate reform proposals

In light of these problems, it is no coincidence that the debate on the reform of the federal system has gained a new drive during the last years. Politicians and experts have blamed cooperative federalism for political stalemates and have pleaded for a transformation towards a "competitive federalism".[26] This term covers two types of proposals: On the one hand, it summarizes pragmatic considerations for a revision of the allocation of power between tiers of government, a sorting out of fiscal responsibilities and a reorganization of territorial boundaries.[27] On the other hand, the term "competitive federalism" suggests a new model for modernizing government based on an economic theory of federalism.[28] The fundamental idea guiding these proposals is the principle of "fiscal equivalence". Governments should finance all tasks they are responsible for, and they be accountable for their own policies. In the economic model of federalism, this implies a clear separation of responsibilities between levels of governments and the connection of spending power and tax power.

It is not my intention to comment in detail on these proposals from a theoretical point of view. From the preceding analysis on the imbalances of German federalism it follows that the federal system needs to be modernized. However, we have to ask whether the model of a competitive federalism is adequate to solve the existing problems and whether such an institutional design can be implemented in the specific German political system. Bearing in mind the interdependence between institutions, politics and policies, we have to realize that a radical transformation towards a "competitive federalism" is neither feasible nor desirable.

It is not feasible, because the weak *Länder* will reject it. A competitive federal system based on the economic theory of federalism would intensify resource inequalities among the *Länder*. Furthermore, it would have considerable redistributive effects. Therefore, the Eastern *Länder* (and some weak Western *Länder*, too) cannot reasonably be expected to agree. Without their approval, the reform is doomed to fail.

The currently predominating model of a competitive federalism is not very attractive, either.

- First, it provokes input-oriented policy-making. *Länder* governments would (according the principle of fiscal equivalence) bear the costs and receive the benefits of their policies, and actually this should motivate them to make efficient decisions in the best interest of their constituency. But, as we can learn from the American experience, these economic orientations produce a bias in policy-making: Measures to improve the tax base (industrial policy, technical infrastructure) are supported at the expense of education and social services and short-term-oriented decisions are fostered.

- Second, pure economic competition increases rather than decreases regional disparities, in particular if the initial conditions of the *Länder* are different.

- Finally, the model is not supported by a political consensus on distributive justice that can replace the normative basis of the welfare state. In Germany, it is in the foreseeable future quite unlikely that the principle of equivalent living conditions will be abandoned entirely. Hence inequalities caused by competitive federalism will hardly be accepted by affected citizens or their representatives.

5. Fair competition in a cooperative federal system – an alternative design for modernizing German federalism

This does not mean that in modernizing federalism unitary policy-making in cooperative federalism should necessarily be restored or maintained. Decentralization, autonomy of *Länder* and competition make sense if they contribute to a *fair competition*.[29] Without going into detail, I suggest the following elements of a modernization policy that are essential for achieving fair competition among regions and *Länder*:

- Of fundamental importance are ongoing transfers to economically depressed *Länder* in order to improve their start-off conditions. These transfers must be based on a new consensus on a conception of distributive justice, which emphasizes the principle of need instead of equality or equity/equivalence (This reconsideration of the normative fundament of fiscal federalism is exactly what the Federal Constitutional Court stipulated in a recent decision on this matter). The existing system of fiscal equalization should be overhauled, but not entirely abolished. If the principle of need provides the basis of redistribution, a continuous review of fiscal transfers with regard to changing problems and policy goals is required. Therefore, not only the substance, but also the institutional framework of intergovernmental revenue sharing and transfers has to be reformed.

- In most policies, a devolution of legislative powers is not necessary. Decentralization stimulating competition can be achieved by further deregulation in federal policies and by reducing the substance of federal laws to "standards" and rules for inter-regional competition. This way, the *Länder* governments can gain more flexibility in implementing the federal law (be it by passing laws at the *Länder* level or by administrative decisions)

- The *Länder* governments should better use their powers in decentralized policies such as regional planning, regional economic policy, active labor market policy, education, regional transport, social services, etc., to compete for best practices.

A modernization of the federal system in this sense is possible within the existing institutions of cooperative federalism. It does not necessarily require a reallocation of powers through an amendment of the Basic Law. Decentralized competition for best practices is encouraged by a more regionalized party system. In order to win elections, *Länder* governments have to improve the quality of regional policies rather than meddling in federal policies. And in the long run, this kind of output-oriented fair competition is even susceptible to reducing regional disparities.

Notes

1   Hans Herbert von Arnim, *Vom schönen Schein der Demokratie*, München, Droemer, 2000.

2   Ursula Männle (ed.), *Föderalismus zwischen Konsens und Konkurrenz*, Baden-Baden, Nomos, 1998.

3   Fritz W. Scharpf, "The Joint-Decision-Trap. Lessons from German Federalism and European Integration", *Public Administration*, vol. 66, 1988, 239-278; Fritz W. Scharpf, *Games Real Actors Play: Actor-Centered Institutionalism in Policy Research*, Boulder, Westview Press, 1997.

4   Arthur Benz, "From Unitary to Asymmetric Federalism in Germany: Taking Stock after 50 Years", *Publius. The Journal of Federalism*, vol. 29 (Fall 1999), 55-78.

5   Rainer-Olaf Schultze, "Statt Subsidiarität und Entscheidungsautonomie – Politikverflechtung und kein Ende: Der deutsche Föderalismus nach der Vereinigung", *Staatswissenschaften und Staatspraxis*, vol. 4, 1993, 225-255.

6   Arthur Benz, "From Unitary to Asymmetric Federalism in Germany: Taking Stock after 50 Years", *Publius. The Journal of Federalism*, vol. 29 (Fall 1999), 55-78. Thomas Bräuninger and Thomas König, "The checks and balances of party federalism: German federal government in a divided legislature", *European Journal of Political Research*, vol. 36, 1999, 207-234; Ute Wachendorfer-Schmidt, "Gewinner oder Verlierer? Der Föderalismus im vereinten Deutschland", in Roland Czada and Hellmut Wollmann (eds.), *Von der Bonner zur Berliner Republik. Zehn Jahre deutsche Einheit* (special issue of *Leviathan*, vol. 19), Opladen, Westdeutscher Verlag, 2000, 113-140.

7   Gerhard Lehmbruch, *Parteienwettbewerb im Bundesstaat. Regelsysteme und Spannungslagen im Institutionengefüge der Bundesrepublik Deutschland*, Opladen, Westdeutscher Verlag, 2nd ed., 1998.

8   Gerhard Lehmbruch, "Institutional Linkages and Policy Networks in the Federal System of West Germany", *Publius. The Journal of Federalism*, vol. 19 (Winter 1989), 235.

9   Manfred G. Schmidt, *Thesen zur Reformpolitik im Föderalismus der Bundesrepublik Deutschland*, ZeS-Arbeitspapier Nr. 4/2000, Bremen, Zentrum für Sozialpolitik der Universität Bremen, 2000, 4.

10 Arthur Benz, "Intergovernmental Relations in the 1980s", *Publius. The Journal of Federalism*, vol. 19, (Fall 1989), 203-220.

11 Fritz W. Scharpf, Bernd Reissert and Fritz Schnabel, *Politikverflechtung. Theorie und Empirie des kooperativen Föderalismus in der Bundesrepublik*, Kronberg/Ts, Scriptor, 1976.

12 Wolfgang Renzsch, *Finanzverfassung und Finanzausgleich*, Bonn, Dietz, 1991.

13 Charlie Jeffrey, "The Non-Reform of the German Federal System after Unification", *West European Politics*, vol. 18, 1995, 252-272.

14 Arthur Benz, "Verfassungspolitik im kooperativen Bundesstaat", in Karl-Heinz Bentele, Bernd Reissert and Roland Schettkat (eds.), *Reformpolitik*, Frankfurt a.M./ New York, Campus, 1995, 147-164.

15   Roland Czada, "Schleichwege in die Dritte Republik", *Politische Vierteljahresschrift*, vol. 35, 1994, 245-270.

16   Roland Czada, "Schleichwege in die Dritte Republik", *Politische Vierteljahresschrift*, vol. 35, 1994, 245-270; Klaus H Goetz, "Kooperation und Verflechtung im Bundesstaat", Rüdiger Voigt (ed.) *Der kooperative Staat*, Baden-Baden, Nomos, 1995, 145-166; Gerhard Lehmbruch, "Die deutsche Vereinigung. Strukturen und Strategien", *Politische Vierteljahresschrift, vol.* 32, 1991, 585-604.

17   Uwe Leonardi, "Deutscher Föderalismus jenseits 2000: Reformiert oder deformiert", *Zeitschrift für Parlamentsfragen*, vol. 30, 1999, 135-162.

18   Klaus H. Goetz, "National Governance and European Integration: Intergovernmental Relations in Germany", *Journal of Common Market Studies*, vol. 33 (1), 1995, 91-116.

19   Oskar Niedermayer, "Das gesamtdeutsche Parteiensystem", in Oscar W. Gabriel, Oskar Niedermayer and Richard Stöss (eds.), *Parteiendemokratie in Deutschland*, Opladen, Westdeutscher Verlag, 1997, 106-130.

20   Gert-Joachim Glaeßner, *Demokratie und Politik in Deutschland*, Opladen, Leske + Budrich, 1999, 597.

21   David Patton, "The Rise of Germany's Party of Democratic Socialism: ‚Regionalised Puralism' in the Federal Republic?", *West European Politics*, vol. 23, 2000, 144-160.

22   Peter Lösche and Franz Walter, *Die SPD. Klassenpartei – Volkspartei – Quotenpartei*, Darmstadt, Wissenschaftliche Buchgesellschaft, 1992; Josef Schmid, *Die CDU: Organisationsstrukturen, Politiken und Funktionsweisen einer Partei im Föderalismus*, Opladen, Westdeutscher Verlag, 1990.

23   Richard Stöss, *Stabilität im Umbruch. Wahlbeständigkeit und Parteienwettbewerb im "Superwahljahr" 1994*, Opladen, Westdeutscher Verlag, 1997.

24   Gerhard Lehmbruch, "Institutionelle Schranken einer ausgehandelten Reform des Wohlfahrtsstaates. Das Bündnis für Arbeit und seine Erfolgsbedingungen", in Roland Czada and Hellmut Wollmann (eds.), *Von der Bonner zur Berliner Republik. Zehn Jahre deutsche Einheit* (special issue of *Leviathan*, vol. 19), Opladen, Westdeutscher Verlag, 2000, 89-112.

25   Thomas Bräuninger and Thomas König, "The checks and balances of party federalism: German federal government in a divided legislature", *European Journal of Political Research* 36, 1999, 207-234.

26   Ursula Männle (ed.), *Föderalismus zwischen Konsens und Konkurrenz*, Baden-Baden, Nomos, 1998.

27   Heidrun Abromeit, *Der verkappte Einheitsstaat*, Opladen, Leske + Budrich, 1992; Arthur Benz, "Reformbedarf und Reformchancen des kooperativen Föderalismus nach der Vereinigung Deutschlands", in Wolfgang Seibel, Arthur Benz and Heinrich Mäding (eds.), *Verwaltung und Verwaltungspolitik im Prozeß der deutschen Einheit*, Baden-Baden, Nomos, 1993, 456-475; Heinz Laufer and Ursula Münch, *Das föderative System der Bundesrepublik Deutschland, München*, Landeszentrale für politische Bildungsarbeit, 1997, (also published 1998 by Leske + Budrich, München).

28 Sachverständigenrat, *Jahresgutachten des Sachverständigenrates zur Begutachtung der gesamtwirtschaftlichen Entwicklung*, Bundestags-Drs. 11/8472, 1991, 210-216.

29 Bertelsmann-Commission "Governance & Constitutional Policy", *Disentanglement 2005. Ten Reform Proposals for Better Governance in the German Federal System*, Gütersloh, Bertelsmann Foundation Publishers, 2000, 18.

American Federalism: The Changing Dynamics of Intergovernmental Relations

William T. Pound

"Devolution of authority" from the federal government to the states is often cited as the operative concept in American intergovernmental relations at the present time. While change is taking place, both in the relationships between the national government and the states and in state-local relations, one can argue whether this is in reality devolution or simply another in a long series of adjustments in the flexible American federal system.

In the Winter 2000 issue of the *Brookings Review* Professor Martha Derthick wrote, "American federalism is a highly protean form, long on change and confusion, short on fixed, generally accepted principles."[1] After assessing recent United States Supreme Court decisions, changes in welfare and education programs, and the tortured history of the two recent Executive Orders on Federalism issued by President Clinton which went from a sweeping assertion of federal authority in the original (EO130883) to an emphasis on constitutional principles, maximum administrative and policy-making direction to the states, and state consultation as to need for and the development of national standards in its successor (EO13132) Professor Derthick commented:

"One can cite the original order as evidence of the imperious attitudes that high federal officials actually bring to intergovernmental relations, or one can cite the revision as evidence of the continuing power of the states. In studying American federalism, the analyst is forever asking whether the glass is half-empty or half-full. That is the appropriate question as the century turns, and the answers are to be found more in the day-to-day operations of intergovernmental relations than in either Supreme Court decisions or executive orders. It requires a blind eye to call ours an era of devolution. But even with two sharp eyes, it is hard to detect a plain answer. Everywhere one looks, the answer remains murky and many-sided."[2]

From the perspective of American state government and, in particular state legislatures, the observation that the glass of American federalism is both half-full and half-empty is appropriate. What is clear is that we have moved toward a more balanced federalism in recent years as opposed to being either more Washington or more state-dominated as has been the case at times in the past. Whether this will continue is uncertain and depends on many factors. Among these are international developments, globalization with its centralizing tendencies, economics, the U.S. Supreme Court and the response and performance of American federal and state governments to problems of the early 21st century.

This move toward a more balanced federalism has many elements, not the least of which is stronger public support for state and local government and a political climate which supports action at the state and local level and exhibits distrust of the national government. While it can be argued that the American public does not clearly understand the roles and functions of the various levels of government, they do understand that they can have most impact on the decisions of the governments closest to them. The mingling of roles and functions in American federalism (or marble cake federalism), which has accelerated in recent years, contributes to public misunderstanding of which government does what.

The changing dynamics of American federalism include both increased program flexibility in the management of several public policy areas, such as welfare, education and environment, and greater federal involvement in traditional areas of state authority, such as law enforcement and criminal justice. The welfare reform legislation of 1996 – Personal Responsibility and Work Opportunity Demonstration Act – and the Educational Flexibility Partnerships Demonstration Act of 1999 are often cited as key components of devolution. Both established frameworks within which federal aid would go to the states, free from the often cumbersome and detailed conditions which had previously applied, and from which the states often sought waivers – normally a very time consuming process. Program authority was essentially decentralized. In fact, these Congressional actions recognized that the states were already experimenting with these programs under specific waivers from these existing requirements. Both acts require that the executive and legislative branches of state government be involved in program decisions. This would likely not have been the case twenty years earlier. The result in welfare has been much greater program flexibility, more experimentation and the spreading of innovation among the states, reduced welfare expenditures, and a growing concern by states over the stability of the federal financial commitment to the program. Congressional budgeters in each of the past two years have seriously considered reclaiming unused Temporary Assistance to Needy Families funds committed to the states as a key component of the welfare reform legislation. Congressional authorization of welfare reform and TANF is required in 2002 and will provide a key test of the viability of devolution.

Education and criminal justice are policy areas with a more mixed and contradictory picture. Both are policy areas of primary state jurisdiction with strong traditions of local administration and control. Even with a growth in federal assistance programs in these areas the overwhelming amount of funding comes from the states and their local entities. In education about 93% of total funding is provided by state and local government. Similarly, the bulk of financing for law enforcement and the actual enforcement of laws takes place in the states.

While the states were successful in obtaining passage of the Unfunded Mandates Reform Act in 1995, which has both slowed the imposition of unfunded mandates and modified the manner in which Congress considers them, there is an accelerating Congressional tendency to preempt the states and interfere in the way states use their powers. Recent examples include proposed health maintenance organization restrictions in the Patients' Bill of Rights which will preempt health care regulations in many states and various provisions in juvenile justice legislation which would limit state discretion in the prosecution of juveniles and federalize a variety of crimes. Recently enacted financial services legislation transfers more regulatory authority over banking and insurance from the states to the federal government. Federal proposals for electricity deregulation would supersede state approaches to this issue, which have to date been enacted in nearly half of the states. No area, not matter how large or small, seems immune from Congressional reach at the present time.

A primary force in the movement for preemption is the business community and the trend toward globalization of economic activity. There are reasonable arguments for more uniformity in areas of commercial regulation and pressure from international business to reduce the complexity and diversity of state law. States recognize this and have moved aggressively toward deregulation in many business areas. States take the position that regulatory policy be developed on a consultative, rather than preemptive, basis. Preemption results in a sweeping away of often reasonable state regulatory policy, often for no better reason than that a more favorable policy in a particular situation can be achieved at the federal level than in the states. Little attention is paid to federalism as a governing principle. Interests of both the right and left find Congress a more friendly and convenient arena than the fifty state legislatures. Political considerations and campaign fundraising overcome the traditional allocations of authority in American federalism.

A related trend is the tendency for international agreements, particularly on trade policy, which are the province of the federal government, to override or preempt state laws. The effect of globalization is to preempt by treaty or create pressure for statutory preemption and frustrate the reach of state regulatory and tax policy. The growth of electronic commerce also promises to have a major impact on these policies in the next few years.

Some of the most significant adjustments in the state-federal relationship have come through recent decisions of the United States Supreme Court. After more than half a century of justifying expansion of the national government, particularly through the commerce power, a narrow majority of the Supreme Court has applied a more restrictive view of Congressional power and of the need for the Courts to defer to Congressional policy determinations. In a recent series of federalism cases, the Court has much more often come down on the side of the states in decisions involving the long dormant Tenth Amendment or Congressional assertions of action under the Commerce Clause of the Constitution. These decisions have established greater deference to state action and stricter standards for the preemption by Congress of state authority. The subjects of these cases have been diverse: *United States vs. Lopez*[3] overturned federal law prohibiting carrying a firearm near a school; parts of the Brady gun control laws which covered state action were struck down in *Printz vs. United States*[4], and most recently the Court has ruled the states immune from suits in federal court alleging patent and trademark law violations[5] and for violations of the Age Discrimination in Employment Act[6].

The Supreme Court as currently composed seems likely to continue this trend. Most recently the Court has limited Congressional expansion of federal criminal law in *United States vs. Morrison*[7] where victims of sexual assault had been given the right to sue their attackers in federal court and rejected assertions of broad regulatory authority by the federal government under the Clean Water Act in *Solid Waste Agency of Northern Cook County vs. United States Army Corps of Engineers*[8].

If globalization leads to greater centralization and expanded national or international authority, other trends are leading to expanded state power vis-à-vis their local units. There are clear trends in most American states for the state to exercise expanded authority and responsibility over functions once primarily local in control. Examples of this can be found in education, growth policy and environmental management, transportation and health. Several factors explain this. The greater fiscal capacity of states is one. Problems that are broader than a single unit of local government and require larger scale solutions are another. The quest for equity in treatment for all citizens, especially in education finance, is another. And as the states financial role in achieving equity and offsetting local variations grows, so does the tendency for the states to dictate policy and make the rules.

The role of the states in American federalism may thus be seen to have expanded both from assumptions of local authority and devolution of federal power. Devolution is taking the form of establishing a federal framework or standards within which the states have considerable latitude to develop policy. The result is considerable state or regional variation which, in turn, may lead again to pressure for federal standardization.

Policy innovation today primarily occurs in the states, consistent with Justice Brandies invocation of states as "laboratories of democracy". One need only look at health policy to see this. After the failure to create a national health care system, innovation and experimentation is spreading among the states. As innovations become widespread, they will be woven by the Congress into national policy. Similarly, changes in education policy are occurring in the states. The tensions between federal and state governments in this policy environment are exemplified by several problems:

- the tendency of the federal government to impose standards or controls while providing only a minor financial commitment. The special or handicapped education program is an example.

- the tendency to provide only temporary financing for what will become permanent programs. More police officers on the streets and teachers in the classroom are examples.

- when Congress moves to nationalize an area of state action, there is often a tendency to overly sweeping preemption and standardization which results in the loss of state flexibility.

The future of American federalism depends to a great extent on the changing patterns of fiscal federalism and the revenue sources available to the states – contrasting patterns emerge in this area. State and local spending and employment are growing much faster than at the federal level in the 1990s. States have recently experienced the most favorable budgetary situation in memory. Record surpluses have made possible both program and service expansion and tax cuts. Yet an examination of state revenues indicates that their growth rate in a strong economy lags that of federal revenue. Revenue growth rates in recent years approximate nine to ten percent for the federal government, seven to eight percent for states and five percent or less at the local level. The state revenue system is heavily dependent on sales taxes, which are geared to a manufacturing rather than a service economy. The growth of electronic commerce and remote sales is another problem for states. Due to the Supreme Court decisions in *Bellas Hess* and *Quill*[9] the states are unable to enforce the collection of sales and use taxes on remote commerce where the seller lacks nexus in the state. This situation could be solved by Congressional authorization for such state tax collection on interstate sales. However, Congress has not given indication of a willingness to grant such authority to the states.

The greatest threat to American federalism at present is in the preemption by Congress of parts of the state revenue base. The Internet Tax Freedom Act, passed in 1998, preempted state and local taxation of internet access for three years and created an Advisory Commission on Electronic Commerce to study this issue. This commission, composed of federal, state and business representatives, was unable to achieve the required majority for most of its recommendations, which were pro-business and detrimental to the states. At stake are both taxation of the means of electronic commerce and taxation of internet and remote sales. As the volume of internet commerce grows, the viability of the state sales tax system will be undermined.

Current proposals in Congress would extend the moratorium on internet access taxes and, at the extreme, prohibit state taxation of electronic commerce. At the same time, a coordinated effort is underway in the states to simplify, remove barriers to collection and make more fair the state sales tax system, so that the burdens on retailers in collection will be largely eliminated. If the states are successful in cooperatively creating and adopting such a streamlined sales tax collection system, it might be authorized by Congress or the Supreme Court might determine that the state barriers to commerce created by attempts to collect sales and use taxes have been eliminated.

This effort will have much to say about the future of American federalism. Should Congress preempt a significant part of the state revenue base, the states will be weakened and increasingly dependent on federal aid and control. If the states succeed in solving this problem, with or without the assistance of Congress, it will be a significant indicator of their vigor and ability to work cooperatively together to maintain their role in American federalism. Though there were continued attempts to prompt state authority in Congress during the past year, they have largely failed. The new Bush Administration suggests that it will take a much more cooperative approach to federalism, giving states discretion within the broad outlines of federal programs in education, environment and social welfare. Policy innovation in health and other areas will continue to occur primarily in the states, especially given the close, sharp partisan division in the American national government.

Notes

1 *Brookings Review*, "American Federalism-Half-Full or Half-Empty", (Winter 2000), 24.

2 *Brookings Review*, "American Federalism-Half-Full or Half-Empty", (Winter 2000), 27.

3 *United States vs. Lopez*, 524 U.S. 549, 1995.

4 *Printz vs. United States*, 521 U.S. 98, 1997.

5 *Florida Prepaid Postsecondary Education Expense Board vs. College Savings Bank*, 527 U.S. 627, 1999.

6 *Kimmel vs. Florida*, 528 U.S. 62, 2000.

7 *United States vs. Morrison*, 120 S.Ct., 1740, 2000.

8 *Solid Waste Agency of Northern Cook County vs. United States Army Corps of Engineers*, 69 USLW, 4048, U.S. January 9, 2001.

9 *National Bellas Hess vs. Department of Revenue of the State of Illionois*, 386 U.S. 753, 1967; *Quill vs. Heitkamp*, 504 U.S. 298, 1992.

The Revival of German Federalism:
Two Examples

Ursula Männle

1. The Devolution of Legislative Power to *Land* Level

1.1. Sunday Speeches

"The principle of subsidiarity is not only valid for the inner order of European institutions. Its benefit has to be rediscovered within the order of our own country as well. ... But a new agreement is missing that regulates what has to be established by uniform federal law and what lies within the self-determination, the imagination and discretionary power of the *Länder*. ... If the *Länder* get enough leeway to experiment courageously, new ideas will get a chance, too."[1]

The reform of the federal system of the Federal Republic of Germany is playing a predominant role not only in scholarly discourses but also in speeches held by politicians. The former President of the Federal Republic of Germany, Roman Herzog, demanded a new distribution of powers. Inaugural speeches of newly elected Presidents of the *Bundesrat* regularly focus attention on the extensive abuse of federal competencies as well.[2] Devolution of legislative competence to the *Länder* – that is what is demanded unanimously. "Against the ossification of our country - for the revival of federalism" is the title of an essay by the Friedrich-Naumann-Foundation. It demands a revival of federalism which grants more independence and autonomy to local administrative units.

"What is called for now is real and strengthened competition among the federal states. This is playing a significant part in the system of checks and balances of a divided and subsidiarily organised state authority and is indispensable as a principle of decentralisation."[3]

This view was also expressed on the occasion of the festivities for the 50th anniversary of the Parliamentary Council's first session:

"[W]e have got a system which is actually supposed to be very flexible because of federalism due to decentralisation and relocation of decision-making power and responsibility; but in reality it has become a system which is incredibly rigid and interwined. ... Today we all agree on the fact that this development was a mistake, that the reorganisation of federalism in Germany by a disentanglement of competencies of the federation and of the *Länder* is probably more important than everything else."[4]

Politicians of all parties have the same opinion: the sharing of competencies between federation and *Länder* has turned into a confusing network not only between federation and *Länder*, but also among *Länder* themselves. This is restricting the ability to act and mixes the respective responsibilities and competencies.

Already the discussion about Article 5 of the Unification Treaty, which says that changes in the Basic Law (following unification) have to be considered especially carefully with regard to the relationship between the federation and the *Länder*, showed clearly that a redistribution of competencies in favor of the *Länder* would encounter the resistance of the federal legislator. The line was drawn beyond any party boundaries between federation and *Länder*.

It was Dr. Hans-Jochen Vogel, the chairman of the parliamentary group of the Social Democrats at that time, who contributed to a compromise that meant a success for the *Länder*.

1.2. A Suggestion's Odyssey

In order to strengthen the federal principle of the Federal Republic of Germany, the federal legislator revised, among other things Article 72, paragraph 2 and Article 75 of the Basic Law in 1994.

According to this revision the federation can now make use of the constitutional provisions for concurrent legislation and the framework legislation only under strict conditions. The federation now has to demonstrate that the intended revision is necessary: either in order to create "equivalent" (not "uniform" anymore) living conditions within the federal territory or to preserve the unity of law and economy in the federation's interest. But the hope that this regulation would reduce the amount of federal laws has not yet been realized. I am not familiar with any case where a weighing process of that kind led to a reconsideration of a federal law. The federal legislator continues to produce industriously.

As stated in Article 72 of the Basic Law, legislation which was enacted before November 15, 1994, continues to be valid as federal law according to Article 125 a, paragraph 2, of the Basic Law. However, federal law can provide for its replacement by *Land* law (so called "opening clause", Öffnungsklausel). This can be considered as a success for the *Länder* and for federalism. But it can only remain a success for the *Länder* if these newly created opportunities will be seized. Neither the federal government nor the *Bundestag* have been willing to leave federal jurisdictions to the *Länder* legislatures for the purpose of change. So it was up to the *Länder* themselves to take the initiative. "It would not be consistent after the *Länder* had been complaining for years about not having enough legislative power, to use their newly acquired opportunities now only hesitatingly or not at all.[5] The willingness to become more active, however, has not been all that great. Already on May 18, 1995, Bavaria brought a suggestion to the leaders of the State and Senate Chancelleries in order to gain as broad a basis as possible among the *Länder*: it suggested the introduction of a task force which was to prepare a joint *Bundesrat* initiative. This suggestion was turned down and Bavaria was asked instead to carry out the relevant preparations for a possible future initiative in the *Bundesrat*. That is why Bavaria has compiled extensive papers already in 1995 and 1996, listing topics for which an opening clause can be applied. The starting points were initially those areas in which competencies for the *Länder* were demanded during negotiations of the Joint Constitutional Commission established in 1993, but not achieved (e.g., right of assembly, public welfare, real estate transactions, property law, economic viability of hospitals, waste disposal, prevention of air pollution, noise pollution reduction, civil service legislation and higher education). The reports of interministerial teams were discussed repeatedly and very controversially in the Bavarian Cabinet. It became evident that the respective ministries hesitated to claim competencies for themselves, and there was a tendency to keep the federal regulations in many areas. Only a personal decision by the Bavarian Minister-President resulted in concrete suggestions for devolution and in the elaboration of a bill as a Bundesrat initiative. The details were presented by the Bavarian Minister-President in his speech in the *Land* Parliament on November 29, 1996.[6] Supported by a previous statement by the parliamentary group of the Christian Social Union[7] he demanded the return of policy-making competencies in favor of the Bavarian *Land* Parliament, which he claimed to be a matter of bipartisan concern. The Bavarian initiative was taken up at the conference of Minister-Presidents on May 20, 1997. A task force - open to all *Länder* - was set up to work out a joint proposal. Despite a lot of effort this team could not come to an arrangement on central issues. It was decided to dispense with a *Länder* initiative, as the few topics of consensus in the end would not have served the aim of strengthening federalism. As a result the states of Baden-Wuerttemberg, Bavaria and Hesse introduced a bill in the *Bundesrat* on January 19, 1998, which was based on the original Bavarian proposal. The debates in the committees of the *Bundesrat* were a fiasco. The committees defeated the motion in all major points. The Minister-Presidents agreed to postpone the final debates in the Committee on Legal Affairs to avoid the initiative's failure. This confirmed the accusation that there was no real interest in the devolution of legislative powers. Nothing happened for quite some time. After that the Bavarian Minister-President appealed again emphatically to his colleagues in all German *Länder* and tried to gain support for the essential points of the bill. A watered-down version then passed in the *Bundesrat* on October 15, 1999. And finally, after years of discussions and preparations as a first step a bill was introduced in the process of federal legislation that provided for opening clauses for the *Länder* legislatures in rather minor areas.[8] At first the bill was put on ice in the *Bundestag* on recommendation of the federal government. The federal government referred to a governmental commission that would officially start their deliberations about reforms concerning financial equalization between the *Länder*, revenue sharing and the distribution of responsibilities between the Federation and the *Länder* in the spring of the year 2000. Only after these talks had been successfully completed would the bill be placed on the agenda of the *Bundestag*. Whether this will take place in this legislative term or in the next

164

remains to be seen. I personally do not expect any significant progress in the near future, as the *Länder* are completely divided among themselves concerning financial equalization between the *Länder*. The Federation will certainly know how to make use of this situation.

1.3. Assessment

The intention of the promoting politicians was clear: strengthening federalism by giving more competencies to the *Länder*. The result: a bill that leaves doubts whether it will reach the goal of making the *Länder* competitive and self-confident partners with the Federation, a requirement for the modernization of governance. But these goals have been undermined by bureaucratic maneuverings. Reinhold Bocklet, Bavarian Minister for Federal Affairs suggested this in his speech in the *Bundesrat*, when he complained about the fact that in the committee deliberations the experts had obviously been successful.[9] But the decision ought to be first and foremost a decision about policy guidelines. At some point, the German President Roman Herzog had put the truth into poignant words. Most of the work of the *Bundesrat* is done in the committees, which usually do not consist of state ministers but of ministerial state officials. The Federation's ministerial bureaucracy is opposed by "the controlling power of the state's ministerial bureaucracies. I do not know of any country on earth where powerful bureaucracies have been able to gain such control."[10] It is quite understandable that they do not like this power taken from them. The civil service machinery refuses by any means to have its power reduced, to have its influence handed over to *Länder* parliaments. The term "executive federalism", which is often used to characterize German federalism, is absolutely justified. It is a politician's duty to establish general policy guidelines[11], while implementation and detailed regulations are the duties of the civil servants. This proves the bureaucracy's power of persistence, and that they have more leverage. The cooperation between federal and state bureaucracy - nowadays additionally intensified by its European version - functions very smoothly.

But it would be too easy to blame the failure of substantial reforms in the allocation of responsibilities only on the bureaucracy. *Länder* politicians also hesitate to take over responsibilities. They are afraid of the consequences of competititon, they do not think they are up to that financially, nor do they want to widen the gap between the *Länder*. Participation in the Federation's decision-making process is considered to be more important than their own legislative competencies. Co-determination in the *Bundesrat* is regarded to be of higher value than self reliance of the *Länder*. Competitive federalism demands more political responsability instead of plain administration. Delegating political competencies means dividing governmental sovereignty between the jurisdictions of the Federation and the *Länder*. The majority of *Länder* do not yet support this and this not only because of financial reasons.

2. Strengthening *Länder* Parliaments

2.1. Regaining of Powers

Parallel to the efforts of the Bundesrat, *Länder* parliaments became active as well. They were the losers of centralization and had noticed that the extension of the involvement in the decision making process of the Federation resulted in a power shift favoring the *Länder* governments. For a long time *Länder* parliaments did little to counter the undermining of their powers. Frequently they only had the opportunity to rubber stamp arrangements already reached elsewhere.[12] They could not directly influence decisions of the *Bundesrat*. In contrast to the Basic Law's intentions, *Länder* parliaments were prevented from the execution of essential legislative powers. As a result the basic function of federalism - to safeguard democracy and to ensure the responsiveness to the citizens' concerns - was clearly weakened. Therefore two *Länder* parliaments established study commissions to prepare suggestions how to strengthen *Länder* parliaments. The commission in Hesse has been working on this topic for two parliamentary terms by now and has submitted an interim report.[13] In February 1998 the Bavarian parliamentary group of the Social Democrats demanded to set up a study commission "Reform of Federalism - Strengthening of *Länder* Parliaments". The Bavarian parliament followed this request and decided on November 26, 1998, to set up a study commission. Its concrete tasks and its composition were subsequently decided on July 8, 1999. But it is not only the *Bundesrat* that takes a long time to decide because of difficult decision-making processes and different interests. Even such a joint request by all parliamentary groups of the Bavarian parliament, which supposedly is in everybody's own best interest, took one-and-a-half years until it was translated into action.

2.2. The study commission's mission

The Bavarian commission consists of 15 members - eight members of parliament according to the size of the parliamentary groups and seven scholars as experts. The study commission's task is manyfold, four large subject areas with many issues and details have to be worked on. These include federalism and supranational politics, federalism and domestic politics, federalism and public finances, and federalism and local government. For these areas the commission is to deliver concrete recommendations. It is already clear that the report probably will not be completed as scheduled (June 30, 2001). The deliberations are - contrary to the traditions in the Bavarian parliament - not open to the public. There are no completed papers yet on any of the topics. An interim result was reached on "Federalism and domestic politics" including the complex questions concerning the future of German federalism. Questions of detail concern - apart from the devolution of legislative power and the reduction of entangled competencies - the *Land* parliaments' decision-making powers. Which participation rights are within the framework of the Federal Constitution? For instance a binding mandate for the representatives of the *Länder* governments in the *Bundesrat*, issued by the *Länder* parliaments? Which participation rights are politically desirable? These are questions that have aroused great controversy and where the self-confidence of parliamentarians clashed with the defensive tendency of the bureaucracy.[14] The aim of the Bavarian study commission is an order of federalism that connects national unity with a certain degree of regional economic, social and cultural diversities within the territory of the Federal Republic. Competition, combined with the adjective "solidaric", and the acceptance of flexible regulations are positively emphasised. Transparency of governmental decision-making processes in connection with the hope for stronger citizen participation is demanded.

2.3. General aims

There is general agreement on the following reform measures:

Disentanglement: A definite assignment of legislative competencies to the different levels of government without the opportunity of gridlock will strengthen the political ability to act and will make political decisions transparent again.

Subsidiarity: The assignment of tasks to the lowest possible governmental level will enable efficient solutions and foster acceptance and responsiveness to citizens concerns.

Solidaric competition: Competition of the *Länder* for the best political solutions will strengthen the innovative potential of politics; but it has to be prevented that structurally weak regions end up in a ruinous competition of locations.

Transparency: A clear demarcation of tasks will make it more difficult to shift responsibility or costs and will make it easier to attribute and control political decisions.

These general aims are supplemented by a variety of specific suggestions which require changes of the Basic Law in order to be realized: Prioritization of *Länder* legislation, reductions in the catalogue of concurrent legislation, changes in the framework legislation, extension of deadlines for comments of the *Bundesrat* (in order to give *Länder* parliaments the opportunity to intervene on the *Land* level in time). The Bavarian state government is required to start the necessary initiatives in the *Bundesrat*. Initiatives of this kind have had very limited success, as has already been shown in the first part of this chapter. In order to achieve unity in these fundamental questions we need a closer network between *Länder* parliaments and consultation with Members of the *Bundestag*. Especially the latter have to be won over to achieve changes, since the *Bundestag* has already been forced to give away competencies to the European Union. A further reduction of competencies of the *Bundestag* does not have good prospects of success at the moment. Maybe it is possible to use the widespread indignation of the Members of the *Bundestag* about the influence of the *Bundesrat* in favor of *Länder* parliaments. Members of the *Bundestag* might perhaps form an alliance with members of *Länder* parliaments against the respective bureaucracies. This is certainly a utopian dream and it also depends on the fact whether somebody is a member of the ruling party or the opposition.

2.4. The future role of the *Länder* Parliaments

Of central importance, therefore, are the demands of the *Länder* parliaments upon their own executives. The Bavarian study commission is presently discussing a legal provision that would require the Bavarian government to inform the parliament of important matters. The way the *Land* parliament is currently informed and integrated in plans of the *Land* government on the European and federal level is insufficient. A suggestion for changes in the Bavarian Constitution has been worked out. It demands, among other things, the information about intended legislation, about intended inter-state compacts, matters of the *Bundesrat*, contents of administrative agreements, information about the co-operation with the Federation, the *Länder*, the regions, other countries, international institutions and in matters concerning the European Union. The *Land* parliament should get the chance to state its position which will be considered. In urgent cases the position of the whole parliament shall be replaced by a report of the responsible committee. These are far-reaching demands which are supplemented by the suggestion of a legal base for the need to inform the parliament.

The Bavarian study commission is a bit more restrained on the question whether the parliament can issue a binding mandate to the *Land* government concerning decisions in the *Bundesrat*. Here the study commission holds the opinion that successive *Länder* parliaments - according to federal and Bavarian constitutional law - are neither allowed to give instructions to the *Länder* government's representatives in the *Bundesrat* nor are they allowed to oblige *Länder* governments to give certain instructions. But in all discussions the study commission's members add very wisely that the *Länder* governments are still acting within the framework of parliamentary responsibility. Those who know about the connection and dependence between the major party group and the government also know that this means there will be no change. The government rules the parliament the same way as before.

2.5. Prospects of success

The study commission is also going to suggest various other proposals concerning the reform of federalism. It is only possible to translate into immediate action those which deal with the relationship between the government and parliament in Bavaria and those concerning the relationship between *Land* and local governments.

If these suggestions are implemented convincingly, the transformation on the federal level will be taking place with greater authority as well.

Notes

1 Roman Herzog, speech in St. Paul's Church in Frankfurt a.M. on May 18, 1998, *Bulletin Presse und Informationsamt der Bundesregierung*, Bonn, (May 25, 1998), Number 34, pp 401-404.

2 E.g., Erwin Teufel, Minister-President of Baden-Württemberg in the Bundesrat on November 2, 1996, *Kompetenzen erweitern - Eigenverantwortung stärken. Die Länder als Garant des Föderalismus, Bundesrat* (ed.), Bonn.

3 *Wider die Erstarrung in unserem Staat – für eine Erneuerung des Föderalismus*, Friedrich-Naumann-Foundation on February 4, 1998, Königswinter, Bonn.

4 Dr. Klaus Dohnanyi, former Mayor and President of the Sente of the Freie Hansestadt Hamburg on September 1, 1998. Interview DLR-Berlin in Fernseh/Hörfunkspiegel Inland II, Presse und Informationsamt der Bundesregierung, Bonn.

5 Paper on the occasion of the introduction of an interministerial task force of the Free State of Bavaria; (March 24, 1995). Notes by Dr. Schön, Department Head in the *Bayerische Staatsministerium für Bundesangelegenheiten und Bevollmächtigter des Freistaates Bayern beim Bund* to his colleagues in the Bavarian ministries.

6 *Föderalismus durch Wettbewerb stärken. Kompetenzen für Bayern zurückgewinnen*, speech by Minister-President Dr. Edmund Stoiber in the Bavarian Parliament on November 29, 1996, *Landtagsprotokoll*, 63. Sitzung, 4568ff.

7 *Mehr Aufgaben und Gestaltungsmöglichkeiten für die Länder. Die neue Öffnungsklausel des Grundgesetzes nutzen*, Paper adopted during the meeting of the parliamentary group of the CSU in Banz, (September 1996).

8 E.g. the initiative for the devolution of legislative competencies in the area of civil service legislation failed.

9 *Bundesratsprotokoll* of October 15, 1999. 743. Sitzung, 375f.

10 Roman Herzog, speech, "Zum 50. Jahrestag der Konstitutierung des Landtags Nordrhein-Westfalen", on October 2, 1996 at Düsseldorf, *Bulletin Presse- und Informationsamt der Bundesregierung*, number 83, Bonn, (October 21), 1996,897-901.

11 E.g. *Modernisierung des Föderalismus - Stärkung der Eigenverantwortung der Länder. Baden-Württemberg, Bayern und Hessen zur Notwendigkeit einer leistungs- und wettbewerbsorientierten Reform des Föderalismus*, Bonn, (July 8, 1999). The positions on these questions of legislative competencies, the strengthening of the *Länder's* tax autonomy, the reduction of matching funds financing and the reform of financial equalization between the *Länder* are explained on 49 pages.

12 Especially in the field of education, which is exclusively within the legislative power of the *Länder*, but where *Länder* parliaments only "give their blessings" to decisions by the *Kultusministerkonferenz* (Standing Conference of Ministers of Education and Cultural Affairs of the Länder of the FRG).

13 *Zwischenbericht der Enquetekommission "Künftige Aufgaben des Hessischen Landtags an der Wende zum 21. Jahrhundert*, Hessischer Landtag Drucksache 14/4365, Wiesbaden, (December 14, 1998).

14 Civil Servants from different Ministries, especially from the State Chancellary, follow the deliberations as observers and frequently "support" the Members of the ruling parliamentary party with well worded papers.

III. Fiscal Transfers and Local Government Reform

Introduction

Carola Kaps

As the United States has started much earlier on the path to "Reinventing Government", it is small wonder that there are already tangible results; moreover, progress is made easier by the fact that U.S. states have their own tax revenues and are much less dependent on fiscal transfers from the central government. Even though, progress has not been easy. Washington has increasingly delegated responsibility for various public tasks to the States, demanding certain results but leaving it up to them how to deliver. This result oriented strategy does away with burdensome, often unnecessary regulations and gives the States and communities freedom to choose a course of action which corresponds best to their specific needs and cirumstances. Though the States have often complained about Washington's preference for unfunded mandats - handing over responsibilities without proper financial means - , the overall flexibility allowed by the federal government has openend the door to innovation and creativity in federally mandated programs and problem solving.

As Howard Rosen points out in his contribution about the fiscal relationship between the federal government and the states, not only have the states become the social laboratories of the nation, the most exciting economic development takes place on the local and state level as well. With only 20 %

of state and local expenditures being funded by fiscals transfers from Washington, the states rely for most of their expenditures on their own fiscal revenues. As competition is as American as apple pie, tax rates are by no means equal across states as is true for the level and quality of public services.

Merl M. Hackbart and Robert J. Eger III underline that state and local governments are more and more run like businesses, complete with change in management practices, customer orientation and increased risk taking. They claim however, that Washington's "Reinventing Government" campaign had much less impact on this development than the desire for change and more competition on the state level as well as within state agencies. Another important element of this change agenda is the general and deeply ingrained animosity to the state within the American public which hates taxes, demands constant justifications on how tax dollars are spent and insists on costefficiency and public thrift.

In Germany, fiscal reform and the rebalancing of revenue among the *Länder* is only just beginning and is surrounded by tremendous controversy and torn by conflicting views. As Ernst Ulrich von Weizsäcker, member of the Fiscal Committee of the *Deutsche Bundestag* explaines, the demands for financial equalization (*Finanzausgleich*) and equivalency of living standards among the fifteen *Länder* make a already complicated tax system even more complicated; furthermore, the quite open egotism of the *Länder* does little to enhance the prospect for meaningful change. However, reform is imparative and needs foremost to address the incentive structure which so far is heavily weighted against labor making it too expensive. At the same time Weizsäcker makes the case for an ecological taxreform, as misuse of resources and waste needs to be stopped.

Wolfgang Renzsch confirmes, that the current budgetary crisis and the demands of European integration make reform of the federal system unavoidable; however, the level of pain is still too low to generate action. Moreover, he considers Germany quite unable to travel the road to a competitive federalism. Change will be more incremental and will stress a more cooperative form of federalism, within which the Länder should gain more freedom from federal regulation and should therefore be more flexible on how to deliver their services.

Whereas the reform of the federal system and the accompanying reform of fiscal tranfers move along in a snails pace, lots of modernizing is going on in local governments. To increase transparency in cost and performance in the public sector governments have tried to borrow from the private sector the concept of cost and result accounting. This has, however, proven inadequate for the public sector because the filter of the market is missing for the public sector. As Bernd Adamaschek from the Bertelsmann Foundation explaines, comparative accounting is doing the trick in adding the market function to the cost and result accounting. In keeping local governments constantly on their toes the media has an important role to play as corrective and competition enhancing force.

Federal and Sub-Federal Fiscal Policies in Germany

Ernst Ulrich von Weizsäcker

You may ask why a biologist should ever show a desire to join the parliamentary Fiscal Committee. The answer is actually quite simple. I have been working in environmental policy analysis during the fifteen years preceding my entering the Bundestag. And one thing I discovered for sure: If you put high taxes and levies on human labour and let the use of energy and other natural resources essentially tax-free, you are creating a climate for robotics and not for the efficient use of natural resources. Hence I have been one of the strong advocates for an ecological tax reform, and that if possible internationally agreed or at least harmonised at the level of the European Union.

Well, we made some headway in this regard but are now facing considerable resistance. One of the more prominent Minister-Presidents of the German *Länder*, Dr. Edmund Stoiber of Bavaria, made a series of public attacks on the gasoline taxes. He has three reasons for doing so. One is, that he was against "green" taxes from the outset. The second is the disproportionate rise of crude oil prices in the Euro zone, making fuel taxation particularly unpopular. And the third reason is that Bavaria does not get a penny from the revenue collected at the filling stations.

Which brings me to my main subject of the fiscal structure in Germany. You all know that we have four different levels of taxes in our country:

- European
- Federal
- *Länder* and
- Municipal

In practical terms it is only three because the European taxes are no genuinely separate taxes. It is in effect federal taxes which are later transferred to the European Union.

Fiscal legislation is almost exclusively done at the federal level. But whenever *Länder* taxes are involved in federal legislation, the *Länder*, through the *Bundesrat*, participate in the legislation process. In fact, it has been the Social Democratic majority in the *Bundesrat* which blocked the tax reform proposals that were designed during the last three years of the Kohl government. And now we have an Social Democratic majority in the *Bundestag* and sufficient votes from the conservative camp to block federal legislation. Fortunately, the essentials of the corporate tax reform proposed by the federal government, passed the Bundesrat in July 2000, after a few compromises were formulated to accommodate wishes from some *Länder* ruled by coalitions between Social Democrats and conservatives.

Our constitution which was created under significant U.S. American influence in 1949 and the ensuing fiscal legislation have given the *Länder* considerable powers both for collecting taxes and for the disbursement of revenues. Three of the four biggest taxes are "common taxes" shared more or less between the federal and *Länder* authorities but collected at the *Land* level. The taxman actually operates below the *Land* level at the city level.

The three big common taxes are
- income taxes
- corporate taxes
- and value-added-tax (VAT).

The fourth big tax is the petrol tax which is collected and administered only at the federal level – together with custom duties, insurance taxes and federal monopolies such as the tobacco tax.

Income taxes are shared evenly by the federal and *Land* levels. This apportion was laid down in the Constitution (Article 106 paragraph 3 Basic Law). A federal law also stipulates the percentage of income taxes that goes to the municipalities, currently 15 %.

Pure *Länder* taxes include beer taxes, motor vehicle taxes and inheritance taxes (Article 106 paragraph 2 Basic Law). And the municipalities are allowed to collect a real estate tax and a trades tax (Gewerbesteuer) which is an additional – and hefty – tax for commercial business down to the one-person barber shop (Article 106 paragraph 6 Basic Law).

The VAT which was introduced in the sixties has assumed more and more the role of an important source of income both for the nation and the *Länder*. It's apportionment is not fixed by the Constitution and has actually shifted from federal to *Länder* levels. In 1970 70 % of the revenues were federal, 30 % for the *Länder*. Today it is essentially a 50 – 50 ratio.

However, there are additional equalization mechanisms for all tax revenues in which the *Länder* participate. These mechanisms were introduced to guarantee more or less equal living conditions throughout the country but have come under attack in recent years after the German reunification.

The attack, once again, came from Bavaria. It started the moment Bavaria became a contributing party to the equalization mechanism. Until German reunification Bavaria had been among the receiving *Länder*.

It would be too simplistic to say that Bavaria had only egotistic motives. There are also very sound reasons for criticising the transfer mechanisms. In effect they offered hardly any incentive for individual *Länder* to perform better. To understand this, we should take a somewhat closer look at the redistribution mechanism.

One component is the VAT distribution. The VAT is in effect a consumption tax. It is assumed to be fair that revenues from the VAT should go to the *Länder* more or less on an equal per capita basis. That means *Länder* obtaining from income and corporate taxes less than 92 % of the average per capita revenues get compensated from the *Länder* VAT share to lift them towards the 92 % level. Given the extremely weak performance of the new *Länder*, the Federation decided in 1995 to further subsidize this program using in part the federal portion of the VAT revenues.

A second mechanism of redistribution is the horizontal transfer among the *Länder*. Again 92 % of the per capita average is the magic threshold. Anything left for compensation from the VAT mechanism is completely paid by the rich *Länder*. So that all Länder reach at least 92 %. For the rest, they obtain nearly 40 % of the shortfall between 92 % and 100 %.

The equalization payments by the rich *Länder* are calculated according to the level of their "financial capacity", and involves skimming off for equalization

- 15 % of their financial capacity which is between 100 % and 101 % above average,
- 66 % of their financial capacity which is between 101 % and 110 % above average,
- 80 % of their financial capacity which is above 110 % of the average of all *Länder*.

A factor is applied to these surpluses of the financially strong *Länder* to raise or lower the total volume of payments so it equals the total volume of equalization grants.

Finally, there are a large number of complex rules meant to ensure that the equalization grants and payments which have been determined in this way also fulfil certain subsidiary conditions (e.g. keeping the same order of financial capacity of the *Länder*, avoiding placing excessive burdens on financially stronger *Länder*). The quantitative effects of these so-called guarantee clauses are insignificant compared to the effects of the equalization mechanism described above. The total volume of horizontal financial equalization amounted to just below DM 11 billion in 1996.

Finally, federal grants ("supplemental grants") are made to financially weak *Länder* in order to complement the coverage of their general financial requirements.They are likewise an expression of solidarity, but between the Federation and the *Länder*. The *Länder* receiving supplement grants have a free hand to dispose of the funds as part of their budgetary autonomy.

The total volume of supplement grants (in 1995 approx. DM 25 billion) was considerably expanded under the reorganisation in order to take account of additional special requirements:

- Financially weak old and new *Länder* receive shortfall supplement grants from the federation amounting to 90 % of the shortfalls which remain after the financial equalization among *Länder* (volume in 1996: DM 4,9 billion).

- Besides that over the period 1995 to 2004 the Federation will pay the new *Länder* special supplement grants of DM 14 billion a year in order to reduce special burdens linked to the division of Germany and to compensate the less-than-average financial capacity of the municipalities.

The system is fairly complicated and ultimately leads to a nearly complete equalization of taxes available to the *Länder* in proportion to their population.

Bavaria was joined by Baden-Württemberg and Hesse in demanding a fundamental change of the system. A Supreme Court ruling of November 11, 1999 in favor of these plaintiff *Länder* gives the federal legislators a few years to come up with a new system that contains some significant rewards and penalties for outperformance and underperformance, respectively.

The situation is aggravated by the fact that the federal treasury is in deep troubles due to the demographic situation, high unemployment, unlimited expectations of achieving equality in East Germany, and by the dwindling revenues from capital taxes (owing to high capital mobility). Hence, the Federation will find it nearly impossible to solve the problems by giving a generous contribution to outperforming *Länder*. Whichever reward for the strong Länder will therefore come at the expense of the weak *Länder*.

Let me conclude with a personal remark leading back to my environmental concerns. This unwieldy *Länder* compensation mechanism cannot be said to be ecologically sensible. Rather I sense that the reform of the system should also be looked at from an environmental point of view. But that goes far beyond the scope of this transatlantic endeavour of this book.

Further Readings

Jens Altemeier, *Föderale Finanzbeziehungen unter Anpassungsdruck, Verteilungskonflikte in der Verhandlungsdemokratie*, Schriften des Max-Planck-Instituts für Gesellschaftsforschung, Frankfurt/Main et al., Lang, 1999.

Bundesministerium der Finanzen, *Bund-Länder Finanzbeziehungen auf der Grundlage der geltenden Finanzverfassungsordnung*, 2. Aufl., Dokumentation 3 / 2000, August 2000.

Decision of the Federal Constitutional Court concerning the system of fiscal equalization in the German Federal System, *BVerfGE* 101, 158ff.

Federal Ministry of Finance, "The Economic Situation in the Federal Republic of Germany", *Economic and Financial Reports*, Berlin, Monthly Report 12/2000.

Federal Ministry of Finance, "Facts on Public Finance", *Economic and Financial Reports*, Berlin, Monthly Report 12/2000.

Federal Ministry of Finance, "German Stability Programme", *Economic and Financial Reports*, Berlin, October 2000 update.

Federal Ministry of Finance, "Promotion of Environmental Protection in German Laws on Taxes and on Other Types of Levies", *Economic and Financial Reports*, Berlin, January 2000.

Federal Ministry of Finance, "Guiding Principles of Fiscal Policy. Seven pointers for future-oriented, equitable fiscal policy in a European context", *Economic and Financial Reports*, November 2000, Berlin.

"Gesetz über verfassungskonkretisierende allgemeine Maßstäbe für die Verteilung des Umsatzsteueraufkommens, für den Finanzausgleich unter den Ländern sowie für die Gewährung von Bundesergänzungszuweisungen (Maßstäbegesetz – Maßst.G -)", Bill agreed upon by the Federal Cabinet on February 21, 2001.

Klaus Dirk Henke, *Die Zukunft der Staatsfinanzierung*, Baden-Baden, Nomos, 1999.

Jürgen W. Hidien, *Der bundestaatliche Finanzausgleich in Deutschland: geschichtliche und staatsrechtliche Grundlagen*, Baden-Baden, Nomos, 1999.

Bernd Huber/Karl Lichtblau, *Ein neuer Finanzausgleich. Reformoptionen nach dem Verfassungsgerichtsurteil*, Köln, Deutscher Instituts Verlag, 2000.

Hans Mackenstein/Charlie Jeffery, "Financial Equalization in the 1990s: On the Road Back to Karlsruhe? ", Charlie Jeffery (Ed.), *Recasting German Federalism. The Legacies of Unification*, London, New York, Pinter, 1999.

Organization for Economic Co-operation and Development (OECD), *Managing Across Levels of Government*, Paris, 1997, 32-44 and 179-190.

Wolfgang Renzsch, "Financing German Unity: Fiscal Conflict Resolution in a Complex Federation", in, *Publius. The Journal of Federalism*, vol. 28, (Fall 1998), 127-146.

Wolfgang Scherf, *Der Länderfinanzausgleich in Deutschland: ungelöste Probleme und Ansatzpunkte einer Reform*, Frankfurt/Main, Lang, 2000.

Wissenschaftlicher Beirat beim Bundesministerium der Finanzen, *Stellungnahme zum Finanzausgleichsurteil des Bundesverfassungsgerichts vom 11. November 1999*, Berlin, 08. Juni 2000.

U.S. Federal Transfers to the States:
Devolution and Dollars

Howard Rosen[1]

Introduction

The American style of federalism - the separation of powers between the Federal and state governments - finds its roots in the U.S. Constitution. Subsequent legislation passed by the Congress and approved by the President, as well as decisions made by the courts, have reinforced and clarified this separation. The result is a unique system of responsibilities and transfers, which is specific to the United States. The following discussion of federal transfers to state and local governments in the United States is presented in order to deepen the understanding of the U.S. system, not as a means of comparison with any other country.

In general, the primary means by which the federal government collects revenues is through taxes on personal income and corporate profits.[2] The federal government also imposes a payroll tax to finance Unemployment Insurance, Medicare and Social Security. Traditionally, states have collected their revenue through taxes on commercial sales and corporate profits. More recently, states have begun to introduce income taxes as well. Property taxes have been the primary means by which local governments collect their revenue.[3]

Total (federal, state and local) government spending in the United States equaled about 34 percent of Gross Domestic Product (GDP) in 1999. Federal government spending was 20 percent of GDP, state and local government spending was 10 percent of GDP, and federal transfers to state and local governments, which valued $267 billion in 1999, were 4 percent of GDP. In other words, two-thirds of government spending was performed by the federal government and a third of government spending was financed by state and local governments.

In general, states have the responsibility for public education, police and fire protection, sewage and sanitation, maintaining highways (built by the federal government), Medicare (health insurance for the poor), and some welfare and social services. The federal government has the responsibility for Social Security, Unemployment Insurance, Medicare (health insurance for the elderly), most programs for the poor, disadvantaged and elderly, and large transportation projects, as well as national defense.

There have been three important developments in terms of federal transfers to state and local governments over the last 40 years. First, macroeconomic conditions and changes in economic policies have had a major influence over federal transfers to the states. Second, during the late 1960s and early 1970s, President Nixon used "block-grants" as a means of *increasing* the value of federal transfers to state and local governments. Block-grants are a way for Congress to appropriate money to the states for the purpose of administering programs, as opposed to the federal government funding and administering the programs itself. By contrast, President Reagan used the same mechanism - block-grants - to *reduce* the value of federal transfers to state and local governments. Third, currently, due to an increase in demand for social services, federal funds have become less important relative to the amount of activity supported by state and local governments. State and local governments and private enterprise have taken on more of the burdens of financing traditional federal government responsibilities.

This chapter will provide details on recent trends at various aspects of federal transfers to state and local governments. In addition, information will be provided describing the sources of tax revenue.

There are various models concerning funding sources and administration of government programs. There are numerous combinations of local, state, and federal funding as well as local, state, and federal administration. The following table provides examples of some of the larger programs.

Program	Funding Source	Administration
Education	local	local
Medicare	federal	federal
Medicaid	federal/state	local
Unemployment Insurance	federal	state
Welfare	shift to the states	state

The Structure of U.S. Tax System

Eighty-two percent of all federal government tax revenue is collected through income and payroll taxes. Taxes on corporate income account for 10 percent of all federal government tax receipts. The remaining 8 percent is made up of excise, estate and gift taxes, customs duties and fees, Federal Reserve deposits, and universal service fund receipts. (See Figure 1, page 193).

The structure of state tax system is very different from that of the federal tax system. State taxes are predominantly sales-related and the federal tax system is primarily based on income - both individual and corporate. Forty-eight percent of state tax revenue is derived from sales taxes. Individual income tax makes up 33 percent and corporate income tax makes up 7 percent of state tax receipts. (See Figure 2, page 194).

State taxes are determined by the individual state's legislators and governors. As a result, there is great variety among state tax systems. Some states do not tax direct income, but do tax investment income. Seven states Alaska, Florida, Nevada, South Dakota, Texas, Washington and Wyoming have no income tax. The effective income tax rate in three states – North Dakota, Tennessee, and New Hampshire – is around 1½ percent. Half the states (25) have an income tax which is between 1½ and 2½ percent of income. The income tax rate for the remaining 15 states is between 2½ and 4¼ percent of income. (See Figure 3, page 195).

Similarly, sales tax rates vary by state. Five states – Alaska, Delaware, Montana, Oregon and New Hampshire do not have a sales tax. The remaining 45 states have tax rates which vary from 3 percent to 7 percent of sales. (See Figure 4, page 196).

Taken together, the vast majority of states (38) collect between $1,000 and $2,000 in tax revenue per person. New Hampshire and Utah collect less than $1,000 per person and 10 states – California, Connecticut, Delaware, Hawaii, Massachusetts, Michigan, Minnesota, New Mexico, Washington and Wisconsin – collect more than $2,000 per person. (See Figure 5, page 197).

State taxes vary in terms of their importance to individual states. For more than half of the states (27), state taxes account for between 42 and 57 percent of total state revenues from all sources. Twenty-one states depend on taxes to make up between 29 and 42 percent of total state revenue. For Alaska and New Hampshire, taxes account for between 13 and 29 percent of total state revenue. (See Figure 6, page 198).

Federal Grants to State and Local Governments

The value of federal grants to state and local governments has grown significantly, in real terms, over the last 40 years. Between 1960 and 1978, the real value of federal grants to state and local governments grew fivefold. Federal grants fell by almost 25 percent between 1978 and 1982. The value of federal grants changed very little between 1982 and 1989. Since 1990, federal grants to states and localities grew on average by $11 billion a year, or by 60 percent over the nine years. (See Figure 7, page 199).

A different picture emerges when looking at federal grants to state and local governments as a share of total federal outlays and total state and local expenditures. Federal grants to state and local governments doubled from 7½ percent to 15 percent of total federal outlays between 1960 and 1974, before sliding back to approximately 10 percent until 1990. Since 1990, federal grants to states and local governments have grown from 10 percent back to the peak of 15 percent of total federal outlays. As a share of non-defense outlays, federal grants to states and local governments grew from 15 percent in 1960 to a high of 25 percent in 1974, and then down to 17 percent in 2000. (See Figure 8, page 200).

As a share of total state expenditures, federal grants to state and local governments accounted for 10 percent in 1960, before rising to 25 percent in 1974 and 1980. Since then, federal grants have fallen to 20 percent of total state expenditures. (See Figure 9, page 201).

The growth in federal grants has changed the composition of state and local funding sources. In 1960, federal grants and transfers accounted for 11 percent of total state and local operations. By 1999, federal grants and transfers accounted for 21 percent of state and local resources. (See Figure 10, page 202).

Once again, on a state-by-state basis, the picture is quite varied. Seventeen states depend on federal grants for more than a quarter of their state's budget. In 13 states, federal grants account for between 16 and 22 percent of total state expenditures. (See Figure 11, page 203).

Given their small population and the large amount of federal assistance, Alaska and Wyoming enjoy the highest per capita federal assistance – more than $1,800 per person. In addition, the federal government provides a financial incentive for all residents of Alaska. Twenty-nine states receive between $900 and $1,800 in federal grants and transfers per person. Nineteen states receive less than $900 per person. (See Figure 12, page 204).

Composition of Federal Grants to State and Local Governments

Almost half (43 percent) of federal grants to state and local governments are concentrated in health. This is predominantly for Medicaid. Another 24 percent is concentrated in income security payments. Together, these two items constitute two thirds of total federal grants to states and localities. Funds for education and training, economic development and transportation make up most of the remaining third of federal grants to states and local governments. (See Figure 13, page 205).

Federal transfers to states for income security grew on average by 3½ percent a year from 1960 until 1999. By contrast, federal transfers for health grew on average by 15 percent a year between 1960 and 1989. Since 1990, federal transfers to the states for health have doubled. Federal transfers for all other purposes grew more than 5½ times from $23 billion in 1960 to their peak of $128 billion in 1978. These grants have leveled off since 1978, and are currently valued at $89 billion. (See Figure 14, page 206).

Income Security

The major programs under income security are: Unemployment Insurance, food-related programs, and Family Support Payments. In addition, there are other smaller programs under income security. There has been steady growth in most of these programs over the last several years, except for the Unemployment Insurance Trust Fund.

There has been very little change in the Unemployment Insurance Trust Fund over the last 20 years. In contrast, food-related programs grew by 80 percent since 1980. Family Support Payments grew on average by approximately 1½ percent per year between 1980 and 1996. Other income security programs more than doubled between 1980 and 1999, growing on average by 5 percent per year. These programs include payments for emergency food and shelter, low-income energy, childcare, Native Americans, the homeless and youth. (See Figure 15, page 207).

Medicaid Financing

Since 1975, the federal share of total Medicaid spending has averaged 56 percent. The remaining 44 percent has been financed by the states. Between 1975 and 1989, total medicare funding grew on average by approximately 5½ percent annually. In just 3 years, 1990 to 1992, total Medicaid spending rose by more than 70 percent. Since 1992, the growth in Medicare spending has fallen back to about 4½ percent per year. (See Figure 16, page 208).

Under Medicaid, the federal government must match whatever individual states decide to provide, within the law, for its eligible recipients. There is no limit to the amount of total federal outlays for Medicaid. The federal government's portion of the Medicaid program is determined annually for each state by a formula that compares the state's average per capita income level with the national average. By law, this formula cannot be lower than 50 percent or greater than 83 percent of the national average. states with higher per capita incomes have a smaller share of their costs reimbursed. The federal government also shares in the state's expenditures for administration of the Medicaid program. Most administrative costs are matched at 50 percent for all states. However, higher matching rates (75, 90 and 100 percent) have also been authorized for specific functions and activities. (See Figure 17, page 209).

After income security and health, the next largest area of federal funding is for education and social services. Federal transfers to state and local governments grew on average by a little more than 8½ percent per year from 1960 to 1999. Funding for education and social services peaked in 1978, then fell by almost 50 percent by 1984. Although federal transfers in education and social services have rebounded since 1984, they remain 26 percent lower than their peak in 1978. (See Figure 18, page 210).

Federal grants to states and local governments for transportation have only grown slightly over the 40 year period. The average annual growth of transportation grants have been less than 2 percent a year. Given the large size of individual transportation grants, total grants in this area have fluctuated year-to-year.

Federal grants to state and local governments for community and regional economic development, one of the smallest areas of grants, amounted to approximately $600 million in 1960. Grants in this area grew by an average of 23 percent per year, until peaking at $17.7 billion in 1978. Between 1978 and 1989, federal grants for economic development fell on average by 10 percent a year, before dropping to $5.4 billion. These grants began growing again in 1993. Although federal grants for economic development grew by 77 percent between 1992 and 1999, their level remained below the average level of grants in the 1970s.

Education

The United States has a unique way of funding education. The primary source of funds for education is state and local appropriations. Local municipalities depend on property taxes to finance their share of the education budget. This system of funding is highly inequitable, as areas with higher property values will collect more tax revenues and be able to provide more resources to local schools. Poorer neighborhoods will likely have schools with fewer resources.

State governments attempt to correct for this imbalance in education resources. States depend primarily on sales taxes, and more recently on income taxes, to raise revenue to fund local school districts. It is left up to each state to determine how it wishes to redistribute these resources for education.

The federal governments role in funding education is the smallest of the three. Federal government efforts on behalf of education tend to concentrate on areas for which states and localities are unlikely to provide funding. This includes educational programs for the disadvantaged and students with special needs. Other areas of funding include children and family services programs, foster care and adoption, and training and employment programs.

Federal grants to states and local governments for education for the disadvantaged grew by 32 percent between the 1980s and the 1990s. Funding for special education grew by almost twice that much over the same period. Federal grants to state and local governments for children and family services and foster care and adoption grew by 39 percent and 46 percent respectively, between the 1980s and the 1990s. By contrast, federal grants for training and employment fell by 39 percent over the same time. This may have been due in part to the improvement in the U.S. economy and the falling unemployment rate during the second half of the 1990s. (See Figure 19, page 211).

Total spending on education, regardless of the source of funds, grew on average by 2 percent a year from 1980 to 1996. The distribution of education spending, between the federal, state and local governments has remained relatively constant since 1976. The majority of spending on education – 93 percent – is almost evenly financed by state and local governments. On average, between 1976 and 1996, state governments financed 47 percent of total spending on education. Local governments financed another 46 percent and the federal government made up the remaining 7 percent of total spending on education.

State expenditures on education grew on average by 2½ percent per year between 1976 and 1996. Local expenditures on education grew on average by 1¾ percent per year. Federal expenditures grew on average by less than 1 percent per year. On average, over the 20 year period, increases in state expenditures on education accounted for three-fourths of the increase in total expenditures on education. The remaining fourth was split between the federal government and local governments. (See Figure 20, page 212).

Conclusion

This chapter describes the structure of various funding sources, i.e., federal, state and local tax systems, as well as federal grants and transfers to state and local governments. On the funding side, the federal tax system is primarily based on taxing personal and corporate income. State tax systems have been based on the sales of goods and services, and are currently expanding to include taxing income. Local tax systems have been primarily based on taxing property.

Although states may share a common tax system, their outcomes are likely to differ. States vary in terms of taxing sales versus income, and also have different tax rates. The amount of federal grants and transfers also differs by state. Some grants and transfers are based on need, and others are based on equal distribution. Overall, there is great variety between the states in terms of raising revenues and receiving federal grants and transfers.

Based on the U.S. Constitution, subsequent laws and court decisions, there has been a distribution of responsibilities between the federal, state and local governments. As already mentioned, the federal government has primary responsibility for Social Security, Unemployment Insurance, Medicare (health insurance for the elderly), most programs for the poor, disadvantaged and elderly, and large transportation projects, as well as national defense. States, in general, have the responsibility for public education, police and fire protection, sewage and sanitation, maintaining highways (built by the federal government), Medicare (health insurance for the poor), and some welfare and social services.

In general, there has been an increase in federal grants and transfers to state and local governments since the 1980s. Despite this increases, the federal share of state and local expenditures has remained relatively constant. Spending on health related programs have accounted for a large share of the increase in federal grants and transfers.

Notes

1   The author is grateful to Dan Pollock for his research assistance, including preparing
    the figures for this chapter. The views expressed in this chapter are solely those of the
    author and do not in any way reflect the views of the Joint Economic Committee or
    any member of Congress.
2   Formalized by Article XVI of the U.S. Constitution in 1913.
3   The advent of electronic commerce carried out on the Internet has raised new ques-
    tions concerning the taxation of commerce. Congress has placed a moratorioum on
    any federally-imposed taxation of electronic commerce. For states, sales taxes are a
    very important source of revenue. They have argued that the federally-mandated
    moratorium denies them access to a large and growing tax base. Internet taxation, and
    by which level of government, will be a hotly contested issue over the coming years.

Figure 1

Composition of Federal Tax Reciepts
1999

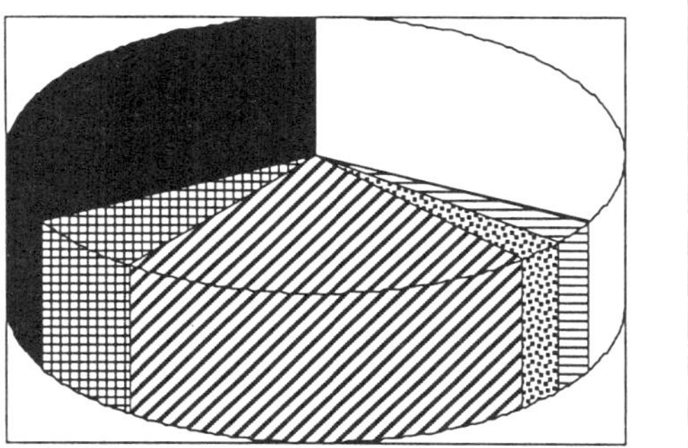

Source: Office of Management and Budget

* Estate and gift taxes, customs duties and fees, federal reserve deposits, and universal service fund reciepts

Figure 2

Composition of State Tax Reciepts

1998

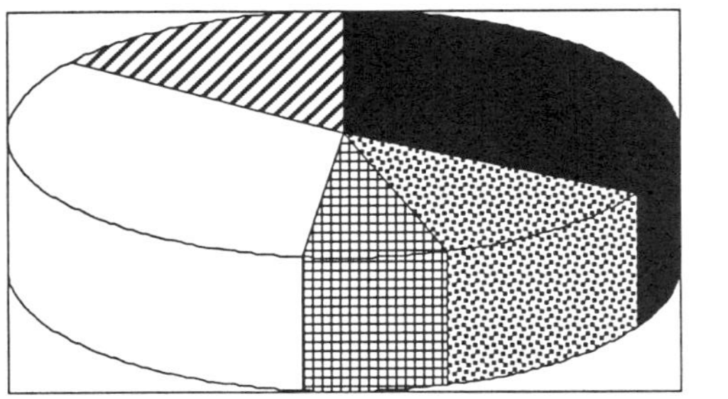

Source: Office of Management and Budget

Figure 3

Average Effective Income Tax Rates by State (1998)

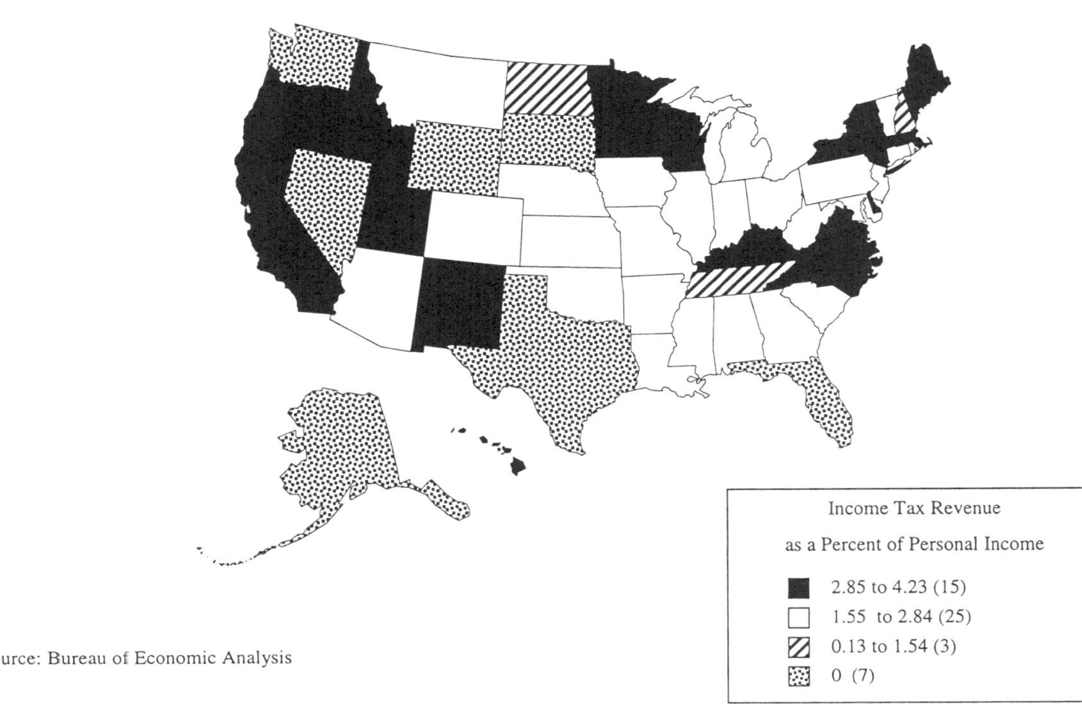

Source: Bureau of Economic Analysis

Figure 4

State Sales Tax (1998)

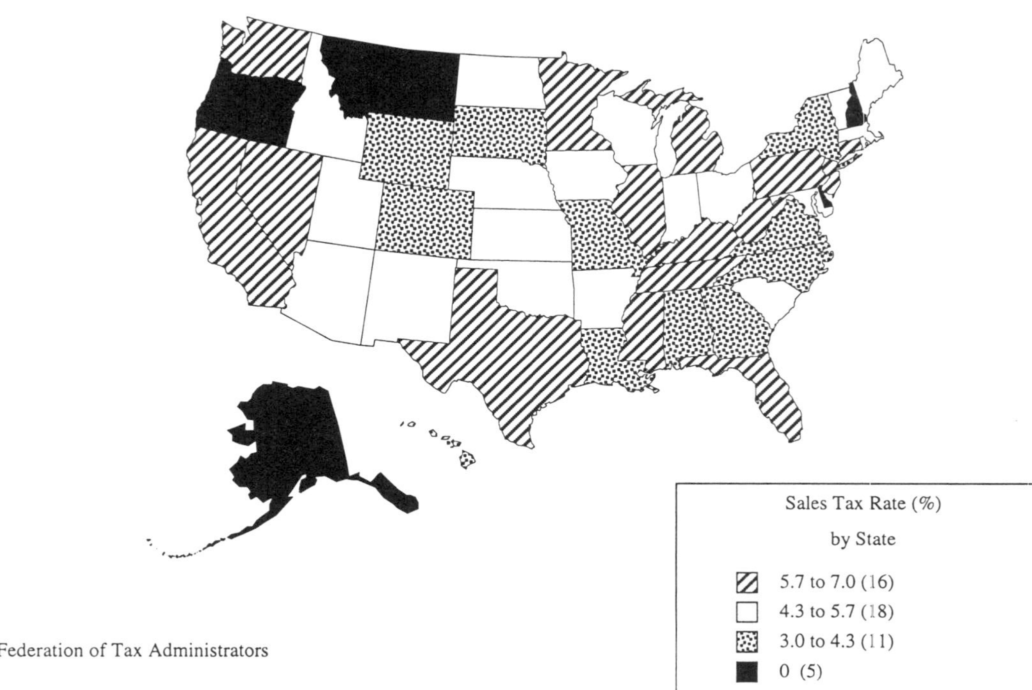

Source: Federation of Tax Administrators

Figure 5

Per Capita Tax Revenue (1998)

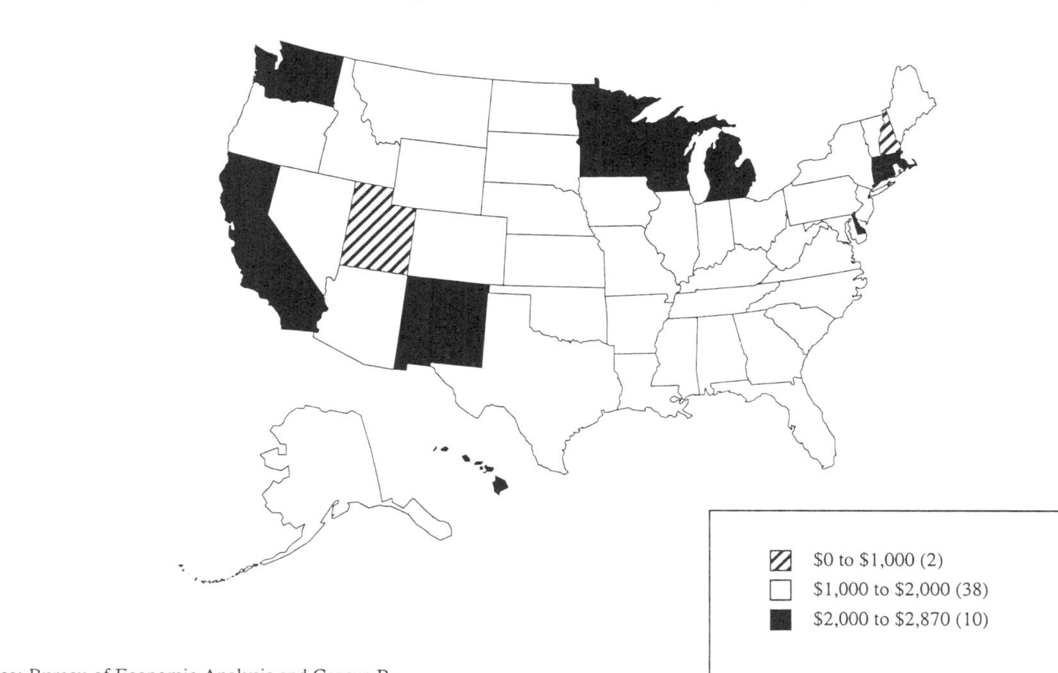

Source: Bureau of Economic Analysis and Census Bureau

Figure 6

Taxes as a Share of Total State Revenue (1998)

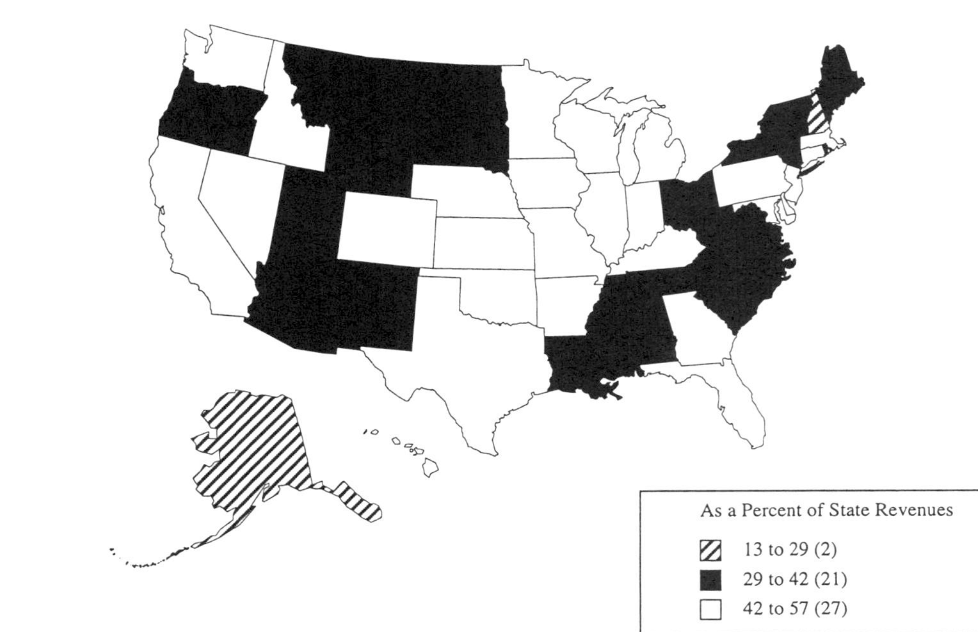

Source: Bureau of Economic Analysis

Figure 7

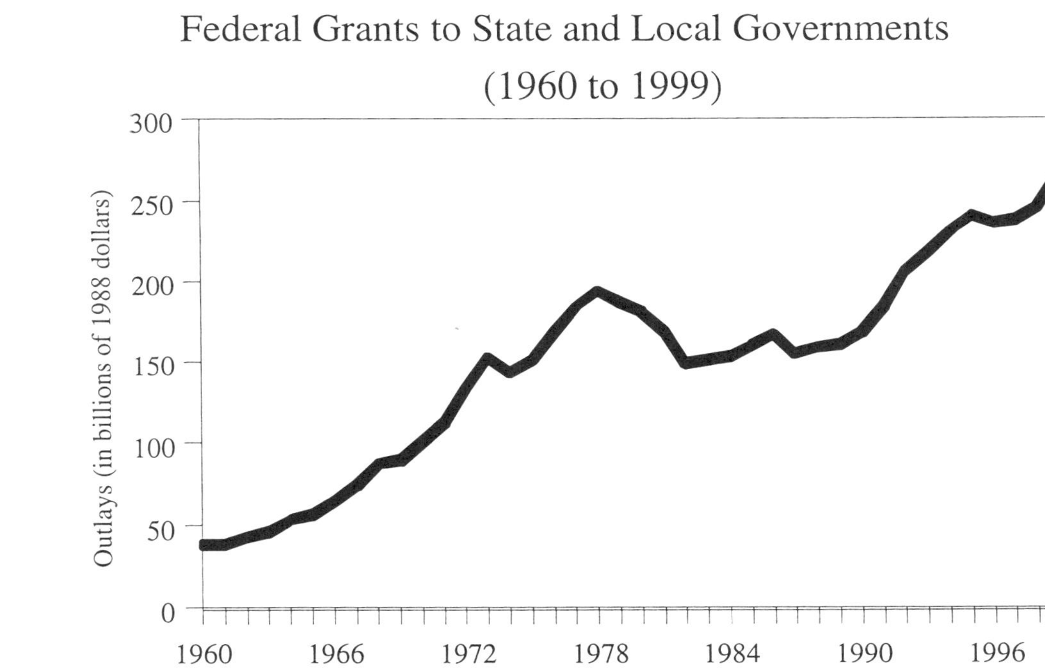

Source: Office cf Management and Budget

Figure 8
Federal Grants to State and Local Governments
(1960 to 1999)
As a Percent of Total Expenditures
25
20
15
10
5
0
1960
1966
1972
1978
1984
1990
1996
Total Federal Outlays
Non- defense Outlays
Source: Office of Management and Budget

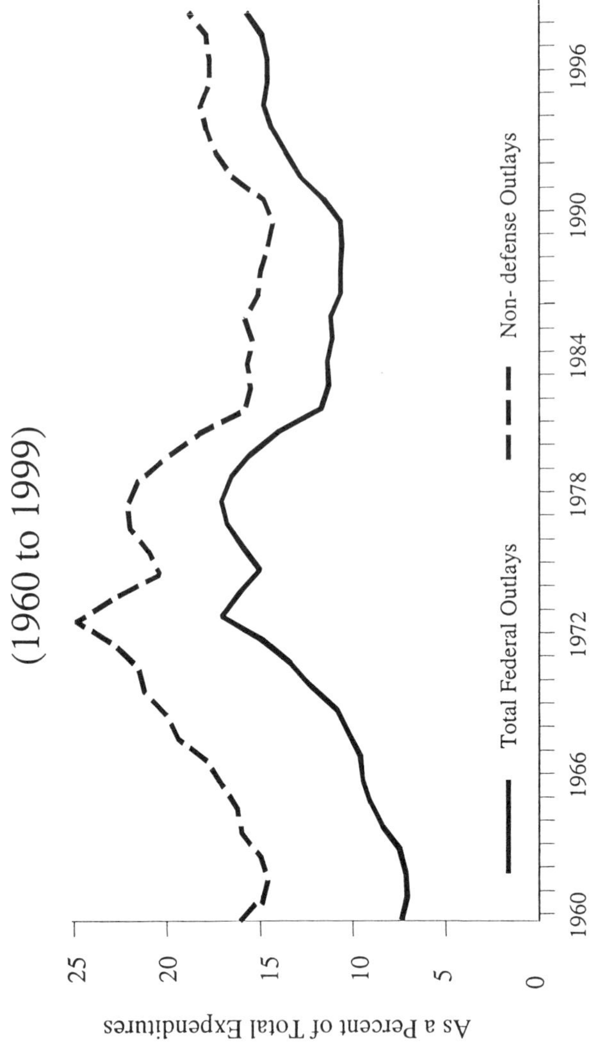

200

Figure 9

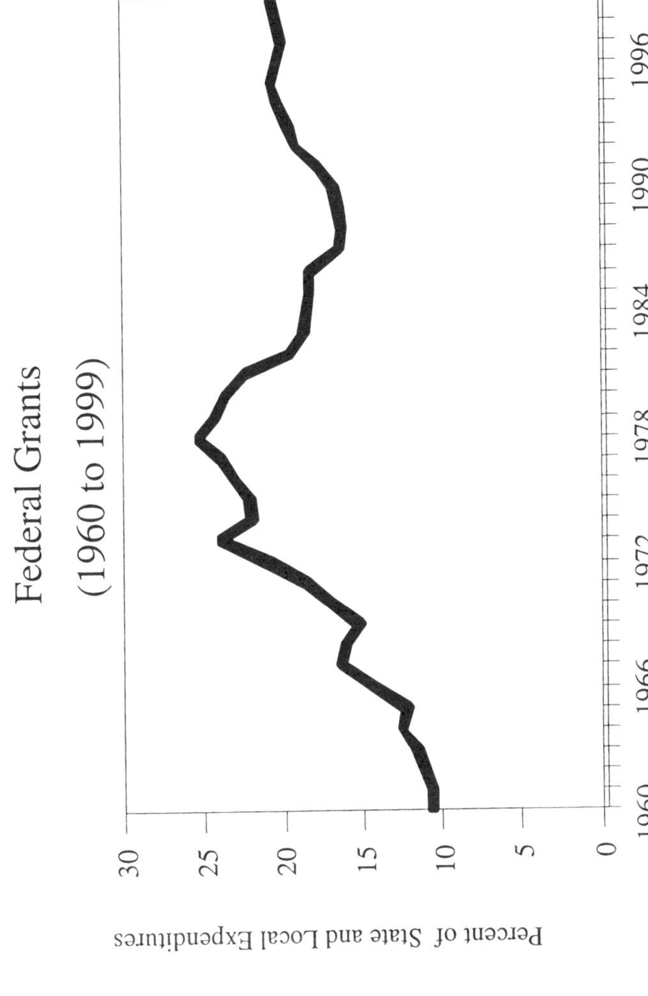

Source: Office of Management and Budget, State and Local Sources and Federal Grants are based on NIPA.

Figure 10

State/Local Funding Sources
(1960 to 1999)

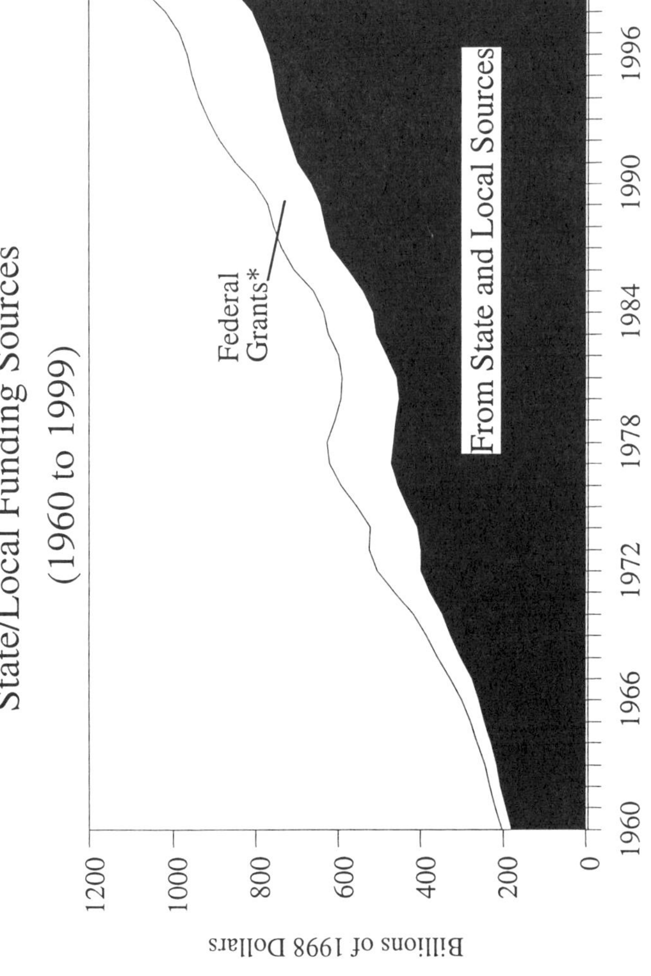

Source: Office of Management and Budget

* NIPA basis

202

Figure 11

Federal Transfers as Percent of State Expenditures in 1998

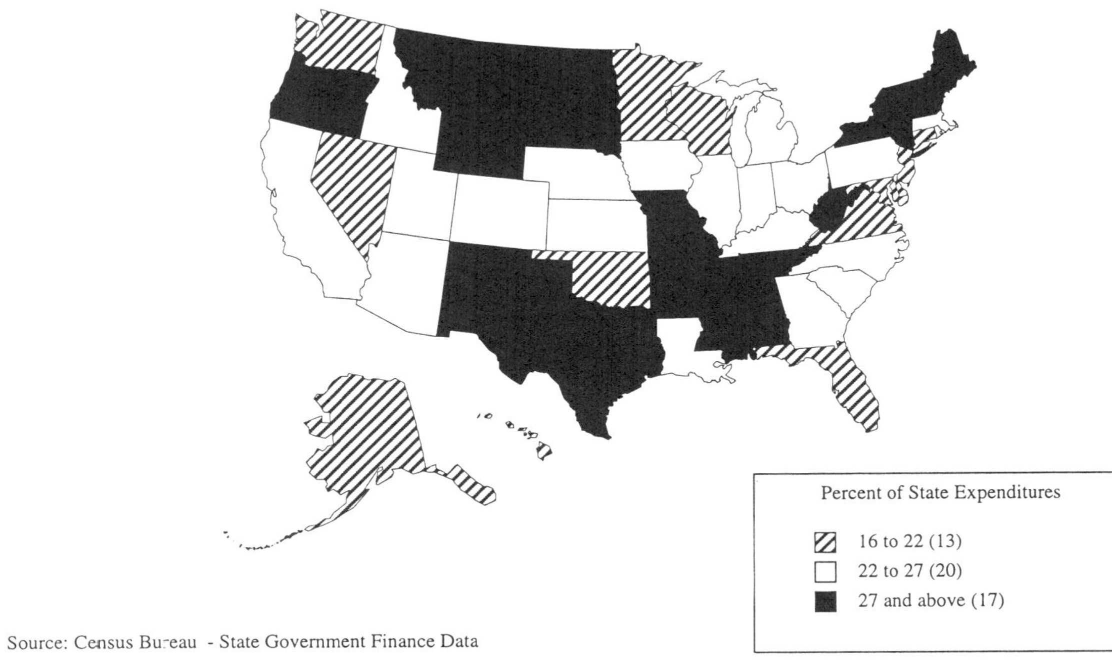

Source: Census Bureau - State Government Finance Data

Figure 12

Per Capita Federal Aid to State and Local Governments (1999)

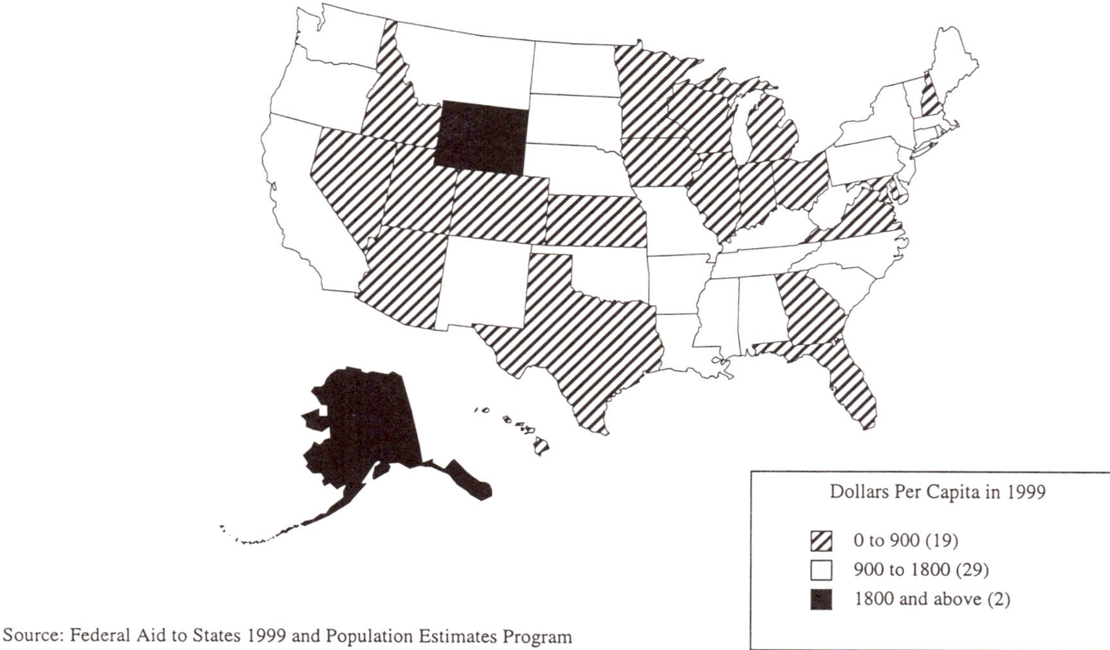

Source: Federal Aid to States 1999 and Population Estimates Program

Figure 13

Distribution of Federal Grants to State and Local Governments by Category in 1999

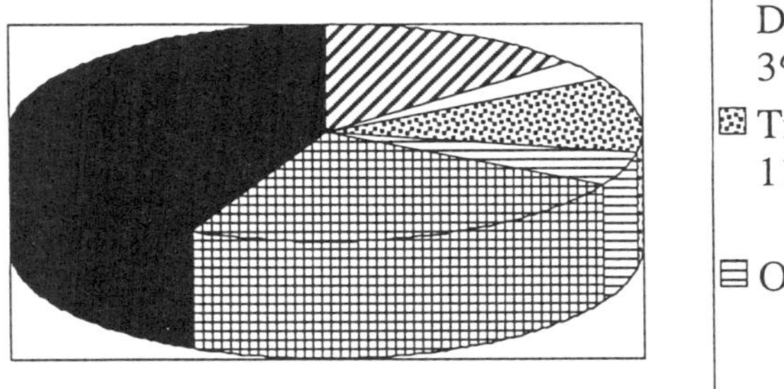

Source: Office of Management and Budget

* Other includes National Defense, Energy, Natural Resources and the Environment, Agriculture, Commerce and Housing Credit, Veterans Benefits and Services, Administration of Justice and General Government

Figure 14

Large Federal Grants
(1960 to 1999)

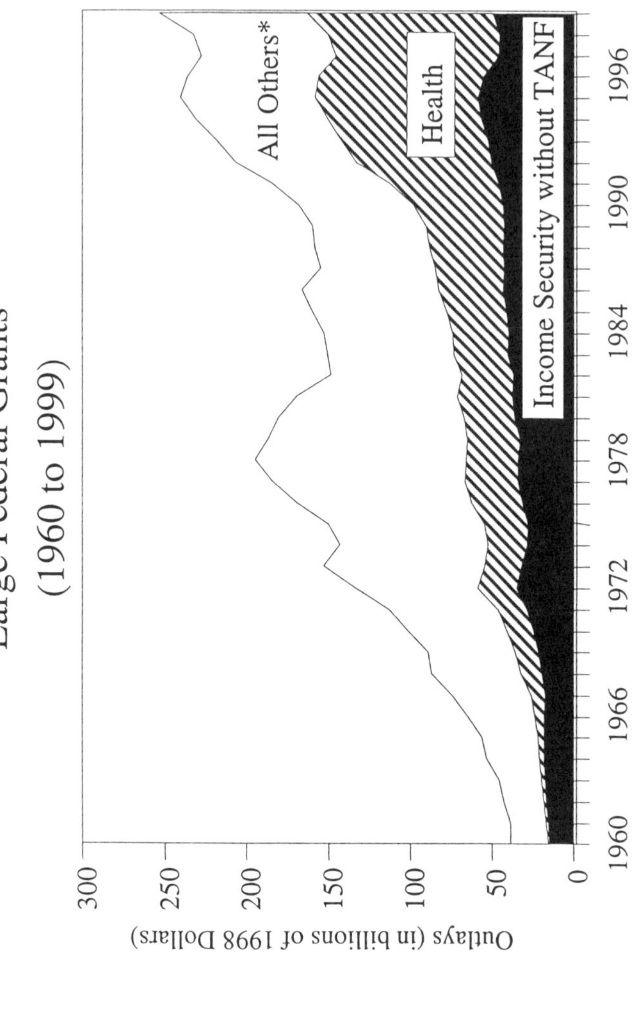

Source: Office of Management and Budget

* Includes Natural Resources, Agriculture, Transportation, Community Dev., Education, Justice and General Government

Figure 15

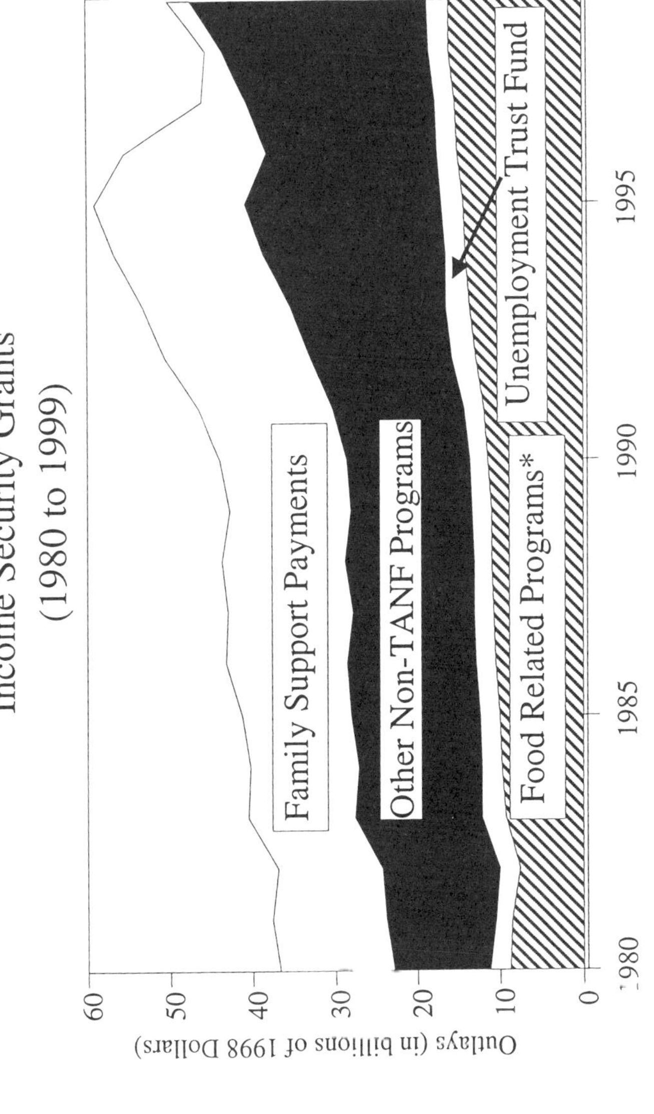

Source: Office for Management and Budget

* Food related programs includes Food Stamps, Supplemental feeding programs and child nutrition programs

207

Figure 16

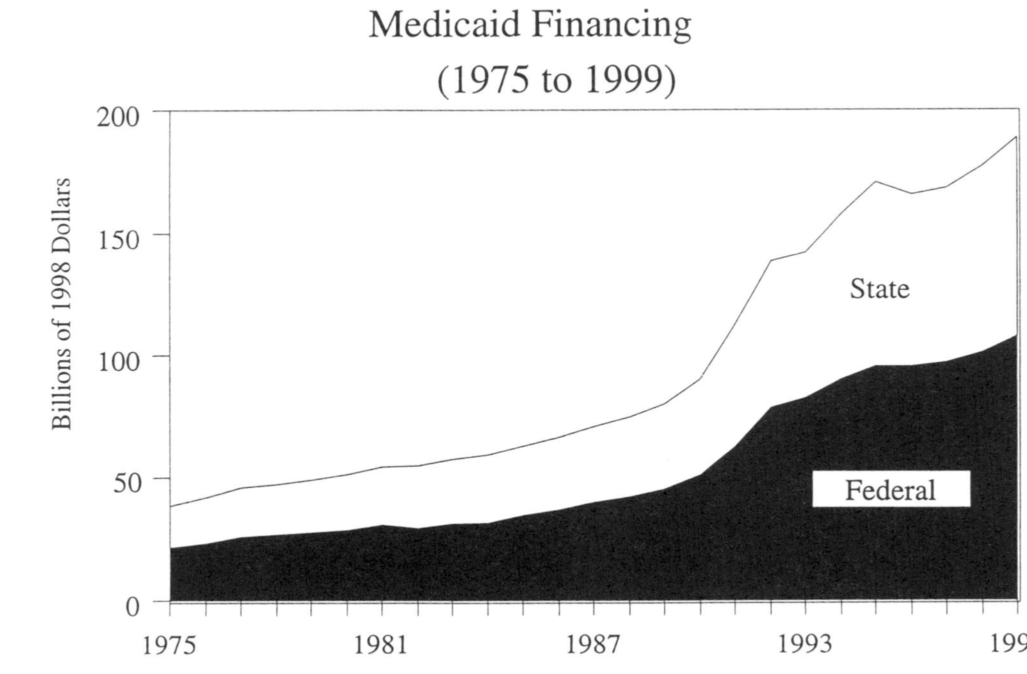

Source: Congressional Research Service

Figure 17

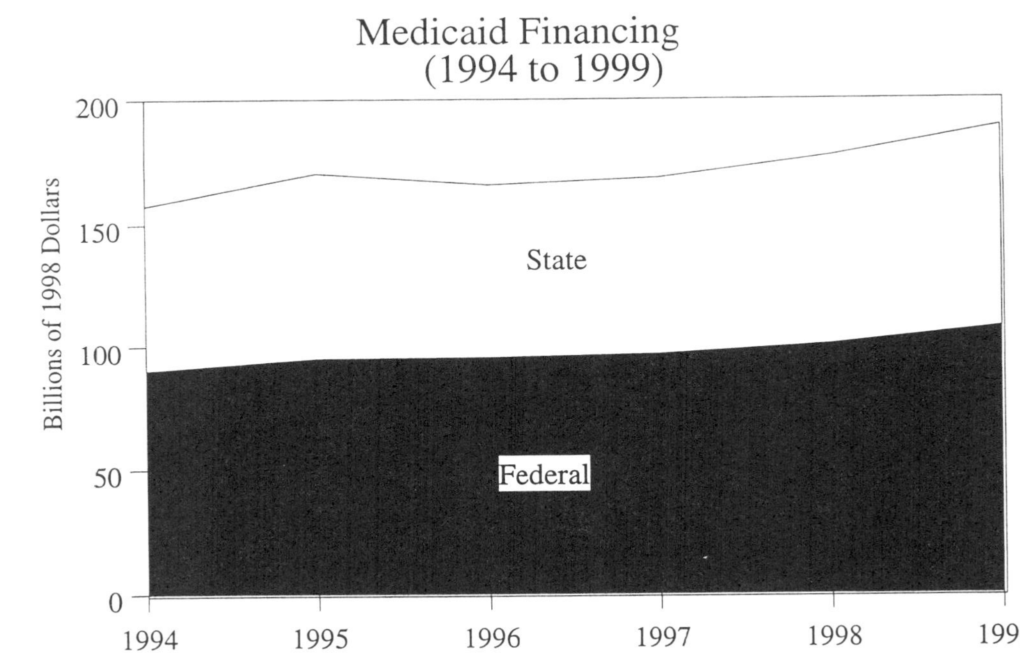

Source: Congressional Research Service

Figure 18

Smaller Federal Grants

(1960 to 1999)

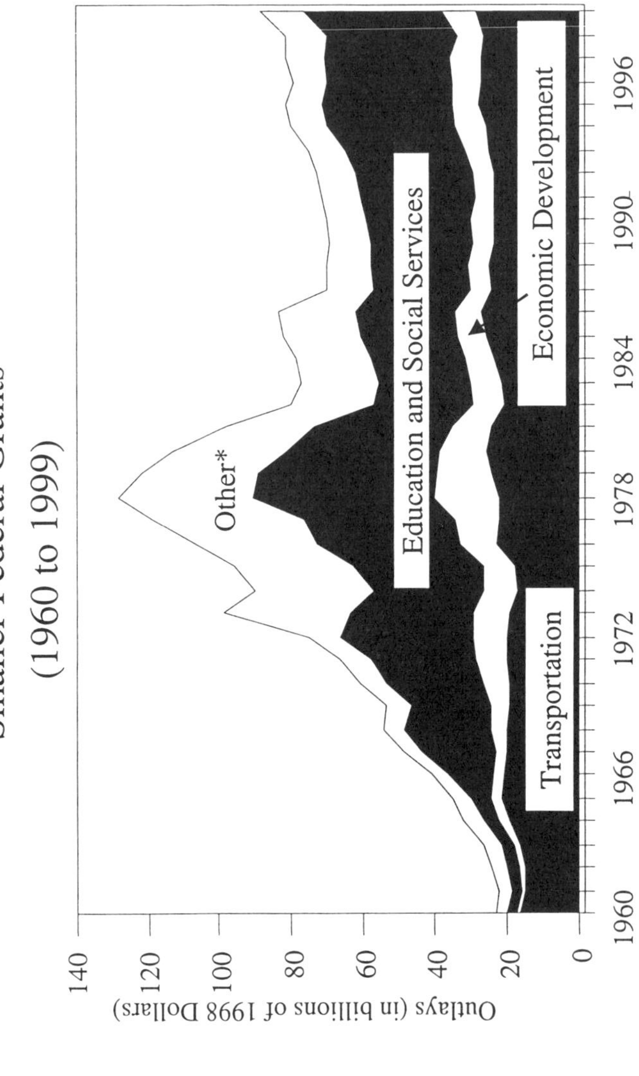

Source: Office of Management and Budget

* Includes General Government, Agriculture, Justice, National Defense, International Affairs, Energy, Commerce and Housing Credit, and Veterans Benefits and Services

210

Figure 19

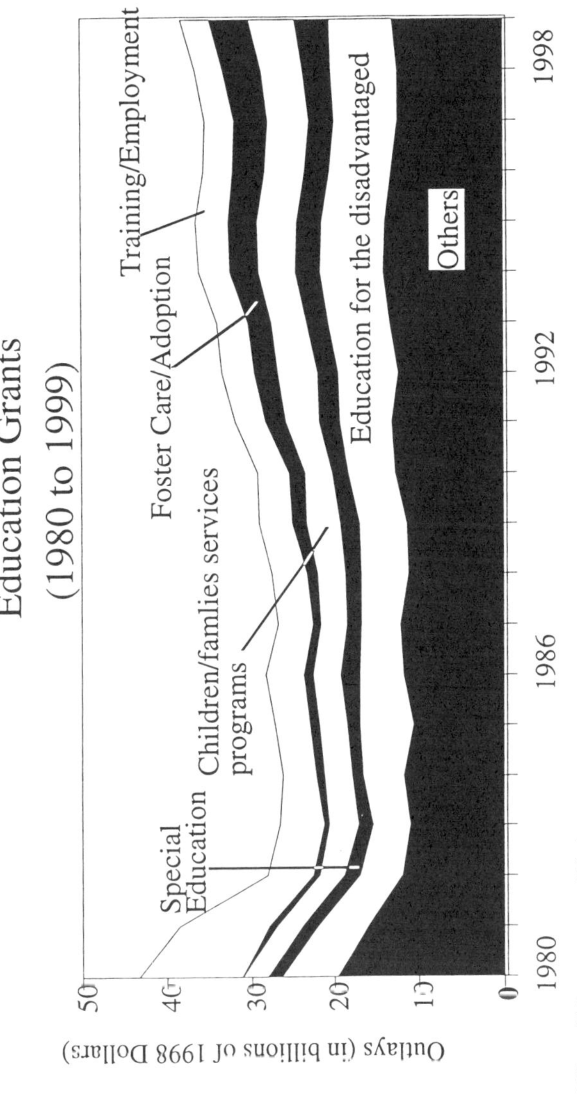

Source: Office of Management and Budget

211

Figure 20

Elementary and Secondary
Public School Financing

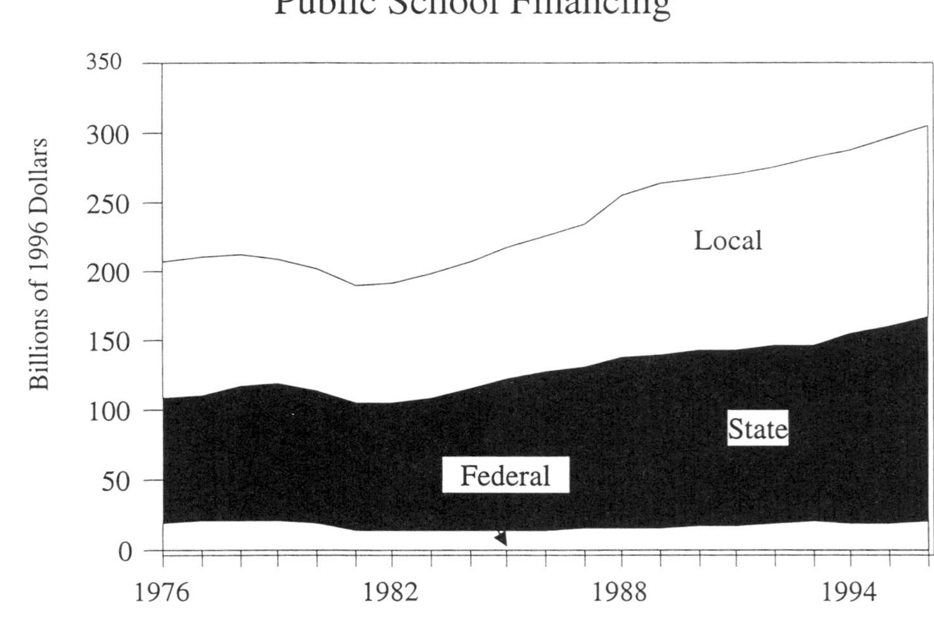

Source: National Center for Education Statistics

212

Why is there no Competitive Federalism in Germany?

Wolfgang Renzsch

The debate about reforming German federalism is not new. It started soon after the implementation of the 1969 "Finanzreform" – one of the most important reforms of intergovernmental fiscal relations. Two books, both published in 1976, pioneered in pointing out the "traps" of German style cooperative federalism. In the theory of interlocking federalism Fritz W. Scharpf and his collaborators[1] drew attention to the political immobility which arises out of joint decision making. Gerhard Lehmbruch[2] focussed on the different modes of decision making within the two chambers of the German federal legislature: decision making by negotiation and by competition. The "incongruence" of both modes will eventually produce political gridlocks. It should be pointed out however, that both depicted dangers, not necessities. Therefore, the question, when do the traps click shut, remained open. Another question would be: what is the price Germany has to pay for avoiding the traps. In this respect it would be quite enlightening to compare the processes of decision making of the failed tax reform in 1998 and of the succesful one in 2000.

After the ice breaking studies by Scharpf and Lehmbruch an extensive debate about the shortcomings and virtues of German federalism started. Numerous books and articles soon filled book shelves. Today I will neither comment nor contribute to this debate. But it would not be unfair to say that among academic observers there is a broad agreement that more flexibility, more competition, more responsibility and less entanglement are needed in order to improve the policy output of the German polity. Media, *Länder* parliamentarians and even a former Federal President have echoed this debate.

However, the real power holders remain comparatively silent. Neither the federal nor the *Länder* governments – except a few – engage themselves in this debate. On the contrary, "practitioners" in the federal as well as the *Länder* administrations often tell about the advantage of cooperative intergovernmental relations. Officials from various departments – finance, economic promotion, research, housing, transportation – report that despite often competing interests they get probably better results by daily administrative cooperation than either autonomous federal or *Länder* administration.[3] Regrettably the opinions of those who operate the system are rarely echoed in academic discussions.

Despite the reluctance of most governments the federal government and *Länder* governments have agreed to start a project called "Modernization of the Federal State". However, the policy of the federal government is unclear and hesitantly still. Among the sixteen *Länder* governments ten are rather reluctant if not opposed to reform. Only four support change. Under these circumstances the prospect for reform is rather limited. Modernization of the federal state is therefore not a question of the best blueprint (drafted by academics) but of political feasibility.

Nevertheless, there is considerable pressure to develop the German federal system. I would like to draw attention to two challenges which will require some adaptation to a changed political environment. These challenges are the *budgetary crisis* and *European integration*. The Federal Republic has responded to neither of them sufficiently. I will start with the budgetary crisis.

The budgetary crisis is essentially home made. It is at least partly caused by the modes of collaborative decision making among the federal and the *Länder* governments. It works well and smooth as long as both orders of governments pursue similar policies, as long as revenues increase and the main issue is how to spend, not how to save tax payers' money. However, when money becomes scarce each order of government tries to solve its problems at the expense of the other. The federal government tries to "devolve" burdens to the *Länder*.

On the other hand, the *Länder* governments request compensation when they are asked to accept decisions the federal government is interested in. The most recent example was the tax reform 2000 when a number of *Länder* governments were "bribed" to accept the reform in the *Bundesrat*.

The origins can be traced back to the second half of the 1960s and the first half of the 1970s. In those days Keynesian models of economic steering which were supposed to create continuous economic growth, were fashionable, and – at least originally – quite successful. It was a time when West Germany modernized its infrastructure. However, quite soon it became obvious that only one part of Keynes' theory worked well – deficit spending – but not the other. Theoretically governments are obliged to pay back debts during boom periods. That part of the model was never carried out for political reasons: It might be difficult to convince a parliament to accept cuts in expenditure when there is no money. However, when there is money, it seems to be impossible to get cuts accepted. The late Franz-Josef Strauß, former Federal Minister of Finance, mentioned once that it would be more difficult to keep parliament from spending surpluses than training a bulldog to ignore beef. Furthermore, the expectations of growth were hardly ever fulfilled. Each slump of the business cycle became more costly to fight, each time the results were less convincing. The revenues of growth never paid for the money spent on this growth. You might remember that two Federal Ministers of Finance, Alex Möller and Karl Schiller, resigned in the 1970s.

At the beginning of the 1980s it was well understood that something had to be done to avoid the trap opened by rising indebtedness and interest payments. The governments were progressively getting into the danger of losing their ability to act because of financial restrictions. The impression that Chancellor Helmut Schmidt was hardly in the position to achieve a turn in public finance was one of the reasons why the Liberals changed coalition in 1982. However, hope for a turn in financial policies was frustrated. Beyond some cosmetic changes Chancellor Helmut Kohl never managed to reduce public deficit spending.

The unexpected German unity increased the calamities of public finance: Expecting a fast and self financing process of adjustment of East Germany to the West, the burdens of unity were at first financed by loans. Therefore, in 1992 the interest rates for the German Mark reached peaks which caused a crisis of the European Monetary System by soaring interest rates. United Kingdom for instance saw itself forced to leave the system in order to avoid suffocating its then starting economic recovery. Later the German federal government changed its strategy and raised taxes and levies. However, it would be short sighted to accept German unity as a main reason for the current public debt of more than 2300 billion marks. According to figures of the federal government the transfer payments to the East have summed up to roughly 4½ to 5 percent of the Gross National Product (GNP) annually in the mid 1990s. At the same time the tax burden was raised by roughly 3½ percentage points. The final net deficit of 1 to 1½ percent of the GNP is without question a heavy burden, however a shallow excuse for the increasing public deficits of those days.

Debts and interest payments are the main reasons for the budgetary crisis the Federal Republic has run into. From 1974 until 1997 the payments for interests on public debts rose from 2.8 percent to 7 percent of the total public expenditure. A further reason for the financial calamities is the rising expenditure for welfare, social security and old age pensions. In the same period of time, 1974 till 1997, the public expenditure for these items rose from 47.2 percent to 51.2 percent of the total. Both categories in sum rose from 50 percent to 58 percent of the total of public expenditure.

On the other hand public investments for the future – education, science, research etc. – are comparatively small. From 1975 until 1997 their proportion of the total public expenditure dropped from 11.3 percent to 9.9 percent. Looking at these figures we have to take into account that a large part, probably the largest part of this expenditure is to pay people working in this field. The average age of the employees has risen considerably resulting in increasing expenditure for their salaries. The German pay schemes for civil service pay a sixty years old person about twice as much as a thirty years old one of the same qualification. The decrease of about one tenth veils much larger cuts in this field.

Overall, the Federal Republic today pays – by comparison – more than many other nations for the past: interest payments, old age pensions and at least parts of social security. The investments for the future are comparatively small. It would not be unfair to say that the generation of the grandparents has lived and will live to a large extent a the expense of their grand children. They have to pay for the debts their grandparents will leave behind – at least as far the public sector is concerned. The foreseeable dynamics of expenditures tend to suffocate the German polity. The trap opened by rising payments for the past is closing. In the private sector, however, the picture is quite different. Tremendous wealth will be inherited during the next years and decades.

The asymmetry between the public expenditure for the past and the future can *partly* be attributed to the modes of federal decision making. The federal government is able to unilaterally reduce expenditure caused by programs administered by federal agencies. Cuts in federal spending often leads to increased expenditure of the *Länder* governments. For example, federal cuts of long term unemployment relieve cause increased welfare burdens of the *Länder*. The *Länder* governments have to cope with these extra burdens. They can pursue budget reductions in those policy areas only which are their sole jurisdiction like education, research and culture.

What is to be done? The easy ways out of the dilemma are blocked. To raise more taxes would make Germany unattractive for private investments diminishing the economic prospects of industry in Germany. Alternatively, to increase loans is no way out either. More public debts might help for the moment, however, they would worsen the budgetary dilemma in the long run. In addition, Europe does not allow an increased deficit spending. Being a member of the European Monetary Union (EMU), Germany has to respect the Maastricht criteria which forbid a public deficit of more than 3 percent of the GNP. Actually, the goal of the EMU is to reduce public deficits further. The federal government wants to reduce its deficit to zero until the 2006.

The second important challenge is the process of European integration. Until about twenty years ago most of the *Länder* felt quite comfortable under the federal umbrella. German federalism provided centralized and uniform regulations with the consent of the *Länder* governments and decentralized policy delivery. The loss of autonomy was compensated for by an increased influence on federal policy. Within a densely populated, fairly homogenous country this loss was not considered politically inappropriate. The weaker *Länder* were quite content that the federation took over tasks which might have overburdened them. Most of the *Länder* governments did not miss legislative powers of their own, the contrary was – and partly is – true: they are quite happy that the federation has taken over this job. They were relieved from drafting laws, and therefore could avoid blame for unpopular decisions. However, within the areas of domestic policies the federation can hardly legislate without the consent of the *Länder*. In practical terms the stronger *Länder* were often able to prevent federal policies violating their interests, or at least influence them considerably. This deal seemed to be of advantage for all: the federal government, especially the federal branch of the governing parties, could extent its area of regulation, the weaker *Länder* were relieved from tasks which might have overburdened them, and finally the stronger ones could use their role as caucus leader within their partisan grouping to exercise an above average influence.[4]

Since the 1980s European integration – in particular the Single European Act – has changed the "terms of trade" for this deal. The governments of the stronger *Länder* started to request more regulative autonomy for themselves. Powers passed over to the federal government should be handed back. Why this change of paradigm?

Due to European integration the German *Länder* experienced a threefold loss of influence.

First, they lost regulative powers which were transferred to Brussels. Since the *Länder* had already lost many competencies to the federal government any further loss was considered as hardly acceptable. This time the loss was especially painful since their consent was no longer required, and not compensated by extended co-determination.

Second, the *Länder* governments lost influence on hitherto federal policies when those were given to the European Union. In these areas the powers of *Länder* in the *Bundesrat* became partly idle.

Third, via Brussels the federal government gained influence in policy areas which used to be under the sole jurisdiction of the *Länder* but were now under European jurisdiction.

This development was heavily criticized by the *Länder* governments, especially by Bavaria and Northrhine-Westphalia. Taking their population and their economic strength into account they both would be comparable to a number of mid-sized member nations of the European Union. Both big *Länder* considered themselves as being able to play an active and a more prominent role in European affairs. In order to do so they created the necessary administrative manpower within their civil service. The smaller *Länder* are hardly in the position to compete with them for this influence.

Rising strength and engagement of the sub-national level of government is one side of the coin of Europe, the other one is the weakening of national governments. The national governments are weakened by a new asymmetry which has occurred between globalized markets and national regimes. The four liberties of the European Single Market – freedom of movement for commodities, people, capital and services – have penetrated national boundaries: boundaries still pose geographical restrictions to national regulation, however, they do not hinder anybody from crossing them, and from leaving the area of a specific national jurisdiction. Markets without borders restrict the political options of national governments considerably. The "big" issues like currency, interest rates, trade policies etc. are regulated by Brussels. These general regulations are the same within the whole Single Market. The "small" issues however, like local infrastructure, access, labor force etc.

are depended on the regional or local decision making. Therefore, competition among nations for investments has largely become competition among regions.

However, the Single Market in Europe has offered new opportunities to the *Länder*. They have started to develop networks with other European regions. It is not surprising that those *Länder* governments which, first of all, are economically strong and play an important role in international markets, and, secondly, employ a comparatively large bureaucracy are the ones which request larger room for decision making of their own. Today more autonomy is asked for especially by Bavaria and Northrhine-Westphalia.

Undoubtedly, the challenges of the budgetary crisis and European integration cannot be ignored for a much longer period of time. The resources which, until now, were allowed to continue on without modernization, will run out eventually; inefficiencies cannot be paid for by revenues of growth any longer. Germany has already become a country of slow economic growth, the expected economic boom in East-Germany after unification did not take place. However, it is very difficult to tell when consequences of non-reform will be painful enough to overcome the politically motivated hesitation against reform.

However, after many years of political standstill the issue of modernization of the federal state has been put on the political agenda for two reasons. First, the Federal Chancellor, Gerhard Schröder, agreed with the Minister-Presidents of the *Länder* in December 1998 to establish a joint working group which is supposed to develop measures for a reform of the federal system. Second, on November 11, 1999 the Federal Constitutional Court decided about the constitutionality of the current system of fiscal equalization. Originally the procedures at Karlsruhe provided an obstacle against the discussion of a reform of the federal system because some *Länder* preferred to wait for the decision of the Court, expecting that the ruling might support their interests. This hurdle has not only been removed, additionally the Court obliged the legislature to examine the whole financial equalization system. The Court did not give precise orders for a new regulation but only for the procedures to be adopted: Within two years general criteria have to be developed which should serve as a yardstick for financial equalization. By the end of the year 2004 a new law concerning the actual equalization has to be passed.

Given the necessity to do something I would like to address the obstacles against reform.

First, I would like to focus on the logical structure of German functional federalism: Federal regulation of the national markets, adopted with the consent of the *Länder* governments which implement federal regulation under their own responsibility, and a federally determined tax system combined with a equalizing system of tax distribution provide a logical system which can hardly be changed in its structures – I am not talking about details here – without destroying its functional relations. Therefore I feel that proposals which suggest changing or removing certain parts of the system, like the role of the *Bundesrat* or the fiscal equalization system based primarily on need, would not improve but destroy the system.

I do not see any opportunity towards a radical change in the direction of a system of jurisdictional or dual federalism. The model of functional federalism has solved the problem of co-ordination between the two levels of government better than most other types of federalism. Article 37 Basic Law – federal enforcement – has never been used against any *Land* government. The financial whip or "golden reign" which in a number of other federations serve to force the states or provinces to adopt policies the federal government is interested in, does not play any important role within the area of German intergovernmental relations. Functional federalism has provided an unusual degree of equalization of living conditions within a geographically small and densely populated country without any relevant linguistic, cultural or religious fragmentation: on election day the electorate never supported regional parties which were hostile towards the given degree of uniformity among the German *Länder*: Do not tell any German car driver to accept five *Länder* traffic regulations instead of one federal when he or she travels from Munich to Berlin. Parties and governments take these expectations into their account: Recently the Conference of the Ministers of the Interior discussed a ban of bull terriers. Despite their own jurisdiction the *Länder* governments were obviously interested in a unitary regulation[5]. Any regulation but a unitary one would easily open loopholes. Allowing loopholes would be considered as politically irresponsible.

Thus, the "race" between decentralizing and centralizing forces resembles the fairy tale race between the hare and the hedgehog: the hedgehog of centralization was already there when the hare of decentralization was still running. It should be acknowledged however, that the tendency towards unitary federalism has been in congruence with an integrated national party system. German parties try to act cohesively over all levels of government, and usually pay little respect to the delimitation of the different tiers of government. The last *Land* election which took place in Northrhine-Westphalia was labeled a "small federal election" by the media.

Unitary cooperative federalism and competition of nationally integrated parties stabilize each other mutually: party competition pushes for unitary solutions. In comparison to the USA German parties tend to act with ranks closed over the different levels of government. The Federal Chancellor and the federal opposition leader both campaigned during the last election of the *Land* parliament in Northrhine-Westphalia. Parties hardly distinguish between different jurisdictions: federal policy issues dominate campaigns at *Länder* level, *Länder* policy issues are discussed at federal level. Additionally, the proportional electoral system fuels the tendency towards unitary policies. Even for parties having regional strongholds it is vital to get some votes elsewhere by offering a broader policy approach than just a regional one.[6] And that is what the electorate expect: disunity will be punished on election day. All these circumstances suffocate regionally differentiated solutions. However, German parties have changed during the last decades. Parties have "federalized" in a sense that regional leaders have gained considerable influence. Consequently, party ideologies have become less important, political issues tend to be beyond "left" and "right", and regional diversity has increased. Therefore, the grip of parties on policy formulation has been loosened. The effect of party competition on the federal system might decrease. However, contradicting positions of relevance between two *Länder* branches or between the federal and a *Land* branch of a party will still be used by competing parties as a "proof" of the disunity of another party and, therefore, its inability to act cohesively.

Despite changes, it seems quite obvious to me that the agencies of political legitimation, the institutional setting and the modes of political competition still restrict the options for change considerably. I do not expect that German federalism will leave the historical path of functional federalism and turn towards a model of competitive federalism.

However, change within the framework of functional federalism is not only possible but is quite probable. I would like to emphasize a change of the historical environment. When fundamental decisions about the federal structure, in particular about federal finance were taken, the political imperative was unity. When the Basic Law was drafted 1948/49 the reemerging German polity had to deal with the challenges of the immediate postwar period. Under the condition of pressing scarcity the basic provisions had to be provided for all. There was hardly any room for differentiation or competing solutions. In 1968/69 when the "Finanzreform" was adopted, the goal was to provide equal standards and opportunities for those regions which suffered from disadvantages. In 1992/93 when East-Germany was financially integrated in the federal system, the East Germans requested to be accepted on equal footing with West Germans. Additionally, it should be remembered that the Cold War put West Germany in competition with Communist East Germany. It will be difficult to explain why Germany has developed an unusually highly elaborated unitary welfare system without taking the East-West confrontation into account.

Although the process of developing East Germany will take another decade or more, the historical circumstances which pushed Germany in the direction of a unitary federalism are gone by now. Instead there are forces which push in the opposite direction. These forces emerge out of the budgetary crisis, and the processes of European integration and economic globalization. Concerning the budgetary crisis some *Länder* have come to the conclusion that federally set standards of their policy delivery can be unnecessarily costly.

One example: Northrhine-Westphalia plans to offer civil servants special retirement schedules at the age of 55 when redundant jobs can be saved. Since the legislation concerning civil servants at all levels of government is under the control of the federation, the government of Northrhine-Westphalia can act only when a federal law has been changed before. The procedure to amend a federal law is not only time consuming but it is also uncertain whether the necessary political majorities can be built. Other *Länder* governments not agreeing with the policy pursued by Northrhine-Westphalia, have already declared their resistance. They are afraid that their civil servants will demand the same privileges. This example illustrates one of the prominent difficulties: Party governments do not necessarily put the common interest of more autonomy first, but also take partisan interests into account, at least as long as they do not violate governmental interests. However, it seems regulations concerning civil servants might be one of the topics which eventually will be handed back to the *Länder* legislatures.

Federal regulation is not only costly for the *Länder* but also provides hurdles for economic progress. In the European Union the general rules are predominantly set at European level. Decisions about investments often depend on local (or regional) conditions. National regulation has lost importance, it can even can become an obstacle for the competing regions. One example: Despite European deregulation, German regulations on artisan trades still provides obstacles for establishing shops or training apprentices. National regulations provide for higher hurdle for new jobs and more job training than European regulations do. Obviously, it is extremely difficult to change federal regulation. Probably, it would be much easier to change such regulations at *Länder* level. Currently we have to wait for the courts to declare German law as incompatible with European law. The regions, in the German case the *Länder*, get interested in regulating the local condition for investment within their areas – at least the stronger ones are. We can expect a change of attitude of the *Länder*, deregulation as a consequence of European law making might open new areas of regulation for the *Länder*.

First indicators of change can be observed already: About three years ago the European guideline on protection of fauna, flora and habitat had to be transformed into national law. In this case the combination of European decisions and budget constraint enforced a decentralized solution: The federal government tried to regulate compensation payments for ecologically motivated restrictions of agrarian production federally. Of course, the compensation was to be paid for by the *Länder* governments. However, the majority of them opposed this proposal and requested *Länder* legislation. Under the pressure that the European guideline was overdue to be transformed into German law, the federal government finally agreed – and the *Länder* saved a lot of money because *Länder* legislation proved to be less costly than federal.

Even the federal government seems to be ready to accept more decentralized regulations. In 1999 some of the *Länder* governments requested a reintroduction of a property tax by a federal law. Other *Länder* governments and the federal government opposed this policy. To come to terms with the *Länder* the federal government offered to open this part of tax legislation to *Länder*. However, none of the *Länder* government requesting the reintroduction of the property tax were interested in *Länder* legislation, they were not ready to take the blame for imposing new taxes on their citizens. Obviously, the federal government proposed land legislation because it expected none of the *Länder* would introduce this tax individually.[7]

Altogether we can observe that the forces pushing German federalism in a unitary direction are decreasing while those force pushing in the other direction are increasing. What are the effects?

I mentioned that a reform of the German federal system has been put on the political agenda. The federal government has declared its inclination for reform – but did not tell what kind of reform. The Federal Constitutional Court requested an overhaul of the whole system of financial equalization until the end of the year 2004 but did not give any hints concerning direction. The heads of the governments of the federation and the *Länder* set up two working groups, one in the hands of the Ministers of Finance. This one is supposed to develop proposal for a renewed equalization system. The other one is in the hands of the Minister-Presidents. This one will discuss constitutional reform including the whole areas of co-financing.

This kind of division of labor will determine the results: The "fiscal conservatives" will avoid any substantial change of the equalization system. In the *Länder* camp we have the "group of ten" defending the given system, and the "gang of four" requesting change towards more autonomy of *Länder*. Two *Länder* are undecided still. Northrhine-Westphalia, currently one of the four, tries to mediate between the two groupings. According to recent information the Federal Minister of Finance favors to keep the present status quo among the *Länder* but advocates some structural change. In the other working group we find the "federative revolutionaries" from the offices of the Minister-Presidents. From this group I expect some proposals to loosen the federal ties which bind the *Länder*, and some proposals to strengthen the legislative powers of the *Länder*. Furthermore, this group might develop a proposal to amend co-financing.

The proper way of reform will be to begin by giving the *Länder* more room for their own discretion, and then to change the system of intergovernmental relations in a second step. The often and correctly criticized development towards increased fiscal equalization follows the tendency towards more and more material unitarization. To get out of the vicious circle of increasing expenditure for equalization and decreasing efficiency it is necessary to change the allocation of legislative competencies first.

What will happen during the years coming? We will not have a fundamental overhaul of the whole federal system. Germany will keep the current type of functional federalism, and will not adopt the American type of jurisdictional federalism. Therefore, there will be no change from cooperative to competitive federalism. A radical change which has been proposed by theoreticians of fiscal federalism has no chance of being accepted by political majorities.

A reform should provide for more efficiency in policy delivery, faster decision making and more flexibility. A remedy would be to disentangle Federal and *Länder* governments in areas where they could easily pursue policies of their own. Co-financing should be reduced and simplified. The regulation of the joint tasks and of various kinds of federal contributions to tasks of the *Länder* could be simplified and reduced to a general claus which would allow the federal government to support ailing *Länder* under specific circumstances. Especially the East German *Länder* will need further federal assistance for the next couple of years.

Concerning the often requested devolution of the power to tax I do not expect any change. Up to now the federal government has not given any hint of readiness to devolve tax legislation. The Federal Minister of Finance argues that European tax harmonization will be the tax issue of the upcoming years, not "parochialization". Neither does the majority of the *Länder* have an interest in tax power. They fear that tax competition would unduly provide advantages for the better off *Länder* and, therefore, the gap between the better off and weaker *Länder* would become wider. Indeed, I feel it is rather crucial to have a functional kind of federalism in which public tasks are predominantly set by the federation (with the consent of *Länder*), however policy delivery has to be financed by the *Länder* under competitive terms.

In the field of intergovernmental fiscal relations we will get a new legislation. Due to the ruling of the Federal Constitutional Court, the risk of failure is much worse than the risk of controlled amendments for all involved. Because the whole business is a no win situation, I expect we will get a reform which will be fiscally based on the present status quo. Looking at the positions the *Länder* governments have adopted it becomes quite clear that ten out of sixteen *Länder* currently oppose any fundamental change. All *Länder* are in a comparatively unpleasant budgetary situation, none of them is in the position to accept considerable redistribution at their own expense. Only a solution which will be close to the given status quo will have the chance of being accepted by the necessary majorities of the federal legislature.

Federal reform will be tricky because it is connected with the issue of devolution of federal legislative powers to the *Länder*. Although on Sunday many politicians of all parties agree on this issue they behave quite differently from Monday through Friday. The 16 Minister-Presidents created a working group which was supposed to draft a proposal to realize the provision of Article 125a of the Basic Law – saying federal law can under certain circumstances be transformed into *Land* law. The results were trivial. We have to accept that there is a huge difference between a general plea for a decentralization of power and building majorities for specific competencies to be devolved.[8]

It is not quite clear yet which objectives the federal government will pursue in this field. Generally speaking, it has only little interest here. Any reform would probably mean less federal influence and less federal power. Yet the federal government is not showing any inclination toward decentralized regulations. It has not perceived that devolution could avoid disagreements among the *Länder*: Why fight over issues like closing hours for shops, regulations for civil servants or fees for universities when a retreat of the federal government would provide peace in federal-*Länder*-relations?

What we can expect might be a piecemeal incremental development which tries to preserve the features of the German model which are worth preserving: successful coordination between the two tiers of government, uniform regulation when politically desired, policy implementation close to the citizen by the local administration. We will certainly not get co-operative decision-making leading to federally uniform standards of policy delivery which has to be financed by the *Länder* governments under competitive terms.

Let me conclude with a proposal which has been put forward recently by Fritz W. Scharpf, and which resembles a procedure practiced in Canada. In the case of concurrent legislation, the *Länder* legislatures should be allowed to override federal legislation with equivalent *Länder* legislation. The federal legislature would have the opportunity to disallow *Länder* legislation without a certain period of time. Canada has had good experiences with an opting-out clause which actually has been seldom used. A constitutional opting-out clause could be pacify the thorny and controversial debate on the devolution of federal legislative powers. It could provide for conflict resolution in the field of federal-*Länder*-relations. There would be a general federal rule, but for those *Länder* which wish a different way there would be an opportunity to do so. Such a clause would allow a kind of flexibility which is unknown to German federalism up to now, however preserve intergovernmental co-operation if wanted. However, the main political parties seem to be rather reluctant to accept this kind of "Sinatra"-federalism[9].

Notes

1   Fritz W. Scharpf, Bernd Reissert and Fritz Schnabel, *Politikverflechtung. Theorie und Empirie des kooperativen Föderalismus in der Bundesrepublik*, Kronberg/Ts., Scriptor, 1976.

2   Gerhard Lehmbruch, *Parteienwettbewerb im Bundesstaat*, Stuttgart et al., Kohlhammer 1976; Gerhard Lehmbruch, *Parteienwettbewerb im Bundesstaat*, 3. Aufl., Wiesbaden, Westdeutscher Verlag, 2000.

3   Two examples: an official of the Ministry of Education and Research of the *Land* Brandenburg reported that the *Land* itself is hardly in the position to run the research institutes located in Brandenburg. Financial and administrative assistance of the federal government is required. Autonomy in this field would imply either "parochialization" or centralization of research policies. Neither is wanted. An official of the Sachsen-Anhalt Ministry of Economic Promotion spoke about coordination of waterways policies. Waterways are partly under federal, partly under *Länder* jurisdiction. Extensive collaboration on a day-to-day base is in the interest of both sides involved.

4   It is quite obvious that Northrhine-Westphalia has become the leader of the caucus of SPD-governed *Länder* while Bavaria has taken over this role for the CDU/CSU-governed ones.

5   *Süddeutsche Zeitung*, May 5, 2000.

6   The PDS, the former Socialist Unity Party, returns roughly 20 percent of the East German votes. That is good for getting elected to the East German *Länder* legislatures, but it does not make 5 percent on federal level. Therefore, it is important for the party to gain 1 or 2 percent in West Germany to overcome the 5-percent-hurdle to get safely represented in the *Deutsche Bundestag*.

7   Quite remarkable was the fact that the *Länder* governments requesting the reintroduction of the property tax were the ones which would have gained less than average. Their interest was to get a federally regulated tax and to profit from the revenues of the better off *Länder* by fiscal equalization.

8   For details see the contribution by Ursula Männle, "The Revival of German Federalism: Two Examples" in this volume, 161-172.

9   Charlie Jeffery, "From Cooperative Federalism to a "Sinatra Doctrine" of the Länder?", in Charlie Jeffery (ed.), *Recasting German Federalism: The Legacies of Unification*, London, Pinter, 1999, 329-342.

Further Readings

Charlie, Jeffrey (ed.), *Recasting German Federalism. The Legacies of Unification*, London, Pinter, 1999.

Heiderose Kilper and Roland Lhotta, *Föderalismus in der Bundesrepublik Deutschland*, Grundwissen Politik, Band 15, Opladen, Leske + Budrich, 1996.

Heinz Laufer and Ursula Münch, *Das föderative System der Bundesrepublik Deutschland*, Opladen, Leske + Budrich, 1998.

Uwe Leonardy, "The Working Relationships between *Bund* and *Länder* in the Federal Republic of Germany", in Charlie Jefferey and Peter Savigear (ed.), *German Federalism Today*, Leicester, Leicester University Press, 1991, 40-62.

Wolfgang Renzsch, "Föderale Finanzbeziehungen im Parteienstaat. Eine Fallstudie zum Verlust politischer Handlungsmöglichkeiten", *Zeitschrift fürParlamentsfragen*, vol. 20, 1989, 331-345.

Wolfgang Renzsch, *Finanzverfassung und Finanzausgleich. Die Auseinandersetzungen um ihre Gestaltung in der Bundesrepublik Deutschland zwischen Währungsreform und deutscher Vereinigung (1984 – 1990)*, Bonn, Dietz, 1991.

Wolfgang Renzsch, "Financing German Unity: Fiscal Conflict Resolution in a Complex Federation", *Publius. The Journal of Federalism*, vol. 28, (Fall 1998), 127-146.

Fritz W. Scharpf, "The Joint-Decision-Trap: Lessons form German Federalism and European Integration", *Public Administration*, vol. 66, 1988, 239-278.

Fritz W. Scharpf, Bernd Reissert and Fritz Schnabel, "Policy Effectiveness and Conflict Avoidance in Intergovernmental Policy Formation", in Kenneth Hanf (ed.), *Interorganizational Policy Making*, London, Sage, 1978.

Reinventing in the American States: Content and Implications

Merl M. Hackbart, Robert J. Eger III

Introduction

In the United States, major reform initiatives have been periodically undertaken to improve government accountability, efficiency or service delivery. Such initiatives have been in response to recognized problems and issues or were undertaken by administrations as they pursued broad themes of reform or service delivery enhancement. In many cases, the initiatives were directed toward improving government processes, through the adoption of business practices, in an effort to run government like a business.[1] Many of these initiatives involved rule bending and entrepreneurship activities.[2] For example, in the early 1900s, financial and budgetary practice improvement initiatives by state and local governments were undertaken in response to widespread concern with financial fraud and abuse. In the 1950s and 1960s, the accountability efforts of the early 1900s were replaced with a greater concern over government "performance". Many of these "performance" initiatives resulted from recommendations of the Hoover Commission reports of the 1940s[3] that stressed outcomes and government performance.

Reform and performance initiatives have also been a favorite subject of Presidential Administrations. For example, the Johnson Administration focused on implementing a government-wide Program Planning and Budgeting System (PPBS) that was designed to more clearly define policy and program goals and performance. In the 1970s, revenue sharing and Management by Objective (MBO) were cornerstones of the Nixon Administration's approach to improved government operations. The Carter administration introduced Zero Base Budgeting (ZBB) and the Reagan Administration pursued management improvement initiatives as well.

While many program improvement, government efficiency, and accountability efforts have started in Washington, state and local governments have been active participants in the change and innovations process. In fact, states have often been the "laboratories" for innovations later adopted by the federal government. Among such state efforts were innovations and change in budgetary practices, welfare reform, privatization of services, infrastructure finance, deregulation, and other change efforts. Many of these innovations were highlighted in Osborne and Gaebler's book entitled *Reinventing Government.*[4]

The "reinvention wave" of the 1990s has many of the characteristics of similar government improvement movements throughout government of this century. Concerns regarding actions of the government agencies which have direct contact with the American public such as the Internal Revenue Service, Department of Interior, and other regulatory and service delivery agencies created an environment which encouraged a rethinking of how government delivers services and performs its responsibilities at all levels of American government. At the same time, President Clinton took office and, like his predecessors, he sought an initiative, which would stress his commitment to improved governance. The reinvention of government movement, therefore, emerged through the confluence of three related trends and initiatives. Included were: 1) an emerging undercurrent of national concern about government efficiency, effectiveness and service delivery; 2) the desire of a Presidential Administration to establish its program of government improvement; and 3) a new theme for government changing how government operates. The "reinvention" theme flowing from Osborne and Gaebler's book captured many of the ideas of previous government management improvement initiatives, but with a new twist - a focus on the citizen as a consumer of government services. The consumer focus added a dimension that had particular appeal and permitted the Clinton/Gore Administration to communicate the idea of improving government operations while, at the same time, making government more responsive to taxpayers and citizens.

The Reinvention Initiative of the 1990s

As suggested, the publication of David Osborne and Ted Gaebler's book entitled *Reinventing Government*[5], which laid out 10 principles that might bring about major reform of government operations, began a new effort to revitalize and enhance government operations. The phrase "reinventing government" quickly caught the attention of public policymakers and administrators as well as academics with its focus on the customer model of government service delivery. The model suggests that government administrators should respond to citizens and taxpayers in the same manner that a business responds and interacts to its customers.

While focusing on the taxpayer as customer theme, the reinvention effort, like similar government improvement efforts in the past, has the major goal of making government work more efficiently or to work better for less cost. In other words, greater efforts to improve the efficiency and effectiveness of government activities are, along with the consumer focus, a major focus of government reinvention. Other author's[6] extended the customer oriented government improvement model of reinvention by focusing on performance as well. In doing so, an even closer tie to previous government management enhancement efforts was established.

Like its predecessors, the "reinvention movement" quickly found itself critiqued by various writers[7] in the 1990s. Frederickson criticizes the "customer-oriented" model proposed in the "reinvention movement". Frederickson suggested that citizens are not customers; rather, they are owners of government who elect officials to represent their interests in the delivery of services. As owners, they can impact the agenda rather than simply reacting, positively or negatively, to the services delivered.[8] John Carroll[9], in an introduction to a series of articles in *Public Administration Review* regarding reinventing government, indicated concerns about the reinvention effort. Citing the writing of Moe[10] and Arnold[11], he indicates "others have been critical (of reinvention), viewing the National Performance Review as a flawed theory, a hodgepodge of recommendations and a superficial manipulation of reform for immediate political advantage". Criticisms, notwithstanding, the reinvention movement clearly drew the attention of public administrators and policy makers in the early 1990s.

Reinvention and the Clinton Administration

The Osborne/Gaebler reinventing government theme was adopted as the centerpiece of the Clinton-Gore Administration's government management improvement effort. In its first phase, the Administration's initiative drew heavily on the Osborne/Gaebler reinvention principles of customer orientation and efficiency and was characterized as "a new customer oriented contract"[12]. The reinvention focus of the Clinton/Gore effort was solidified when David Osborne became a key advisor to Vice-President Gore, who was appointed by President Clinton to lead the effort. Initially named the National Performance Review (NPR)[13], it was later renamed the National Partnership for Reinventing Government.

The first phase of the NPR effort begin on March 3, 1993 when the President charged the Vice-President as the NPR leader and gave the review team (principally civil servants, interns, loaned staff from state and local governments and some consultants) 6 months to carry out their review. The NPR report[14] contained 384 recommendations and 38 specific reports totaling nearly 2000 pages. By December 1993, President Clinton had signed 16 executive orders implementing specific recommendations including a reduction of the federal workforce by 252,000 positions. The NPR created a tracking system to monitor the implementation of over 1,250 action items. Consistent with the consumer orientation of reinvention, customer service standards were generated, performance agreements were promulgated by major agencies, and efforts were undertaken to facilitate communications regarding activities and accomplishments.

In 1995, a second phase of NPR was initiated. In this phase, the focus shifted to analyzing missions and regulatory actions. In doing so, the concept of reinvention was broadened to encompass actions designed to more generally enhance government operational efficiency across the board. As a result, the focus of Osborne and Gaebler's principles seemed to be less important in this phase of the Clinton/Gore reinvention effort. In the regulatory arena, actions were undertaken to eliminate obsolete regulations, and to change the regulatory environment. By September 1995, the second phase effort had identified over 200 new recommendations that could lead to over $70 billion in savings.[15] A major outcome of Phase II was a refocusing of federal agencies on performance and outcomes reminiscent of early federal program management improvement efforts. During Clinton's second term, the reinvention efforts continued but began focusing on smaller organizations such as departments and agencies rather than Cabinets.

The accomplishments reported for the NPR effort are varied and include staffing reductions, eliminating regulations, and other efficiency results. The

NPR reports that: the civilian workforce was reduced by 348,000; 325 reinvention labs have been created; $177 billion in savings have been recognized; 640,000 pages of internal agency rules have been eliminated; over 4,000 customer service standards have been created; and "public trust in the federal government is finally increasing after a 30-year decline".[16]

It should be noted that there is significant disagreement regarding the overall impact of the NPR. The Congressional Budget Office estimated that Phase I savings were overestimated and would amount to only 5 % of the NPR projected savings.[17] Furthermore, Thompson and Ingraham suggest that any evaluation of NPR is complicated due to the diverse nature of the recommendations produced by the NPR. Kettl[18] expressed a similar concern when he suggested: "Assessing the NPR's more fundamental results is difficult because it has pursued radically different, indeed conflicting goals."

Despite the debate regarding probable and actual outcomes, the reinvention wave at the federal level of government has continued throughout the decade of the 1990s under the leadership and support of the Clinton Administration. As indicated earlier, enhanced government management or reform efforts have been pursued by previous administrations as well. Among such efforts were the PPBS initiative by the Johnson Administration, the MBO initiative by the Nixon Administration, and the ZBB initiative of the Carter Administration. Such efforts or "reform waves" were either, initially, fostered by the federal government and continued by the states or vice versa. Other reform efforts had similar wave characteristics[19] with federal, state, and local governments emulating efforts of the other levels of government. Therefore, with the major push for reinvention at the federal government level in the 1990s, a similar "reinvention wave" at the state and local government level could be expected.

Reinvention in the States

As suggested by Osborne and Gaebler's examples discussed in *Reinventing Government*[20] and by other authors as well, reinvention and innovation activities have characterized state government policy and program delivery actions in recent decades. While the nature of such "reinvention efforts" may change due to new themes or management related concepts such as management by objective (MBO), performance related budgeting systems, privatization, and other "waves" or "ripples", the emphasis undertaking efforts to improve state government operations appears continuous.

Various researchers and organizations have analyzed and recognized management and service delivery changes by the states. Included are the innovations awards of the Council of State Governments, the Government Performance Project sponsored by *Governing* magazine in cooperation with Syracuse University[21] and assessment of "reinvention" efforts by the states by authors such as Brudney, Hebert and Wright.[22]

The Government Performance Project involved an assessment of state government operations in five major management areas including: 1) financial management, 2) human resources, 3) managing for results, 4) information technology, and 5) capital management. The project assigned grades for all states for the five management functions. In carrying out the assessment, the evaluation team evaluated the management practices of the 50 states in each of the areas and identified innovations and reinvention initiatives of the states. Among the reinvention/innovation accomplishments were greater flexibility in budgeting, multi-year budget planning, improved fiscal monitoring, appointment of chief information officers (CIOs), standardizing technology, using performance measures and other improved management and service delivery techniques.[23]

The Council of State Governments (CSG), a national organization of the states which represents all three branches of state government, annually recognizes innovation/reinvention activities of the states. The CSG, which provides services to various state agencies and the state legislatures of the states, has held the competition for "best innovation" or reinvention since the 1980s. The awards recognize state and territory innovative or reinvention impacted programs for their creativity, efficiency implication and effectiveness. The program is the only national awards program that focuses exclusively on state programs and policies and selects from these winners based on evaluations by state government leaders. The award winners are selected under a rigorous process. CSG staff evaluate each submission against a criteria designed to select the best and most creative innovations or reinventions. These "top" reinventions are then forwarded to the four geographical regions of the CSG organization. State officials from each region then apply the criteria to select two winners from their region.[24]

As noted, the annual innovation awards are based upon actual program or innovation implementations and include a variety state process and service reinventions. The innovation awards program has identified a variety of innovations and reinventions in economic development, education, environmental policy and health care among others. Among the 1999 Award winners were: 1) Pennsylvania's Compliance Reporting System, 2) North Carolina's Smart Start, and 3) Washington's Human Resource Education & Library Prevention (HELP) Academy.

Pennsylvania's Compliance Reporting System consists of providing an Internet web site that allows residents to investigate business and local governments compliance rates with environmental laws and regulations. The System provides a way to measure overall compliance rates and also to identify areas that need improvement.

North Carolina's Smart Start was modeled after President Clinton's Smart Start proposal on improving the quality, affordability, and accessibility of childcare services. The program provides children age five and under early intervention health care and preventive health screenings.

Washington's Human Resource Education & Library Prevention (HELP) Academy is a training program that was created to reduce the number of cases of sexual harassment, discrimination, and violence in the work place in state government. Results indicate that the program is successful, with evaluations of HELP Academy attendees rating the program 4.5, on a scale of 1 to 5. Over the next few years, the state expects to show a reduction in court and staff costs, damage awards, and state settlements.

A 1999 *Public Administration Review* article[25] report on a survey of 1200 agencies in 50 states focusing on 11 reinvention reforms devised from the major reinvention literature.[26] In their survey agency directors were asked to report on the degree of implementation or change in his or her agency relative to 11 reforms.[27] Their survey found that none of the 11 reforms had been fully implemented (See Table 1) and strategic planning was the only reinvention reform that had been substantially implemented (by more than 39% of the agencies surveyed). Twenty percent of the agencies indicated that they had training programs to improve customer service while only 11.7% reported that they had fully implemented systems for measuring customer satisfaction. Procurement, human resource rules, privatization and flexibility in carrying funds to the next fiscal year had the fewest complete implementations by the states surveyed.

Table 1: State Agency Implementation of Reinvention Recommendations		
Reinvention Recommendation	*Fully* *	*Partially or Fully* **
Training Programs to Improve Customer Service	20.4	81.5
Strategic Planning to clarify Mission Statement	39.3	79.4
Quality Improvement Programs	16.7	76.6
Benchmarks for Measuring Outcomes	14.3	62.0
Decentralization of Decision Making	12.4	54.7
Systems for Measuring Customer Satisfaction	11.7	51.7
Reduction in Hierarchical Levels	16.1	38.8
Greater Discretion in Procurement	5.0	28.9
Simplification of Human Resource Rules	5.2	23.0
Greater Discretion to Carry Over Funds	5.4	21.3
* Percentage of Agency Heads who indicated that the recommendation is fully Implemented ** Percentage of Agency Heads who indicated that the recommendation is either partially or fully implemented		

Source: Brudney, Hebert and Wright, 1999, p. 23

The study also calculated reinvention implementation scores for the states. Scores varied from 1 for New Jersey indicating that all administrators in that state specified that their state had been involved in reinvention to .14 for Alabama (indicating that 14 % of the administrators indicated that they had been involved in reinvention). Among the highest ranked states relative to reinvention effort involvement were New Jersey, Utah, Kansas, Massachusetts, Virginia, Oregon, Connecticut, Arizona, Nevada, and Florida. Using the 11 reinvention principals, the authors also ranked the states across all agencies in terms of reinvention efforts. The state scale averages ranged from 28.3 for Florida to 17.8 for Alabama. The authors observe that perhaps the reinvention wave is more of a ripple and that the reforms suggested by "reinvention" will not be widely and quickly adopted by the states.[28]

Brudney, Hebert and Wright also analyzed factors that enhanced reinvention efforts among the states from their survey results. The authors found that concerted statewide efforts, type of agency (staff or regulatory/elected), interest groups and administrator background were factors influencing reinvention efforts. More specifically, finance and human resource staff agencies tended to be more positive regarding reinvention. They theorized that the staff agencies were more likely to reflect executive leadership (the position of the Governor) on the issue than traditional agencies not directly influenced by the agenda of the executive of the state.

The literature regarding state reinventions has focused on two approaches: 1) identifying and highlighting reinvention and innovation activity (CSG and the Government Performance Project for example) and efforts to determine the use of the Osborne/Gaebler and Barzelay principles by the states. The CSG and Government Performance project indicate a wide variety of innovations and reinventions are occurring while the Brudney et. al., research suggests a modest adoption response by the states to the Osborne/Gaebler and Barzelay principles for reinvention enhancement.

State Government Reinvention: Another View

Following the reinvention compilation efforts of Brudney, Hebert and Wright and the summary work of CSG and the Government Performance Project, this chapter reports on state innovations or reinvention initiatives considered "most valuable" as perceived by key state government officials in the various states. In contrast to the assessment of implementation of the reinvention principles of the Brudney, Hebert and Wright study, the current analysis focuses on specific change or reinvention activities. Reinvention activities are categorized and analyzed relative to goals, origin and impact.

The most significant reinvention / innovation efforts were determined by means of a survey of state officials within the states conducted by the CSG and the Martin School of Public Administration, University of Kentucky.

A survey was sent to the State Budget Director in each state requesting information on the five most significant reinvention efforts in each state based upon the Budget Director's broad knowledge of state programs and policies. The Directors were also asked to provide the following information: 1) goals of the reinvention efforts; 2) the motivating force leading to the reinvention; 3) the nature of the reinvention; and 4) the perceived outcomes of the reinvention efforts. Answers to these questions extend the knowledge gained from the earlier assessment of state reinvention efforts by providing additional insights regarding the motivation and intent of the reinvention as well as the nature and impact of the innovation. Previous research regarding state government innovation and change suggest that goals and motivation may determine whether change efforts (such as reinvention) will be sustained. This research is focused on that issue and may indicate whether the state government reinvention efforts of the 1990s were part of a continuing "wave" or merely a temporary "ripple" as suggested by Brudney, Hebert, and Wright.[29]

As indicated, the reinvention survey was sent to the State Budget Directors of the fifty states. The State Budget Directors were chosen as the preferred respondents due to their broad knowledge and insight regarding state government programs and operations. In addition, Budget Directors are aware of reinvention impacts such as decreases or increases in staff, technology utilization and the like associated with the reinventions.

The surveys were distributed by the Council of State Governments, which is a state government organization recognized for its interest in and research on state government issues including state government management innovations and change.[30] The research staff conducted follow-up telephone conversations with the State Budget Offices and distributed follow-up surveys to enhance participation. Eighteen states or approximately one third of the states responded to the survey, which is comparable to similar studies of this nature. The results of the survey and observations regarding the survey results follow.

Study Results

The survey results analyzed and coded into a database for comparative analysis. The database includes the reinvention effort (See Appendix 1), a description of the effort, the motivating or driving force of the reinvention effort, the principal goals of the reinvention effort, and the outcome or impacted of the reinvention effort. Currently, seventeen states and the territory of Puerto Rico have completed the survey, which renders a response rate of 35%[31]. The eighteen respondents identified 97 reinvention efforts that they classified as the most significant reinvention efforts for their state in the decade of the 1990s.

To analyze the results of the survey, the "reinventions" were categorized into general groups. These groups include family and child services, economic, education, government administration, government finance, government management, health care, public safety, transportation, welfare, environmental, and other. The reinvention efforts are identified under each group heading in Table 2:

Table 2: Reinventions by Grouping	
Group	*Reinvention Effort*
Family and Child Services	Care for Children
	Dept Children Families
	Kids First
Economic	Restructure Economic Development Office
	WY Business Council
	Privatization of State Industrial Insurance System
	Workers Compensation Reform
	Workers Compensation Claims
	One Stop Shopping
	W2 Welfare Reform
	Workforce Development Programs
Education	Higher Education Incentive Funding
	Public School Accountability
	Public School Accountability
	Educational Reform
	K12 Reform
	School Reform
	School Finance Reform
	School Tax Relief
	Merge Community College, Tech College and State Universities
	Reform of Higher Education System
	Scholarship Through Lottery Funding
	Parental School Choice Program
	Library Network

Table 2: Continued	
Group	*Reinvention Effort*
Education (continued)	Network for Education
	Technology for Educational Achievement
Government Administration	Data Center
	Data Center outsourcing
	Electronic Benefit Transfer
	Electronic Benefits
	Use of GAAP
	Government Office of Technology
	Information Technology Resource Management
	Administration Information Network
	Payroll Accounting System
	Project Genesis
	Technological Reform
	Contract Management
	Reorganization
	Review of All State Agencies
Government Finance	Savings Incentive Program
	Capital Budget Reform and Debt Management Guidelines
	Electronic Budget System
	Performance Based Budgeting
	Revenue Estimating Conference
	Electronic Filing of Individual Tax Returns
	Revenue Telephone Filing Program
	Tax Cut program
	Tax Reform
	Cash Reserve and Economic Emergency Funds
	Infrastructure Fund
	Local Mandates Review
Government Management	Governing for Results
	Program Budgeting and Evaluation
	Reorganizing State Government

Table 2: Continued	
Group	*Reinvention Effort*
Government Management (Continued)	Empower Kentucky
	Civil Service System
	Human Resources
	Electronic Personnel System
	Personnel Reform
	Personnel Reform
	Retirement Pension Program
	Voice Response System for Employee Health System
	Development Plan
	Economic Forum
	Government Effectiveness and Accountability
	Strategic Planning Performance Reporting
	Local Government Budget Review Teams
	Statewide Video Conference Sites
Health Care	Connect Care
	Health Care Reform
	Health Care Reform
	Health Choice
	Home Health Care
	Automated Verification and Claims
	Health Care Reform
	Healthier Babies
Public Safety	Computerized Drivers' Licenses
	DNA Databank
	Automated Fingerprint ID
	Harsher Legislation for Violent Offenders
	Privatization of Prison Operations

242

Transportation	Intelligent Transportation Systems
	Five Year Road and Bridge Plan
	Regional Transportation Authority
	DOT Quality Improvements
Welfare	Welfare
	Welfare Reform
	Welfare to Work program
	Work First
	Work First
Other	Tribal Accord
	Automate State Court System
Environmental	Smart Growth
	Wild Land Trust
	Recycling
	Timber Harvest Program

Source: Compiled by authors from CSG/ Martin School Survey

These categories are similar to those used by the Council of State Governments in their "Innovations Awards" publication. The categorizing of the general groups focuses on the type of reinvention the respondents consider as the most important reinvention areas in state government. Furthermore, we classify each reinvention into a group designation that looks at the focus of the reinvention activity. That is, we classify the reinventions into three activities, agency-to-agency reinventions (GOVT), within agency reinventions (AGENCY), and agency to customer reinventions (CUSTOMER). These activities are defined as follows: 1) agency-to-agency reinventions (GOVT) are activities based on improving central services of state government such as personnel enhancements, performance assessments, budgetary and financial management reform, government wide technological innovations and the like. These activities assist in government performance through services that are shared by the agencies; 2) within agency reinventions (AGENCY) are improvements that affect the performance of the agency staff and service internally. These include reinventions such as internal technology changes, internal management and review, coordination activities to improve internal activities; 3) agency to customer reinventions

(CUSTOMER) are activities that directly impact the customers of government. These are service improvements such as privatization and restructuring of customer service delivery.

Table 3 presents the frequencies of the types and activities of the reinventions. Table 3 shows that 32 of the 97 (33%) reported reinventions are categorized as government reinvention and are activities based on improving central services of state government (GOVT). It is interesting that only one-third of the reinventions recognized by the Budget Director's as their top reinventions involve a direct change in government itself, while 51 of the 97 (53%) are focused on the line agencies service to the customer (CUSTOMER). This response may support a continuing "wave" of reinvention, not merely a temporary "ripple" as suggested by Brudney, Hebert, and Wright.[32]

Table 3: Reinventing Category Frequencies				
Category	Frequency	GOVT	AGENCY	CUSTOMER
Economics	8	0	1	7
Education	15	0	1	14
Environmental	4	0	0	4
Family and Child Services	3	0	0	3
Government Administration	14	11	1	2
Government Finance	12	6	1	5
Government Management	17	15	2	0
Health Care	8	0	0	8
Other	2	0	2	0
Public Safety	5	0	2	3
Transportation	4	0	4	0
Welfare	5	0	0	5
Totals	97	32	14	51

Source: Compiled by authors from CSG/ Martin School Survey

Table 4 shows the mean and standard deviation of the motivating or driving force behind the reinvention effort. The question, "Motivating or Driving Force in Reinvention/Innovation Effort", uses a Likert seven-point scale that ranges from least important to most important, with 7 indicating most important. Eighty-six of the ninety-seven reinventions (89%) show that a motivating or driving force was the Governor's platform or policy. This response, with a mean Likert value of 6.12, indicates that the Governor's platform or policy was an important factor.

Table 4: Motivating or Driving Force in Reinvention Effort			
Motivating or Driving Force	Respondents	Mean	Standard Deviation
Governor's Platform or Policy	86	6.12	1.67
Required by Legislation	57	4.42	2.12
Response to Citizens Committee	49	3.49	2.18
Response to Financial Conditions	73	4.37	1.71
Response to Exec/Leg Task Force	57	4.35	2.18
Other	28	6.21	1.69

Source: Compiled by authors from CSG/ Martin School Survey

Table 4 indicates that the Other category was important, with a mean Likert value of 6.21. This category included responses that showed the agency, department committee, industry consumers, local government concerns, the court systems, and Y2K as important forces in the reinvention effort. However, only 29% of the respondents indicated this category as an important motivating factor.

Table 5 shows the mean and standard deviation of the principal goal of the reinvention effort. The question, "Principal Goal of Reinvention Effort/Activity", uses a Likert seven-point scale that ranges from least important to most important, with 1 indicating most important. This question has been reversed scored for comparison to Table 4.

Table 5: Principal Goal of Reinvention Effort/Activity			
Principal Goal	Respondents	Mean	Standard Deviation
Reduce Costs of Government (Efficiency)	77	5.17	1.98
Improve Government Effectiveness (Meet Needs)	90	6.31	1.35
Improve Service Delivery (Response to Citizens)	83	6.14	1.44
Realignment	38	3.08	2.38
Initiate New Program	56	4.09	2.22
Privatization of Services	41	2.61	1.96
Program Restructuring or Merger	48	3.77	2.26

Source: Compiled by authors from CSG/ Martin School Survey

Improved government effectiveness and improved service delivery have a mean Likert value over 6.00, indicating that these are important goals in the reinvention effort. This finding corresponds with Table 3, which showed that 53% of the reinvention efforts were focused on the line agencies service to the customer. Thus, the Budget Director's indicate that meeting needs and responsiveness to the citizen are important goals of their most significant reinvention activities.

Perceived Reinvention Results

A final question asked on the survey was for the Budget Directors to indicate the perceived relative success of the reinvention efforts. The question, Please Evaluate Relative to the Reinvention Goal the Outcomes or Impact, uses an ordinal scale of impact that includes the following choices in order: high impact, moderate impact, limited impact, no impact, and negative impact. This ordinal scale is scored from 1 to 5, with 5 indicating high impact. Table 6 shows the results. Table 5 indicates that reinvention impacted government effectiveness and service delivery the most with means of 4.69 and 4.68, respectively. This corresponds with both Table 3 and Table 5 that indicated a focus on line agencies' service delivery to the customer. Interestingly, 49 respondents indicated a costs savings, however only 13 respondents provide the annual amount of cost reduction. The mean was $901,084,615 and the range of costs reduction was from a low of $600,000 to a high of $9.4 billion. The $9.4 billion was reported by the State of New York with respect to their Tax Cut Program.

Table 6: Outcomes and Impact Evaluation			
	Respondents	Mean	Standard Deviation
Costs Reduction	49	3.94	1.25
Annual Amount of Cost Reduction	13	$901,084,615	$2,581,753,398
Government Effectiveness	83	4.69	0.54
Service Delivery	81	4.68	0.54
Program Realignment	41	3.90	1.18
New Program Implementation	51	4.20	1.00
Privatization of Services Accomplished	30	2.90	1.32
Restructuring or Merger Success	37	3.70	1.33

Source: Compiled by authors from CSG/ Martin School Survey

Implications of Reinvention Efforts

This reinvention survey focused on State Budget Directors and their perception of the most significant reinvention efforts in their state in the decade of the 1990s. While many reinvention efforts have started at the federal government level, states have been characterized as the "laboratories" for innovations that were later adopted by the federal government. In the decade of the 1990s, the "reinvention" movement focused on customer service, that is the constituent perceived as the customer. This characterization of a customer is seen in the survey results that indicate over 50% of the reinventions identified by the respondents are focused on customer service delivery, that is from the line agency to the customer. However, Osborne and Gaebler's reinvention reforms, which can be viewed as internal government reforms, or between agency reinventions, are clearly present in the survey results. That is, 32 of the 43 reinventions (74%) categorized as government, are agency-to-agency reinventions. Moreover, if we include within agency reinventions, 36 of 43 reinventions (84%) categorized as government, are either agency-to-agency reforms or within agency reforms. Thus, it appears that state governments are also reinventing their internal organizations to equip them with the necessary tools and processes to provide enhanced government management. These findings are consistent with the prior literature on reinvention that has theoretically argued that government wide reinvention goes beyond the government itself and indirectly affects the customer. Interestingly, when looking at the reinventions that fall under government itself, only 47% of the total reinventions apply to agency-to-agency reforms or within agency reforms. This is an indication that government may be focused on both the agency with its goals of effectiveness and efficiency and the direct provision of improved customer service.

Brudney, Hebert and Wright theorized that staff agencies were more likely to reflect executive leadership (the position of the Governor) in developing and implementing reinvention actions. Although our results tend to confirm this suggestion, the survey indicates that legislation, financial conditions, and executive/legislative task forces also play roles in motivating reinvention efforts. The principal goals and outcomes of the reinvention effort are focused on improving government effectiveness and service delivery according to the respondents. This is an interesting finding when consideration is given to the question of reinvention as a "wave" or "ripple". Throughout the 1990s the "wave" of reinvention/innovation activities by state governments continued, leading one to theorize that all good government management efforts, whether influenced by the chief executive of a state, the Governor, or the federal government, the President, are but "ripples" on the wave of government change.

Appendix 1

Reinvention Effort	Reinvention Description
Automate State Court system	Centralized and standard system
Automated fingerprint ID	Stores fingerprints optical media
Automated Verification and Claims	Medicaid processing
Cap budget reform and debt mgmt guidelines	
Care for Children	
Cash reserve and economic emergency funds	To be used in times of economic downturns
Civil Service	Abolish civil service provisions
Computerized Drivers' Licenses	Better online id tools
Connect Care	Medicaid patients access to medical care
Contract Mgmt	Master contract system
Data Center	Consolidate agencies and expand info access
Data center outsourcing	Consolidates data centers to a PA vendor
Dept Children Families	Collaboration at local level
Development Plan	Muni and cty master planning
Div of Human Resources	Comprehensive statewide HR policy
DNA databank	
DOT Quality improvements	
Economic Forum	Outside panel input on forecast for revenues
Educational Reform	
Electronic Benefit Transfer	Foods stamps debit cards
Electronic Benefits	Women and children EBT food stamps, prevent fraud
Electronic Budget System	
Electronic filing ind tax returns	
Electronic Personnell System	
Empower KY	Reorg how government operates
Five yr road and bridge	Long range repair plan
Governing for Results	Accountability and improvement of govt
Govt effectiveness and acctability	Strategic planning
Govt office of Technology	Chief Info Officer created
Harsher legislation for violent offenders	
Health Care Reform	Addresses increased cost issues
Health Care Reform	Availability
Health Care Reform	Reduction of uninusred children and adults
Health choice	Health care for low income
Healthier babies	Promote prenatal care for babies

Higher Education Incentive Funding	Increased accountability
Home health care	Local and community health strategies
Info Tech Resource Mgmt	Statewide development of Info tech
Infrastructure Fund	Funding for vertical infrastructure
K12 Reform	Eliminate superintendant and use Commisssioner of Ed
Kids First	Health insurance aid
Library Network	Supports library mgmt and provides online access to resources
Local Govt budget review teams	Mgmt review and consulting services
Local Mandates Review	Financial impact of local legislation
Merge Comm Coll Tech Coll and State Univ	Management of higher ed system
MI admin info network	Management and accting info system
Network for Education	Link public educ at all levels through telecomm infrastructure.
One Stop Shopping	Reorg Dept of Employment offices into regional offices
Parental School Choice Program	Tuition vouchers for low income families
Payroll acctg system	Improve info processing
Performance Based Budgeting	Look at outputs when appropriating funds
Personnel reform	Improve HR functions
Personnel reform	HR lawsuits training
Privatization of Prison Ops	Maximum security
Privatization of state industrial insurance system	
Program budgeting and evaluation	
Project Genesis	To improve customer service
Public Schl Acctability	Assessment program
Public School Accountability	Testing,etc.
Recycling	Recycle contaminated land
Reform of Higher Ed system	with the state's economic development efforts
Regional Trans Authority	Statewide planning and overseeing
Reorg state govt	Overall efficiency and effectiveness
Reorganization	Increased centralization
Restructure Economic development office	Depoliticize the Eco Development function
Retirement pension program	Cost savings
Revenue Estimating Conference	Sets and reviews upcoming fiscal estimates
Revenue telefile program	Personal tax returns via phone
Review of all state agencies	Evaluate current functions and decide what services to

	provide in the future
Savings Incentive Program	Incentive for state agencies to return money to state education savings acct
Scholarship through lottery funding	Merit based college scholarship program
School Finance Reform	Decrease local prop tax and improve per pupil spending equity
School Reform	Core curriculum content stds
School tax relief	tax relief
Smart growth	Incentive based effort to reverse sprawl
Statewide Video Conference sites	Statewide meetings with greater participation
Strategic Planning Performance Reporting	Multi-year plans with goals
Tax cut program	All major taxes cut
Tax Reform	
Tech for Educational Achievement	Access to internet, computer tech, etc. in K-12
Technological Reform	
Timber Harvest Program	Provides material to timber industry
Trans ITS	Technology to improve transportation
Tribal Accord	Prevent issues ending in the court system
Use of GAAP	
Voice response system for employee health sys	Automate enrollment process
W2 welfare reform	Facilitate workforce entry
Welfare	Increase parental responsibility
Welfare Reform	Stop perpetual cash welfare and promote productive activity
Welfare to Work program	Recipients to seek employment
Wild Land Trust	Outdoor recreation needs
Work First	Families on welfare
Work First	Reinvention of traditional welfare system
Workers comp claims	Electronic case file for each claim or dispute
Workers Comp Reform	
Workforce Development Programs	
WY Business Council	Coordinate eco development preserve tourism ag minerals and energy

Source: Compiled by authors from CSG/ Martin School Survey

Notes

1   Linda deLeon and Robert B. Denhardt, "The Political Theory of Reinvention", *Public Administration Review*, vol. 60 (2), 2000, 89-97.
2   Eugene Lewis, *Public Entrepreneurship,* Bloomington, Indiana University Press, 1980.
3   U.S. Commission on Organization of the Executive Branch of the Government, *Hoover Commission Report,* New York, Macmillan Co., 1949.
4   David Osborne and Ted Gaebler, *Reinventing Government*, Reading, MA, Addison-Wesley, 1992.
5   David Osborne and Ted Gaebler, *Reinventing Government*, Reading, MA, Addison-Wesley, 1992.
6   John Jr. DiIulio, Gerald Garvey, and Donald Kettl, *Improving Government Performance: An Owner's Manual,* Washington, DC, Brookings Institution, 1993.
7   Linda deLeon and Robert B. Denhardt, "The Political Theory of Reinvention", *Public Administration Review*, vol. 60 (2), 2000, 89-97; James Fallows, "The Case for Reform", *Atlantic Monthly*, vol. 270 (2), 1992, 119-123; George Frederickson, "Painting Targets Around Bullet Holes", *Governing*, vol. 6 (1), 1992, 13; Paul Glastris, "Paradigm Glossed", *Washington Monthly,* (April 1992), 39-49; *Governing Magazine*, (February 1992); Donald Kettl, *Reinventing Government? Appraising the National Performance Review,* (CPM Report 94-2), Washington, DC, The Brookings Institution, 1994; Ronald C. Moe, "The "Reinventing Government" Exercise: Misinterpreting the Problem, Misjudging the Consequences", *Public Administration Review,* vol. 54 (2), 1994, 111-22.
8   George Fredrickson, "The Seven Principles of Total Quality Politics...", *Public Administration Times,* vol. 17 (1), 1994, 9.
9   James, D. Carroll, "Introduction", *Public Administration Review,* vol. 56 (3), 1996.
10 Ronald C. Moe, "The "Reinventing Government" Exercise: Misinterpreting the Problem, Misjudging the Consequences", *Public Administration Review,* vol. 54 (2), 1994, 111-22.
11 Peri Arnold, "Reform's Changing Role", *Public Administration Review*, vol. 55, 1995, 407-414.
12 Executive Office of the President National Performance Review, *From Red Tape to Results: Creating a Government That Works Better and Costs Less,* Washington, DC, U.S. Government Printing Office, 1993.
13 Executive Office of the President National Performance Review, *From Red Tape to Results: Creating a Government That Works Better and Costs Less,* Washington, DC, U.S. Government Printing Office, 1993.
14 Executive Office of the President National Performance Review, *From RedTapeto Results: Creating a Government That Works Better and Costs Less,* Washington, DC, U.S. Government Printing Office, 1993.
15 National Partnership for Reinventing Government, (April 2000), *http://www.npr.gov.*

16 National Partnership for Reinventing Government, (April 2000), *http://www.npr.gov*, 8.

17 James R. Thompson and Patricia W. Ingraham, "The Reinvention Game", *Public Administration Review, vol.* 56 (3), 1996.

18 Donald Kettl, "Building Lasting Reform: Enduring Questions, Missing Answers", in Donald Kettl, and, John DiIulio, Jr., (eds.), *Inside the Reinvention Machine: Appraising Government Reform,* Washington, DC, Brookings Institution, 1995.

19 Jeffrey L. Brudney, , F. Ted Hebert, and Deil S. Wright, "Reinventing Government in the American States: Measuring and Explaining Administrative Reform", *Public Administration Review,* vol. 59 (1), 1999, 19-30.

20 David Osborne, and Ted Gaebler, *Reinventing Government,* Reading, MA, Addison-Wesley, 1992.

21 *Governing,* (February 1999), *http://www.governing.com/gpp/gp9intro.htm.*

22 Jeffrey L. Brudney, F. Ted Hebert, and Deil S. Wright, "Reinventing Government in the American States: Measuring and Explaining Administrative Reform", *Public Administration Review,* vol. 59 (1), 1999, 19-30.

23 *Governing,* February 1999, *http://governing.com/gpp/gp9intro.htm.*

24 Keon S. Chi, "Privatization", *State Trends and Forecasts,*vol. 2 (2), Lexington, Kentucky, The Council of State Governments, 1993.

25 Jeffrey L. Brudney, F. Ted Hebert, and Deil S. Wright, "Reinventing Government in the American States: Measuring and Explaining Administrative Reform", *Public Administration Review,* vol. 59 (1), 1999, 19-30.

26 Michael Barzeley, *Breaking Through Bureaucracy: A New Version for Managing Government,* Berkeley, University of California Press, 1992; David Osborne and Ted Gaebler, *Reinventing Government,* Reading, MA, Addison-Wesley, 1992.

27 The eleven items used by Brudney, Hebert, and Wright [1999; 22] were: 1) training programs to improve customer service, 2) strategic planning to produce clear mission statements, 3) quality improvement programs to empower employees, 4) benchmarks for measuring results, 5) decentralization of decision making, 6) systems for measuring customer satisfaction, 7) reduction in hierarchical levels, 8) greater discretion in procurement, 9) simplification of human resource rules, 10) privatization of major programs and 11) greater discretion to carry over funds.

28 Jeffrey L. Brudney, F. Ted Hebert, and Deil S. Wright, "Reinventing Government in the American States: Measuring and Explaining Administrative Reform", *Public Administration Review,* vol. 59 (1), 1999, 28.

29 Jeffrey L. Brudney, F. Ted Hebert, and Deil S. Wright, "Reinventing Government in the American States: Measuring and Explaining Administrative Reform", *Public Administration Review,* vol. 59 (1), 1999, 19-30.

30 Keon S. Chi, "Privatization", *State Trends and Forecasts,* vol. 2 (2), Lexington, Kentucky: The Council of State Governments, 1993; Keon S. Chi, "Total Quality Management", *State Trends and Forecasts,* vol. 3 (2), Lexington, Kentucky: The Council of State Governments, 1994.

31 The response rate is calculated by dividing the responses (18) by total number of suurveys (52). The total number of surveys includes the 50 states, the District of Columbia, and the territory of Puerto Rico.

32 Jeffrey L. Brudney, F. Ted Hebert, and Deil S. Wright, "Reinventing Government in the American States: Measuring and Explaining Administrative Reform", *Public Administration Review*, vol. 59 (1), 1999, 28.

Intermunicipal Comparative Performance Measurement: Innovation through Competition

Bernd Adamaschek

The buzzwords of "New Management" are decentralization, budgeting, quality and contract management, Cost and Result Accounting (CRA), etc. "Performance comparison" is rarely used in this context. Apparently, many reformers get along well enough without it, conceding that it is useful, but not necessary. So what is the value of performance comparison in the New Management concept?

A new way of thinking leading to new behavior is intended to establish more result and customer orientation, more effectiveness and efficiency in public administrations. What is at the forefront here is the ability to react flexibly and quickly to the problems and challenges of the outside world and to find answers to them. Changes in the world are accompanied by a self-regulating, continuous improvement process in administration. That is what New Management wants to achieve.

Freedom and accountability

Performance and innovation in this sense are only possible in decentrally organized structures, which are founded on the responsibility, creativity and initiative of their members. Whether we are talking about the commercial sector or administration, the same principle applies: continuous improvement in this sense works best where a

- maximum of self management and
- minimum of central management

are possible. The freedom this creates is the engine for better performance and innovation.

However, freedom brings with it one problem! The more the members of an organization are able to act on their own initiative, the more difficult it becomes for their superiors to take responsibility for this. Despite all the freedom they allow, superiors still have to ensure that the aims of the organization, i.e. the results required, are achieved within the given budget, and they also take responsibility for this. That means the flip side of freedom is the duty to regularly and promptly provide evidence of the "correct" use of this freedom so that all those involved can fulfill their responsibilities. So transparency of performance and the use of resources is the price of freedom!

The core of New Management

Clarity on the achievement of goals, the quantity and quality of administration performance and on the use of resources is necessary not only for decentralization and delegation of responsibility. Other key elements of New Management also depend on it:

- *Quality management*: Concrete details on performance and the use of resources, if possible documented in figures, form the basis for the improvement process. There's good reason for the saying "What you can't measure you can't improve." Transparency is the starting point for the analysis of strengths and weaknesses, for pinpointing causes, recognizing potential for improvements and deciding on optimization strategies.

- *Contract management*: Agreements on targets should name concrete values. Ideally, these are derived from the reports on performance and costs and from the quality management which is built up on the basis of these. They form the contents of contract offers to the higher levels.

- *Checking the target agreements/controlling*: There must be a means of checking target agreements. To ensure this, transparency on the subjects of the agreement is required. That means regular and prompt reporting on compliance with agreed aims is the requirement for contract management and controlling.

- *Council and administration*: The new division of responsibilities between the council and the administration (administration: running operations, political level: strategic control) as well as the delegation of responsibility within the administration require transparency relating to performance and costs. Only where there is transparency can the council perform its new functions responsibly.

- *Administrative culture*: New Management should lead "from a culture of mistrust to an administrative culture." Trust depends not entirely but to a large extent on transparency. That is because trust should not be blind trust. There must be clarity about performance and costs between the various levels of administration and at the interface between the political and the administrative levels. This is the foundation for a cooperation based on trust.

The core of New Management

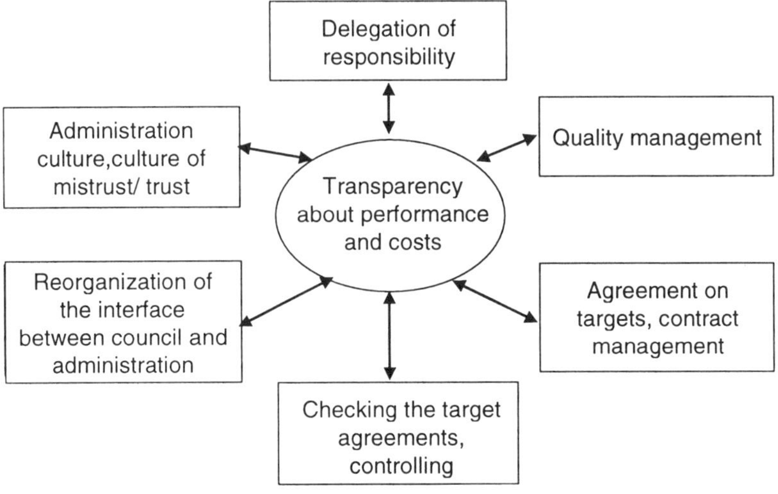

As graph 1 demonstrates, without transparency about performance and costs, the foundation for the main elements of New Management is missing. Clarity about achieving aims, quantities, qualities and use of resources is the core of New Management.

CRA - the solution?

There are many who hope to solve this problem by applying a method, which works well in the private sector: Cost and Results Accounting (CRA). They believe that transferring this method to the public sector will achieve the same success (i.e. controllability) that it does in the private sector.

That is why (almost) all public administrations are currently developing CRA concepts - the graduates in business studies have stormed the strongholds of the traditionalists. Yet the old hands are skeptical about the ability of this "import product" to solve the problem and achieve the same management effects it does in the private sector.

258

To demonstrate that the skeptics have a point, here's a cost and results account for a simple local government task:

<table>
<tr><td>Example:</td><td></td><td></td></tr>
<tr><td>Product group:</td><td>Inhabitants services</td><td></td></tr>
<tr><td>Product:</td><td>Wage tax cards</td><td></td></tr>
<tr><td></td><td>- cost per wage tax card</td><td>DM 9.80</td></tr>
<tr><td></td><td>- number per year</td><td>12,000</td></tr>
</table>

This is the outcome of a cost and results account of the kind routinely compiled in forward-looking administrations. The route to these figures is time-consuming and many people who have to do this work ask themselves whether it is worth it.

Looking at the cost of DM 9.80 for each wage tax card issued, it is difficult to say whether this is good or bad. Transparency is more than just knowing a numerical value. Equally important is being able to correctly interpret it. Whether the production costs of DM 9.80 are reasonable or whether the job could be done more cheaply is a question left unanswered here. The performance (number per year) of 12,000 cards is dictated to the administration from outside. Whether this product quantity is "right" or not, in other words whether there is a need for change here, is also unclear from the number of 12,000. Nor do these figures reflect performance in terms of quality, customer satisfaction, etc. So a whole series of questions remains unanswered, although they are highly relevant for the management of local government services. The figures obtained through CRA are important and certainly not useless. But they are not enough on their own.

The information effect of the market

How can we explain the fact that CRA - so successfully used in the private sector for management purposes - is inadequate in the public sector?
To do this, we have to get down to details: Expressed in simple terms, costs and performance can be defined as follows:

Costs: consumption of factors valued in money terms (use of resources) in order to achieve performance

Performance: sale of goods and/or services valued in money terms.

The situation with regard to costs in public administration is closely comparable to that in the private sector, which is why cost and results accountants concentrate on the cost side and supply at best meager figures on the performance side. There is in fact one essential difference on the performance side. The phrase "sale of goods and/or services valued in money terms" means that CRA assumes market forces are at work. Before the goods and/or services are sold and can be entered as "performance" they have to pass through the filter of the market. Here they must pass all the tests that products in the public sector are spared (because there is no market here). These include price competition, quality competition, service competition, innovation competition, etc.

System links between CRA and the market:

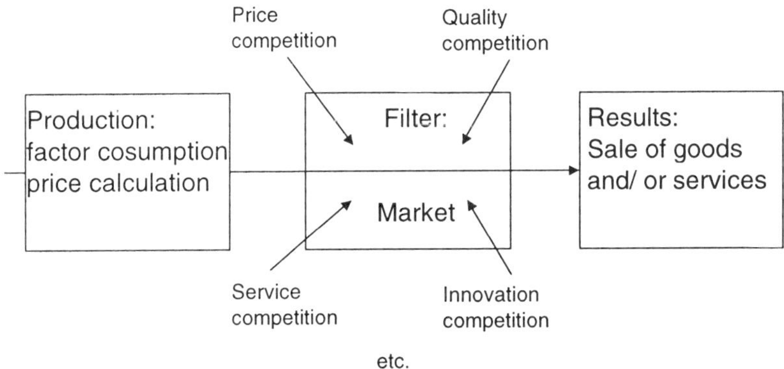

CRA therefore implicitly uses the market as a kind of "external check" which supplies the following information relevant to management:

- the costs/prices are reasonable
- the quality is right
- the customers are satisfied
- the service is right
- the products are innovative
- the company aims have been achieved
- I have to act / do not have to act.

Unfortunately, this extensive information is not available in the public sector, even if it is known thanks to CRA that e.g. the wage tax cards cost DM 9.80 each and altogether 12,000 of them have been issued each year. This may be very interesting. But if the question "good or bad" cannot be answered, the information is useless for management purposes. The belief that introducing CRA can produce the necessary transparency about management-relevant circumstances is based on a failure to realize that CRA in the private sector is systemically linked to the market and only supplies the information relevant to management in interaction with the market. If the method is taken out of this context it cannot work properly.

Three information effects of the market

Unlike the public sector, the market has three different information functions it performs directly through cost and results accounting.

Complete information: The sale of goods and/or services on the market, as reflected in the individual data of a CRA as "performance," is only successful when the products gain a place on the market. This market success depends not only on the price, which appears in the results account multiplied with the quantities as a sum of money. Instead, the product is considered by customers in all its aspects. Take for instance an automobile which has to beat the competition in quality (safety, environment friendliness, space, acceleration, etc.), cost (purchase price, running costs) and various service components (sales, workshop, replacement parts, etc.). "Sale in money terms" of these products in the results account means that the product has succeeded on the market after a complete consideration of all its properties as well as the price. So the money values given in the results account also stand for a whole range of quality aspects which are not and in some cases cannot be expressed in money terms.

Comparative information: This means that the product has been compared to competing products. The decision by customers for the product and the resulting sales tell the manufacturer that the product has a better standard that that of its competitors.

Incentive for optimization: The market indicates whether or not there is a need for management. If the cost and results account produces poor values, this sets off alarm bells. If nothing is done there is a risk of losses or even closure of the business. Without this prospect many companies would not see any reason to improve poor results. The best example for this is that of a monopoly company, which, although it is privately organized and possibly even has an excellent CRA system, tends to perform below its potential because the market is cancelled out and with it the incentive for optimization.

Wherever the market is missing, these three information functions of CRA are also missing. That is why in the public sector CRA will turn into a graveyard for figures unless it is possible to simulate the effects which are achieved by the systemic link between the market and CRA in the private sector.

A threefold supplement to CRA

Where the products from the public sector face parallel offers in the private sector, New Management attempts to establish direct competition with the private sector (contractor-client relationship, issuing invitations to bid with participation by private and public providers, etc.). But there are many areas of public administration where no comparable products are available in the private sector (regulatory, social, cultural administrations; police; internal revenue, etc.). Here it is important to reproduce the information and/or incentive effects of the market by supplementing the system. The point here is not to reverse the introduction of CRA, but to further develop this useful approach. This can be done by reinforcing the systemic context of CRA in the public administration with these three functions:

- complete performance evaluation
- comparative performance evaluation
- optimization incentive.

Complete performance evaluation

Accounts must be provided not only of the cost and quantity patterns of performance but also of the achievement of aims and the quality of administration actions. It is not enough for instance to present the number of fines issued as performance and the cost of a fine as a result in the CRA. Equally important is the question of whether fining drivers for motoring offences has contributed to safety and smooth-running traffic, whether the administration work has been performed correctly and promptly, etc. - in other words whether the task in question has been performed "well".

A special problem in the public sector is customer satisfaction. As a rule in the private sector a good product and a good service are sure ways of securing customer satisfaction, but this is not always the case in the public sector. Take for instance a correctly issued fine or a correct refusal to grant building permission - despite the fact that the goals have been achieved and a high quality has been attained, these services are not always appreciated by the citizen/customer as satisfactory. And yet what counts is that here too citizen satisfaction is actively promoted and - where satisfaction cannot be achieved - at least understanding is created through fair and just actions.

A good example of how to compile a complete picture of performance and the use of resources is provided here by the 4-target-system developed by the Bertelsmann Foundation for local government performance comparisons.

Graph 3

Local government performance comparison: 4-target-system

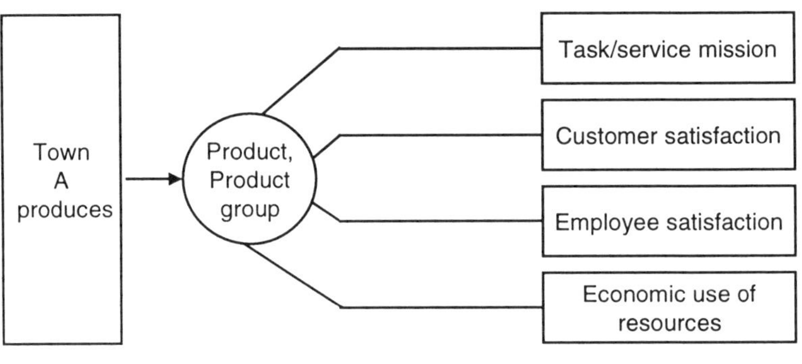

The additional aim included here is employee satisfaction. This is based on the idea that the employees - as the most important and most sensitive resource - should be allocated an equally high management relevance as the money factor. Just as sustainability in finances can only be achieved through financial optimization - expressed in the "economic use of resources" box - in the long term neither a good fulfillment of tasks nor satisfied customers nor economic use of resources can be secured without employee satisfaction.

Comparative performance evaluation

The CRA results for a single administration considered in isolation tell us very little. This also applies in the commercial sector. Anybody who wants to buy an automobile and is offered just one model cannot judge whether the price and the service are reasonable or whether there is a better or cheaper alternative. The same goes for public administration. In the example given earlier of "costs per wage tax card" of DM 9.80, it is not possible to judge whether this value can be improved on or whether it is already an excellent result that needs no further optimization. Only when an administration knows where comparable administrations stand can it correctly assess its own performance.

Example:

City/town	A	B	C	D
Costs per wage tax card in DM	9.80	4.63	20.40	17.50

It is only possible by means of this comparison to see that DM 9.80 (for A) is an acceptable performance (compared to C and D), but that the value can certainly be improved on (see B). If this kind of comparison is made not only for the economic aspect but for all the goals, the CRA is supplemented by the complete and the comparison functions.

This is why e.g. the Bertelsmann Foundation extends its complete performance evaluation according to the 4-target-system to include the values from comparison local governments. This makes it possible to present both a complete and a comparison view of performance and use of resources in a single table.

Local government performance comparison: Business report

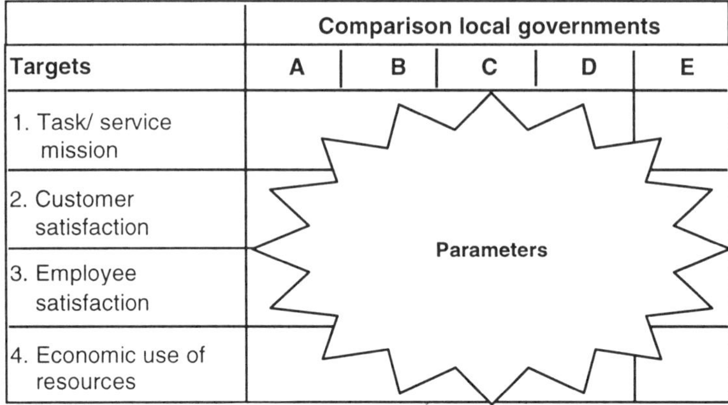

This is the point where the value of performance comparisons in the system of New Management becomes clear. Without a comparison, the information from the cost and results accounting cannot be adequately assessed and the need for management not properly recognized. Without a comparison, CRA in the public sector is incomplete. This proves that this element is not merely an extra that can be included or just as well left out, according to individual taste. Benchmarking in the private sector is an optional extra, but local government performance comparison must be an integral part of the reformer's toolbox. Otherwise the information function of CRA is not fulfilled, and New Management is not complete.

Optimization incentive

Usually a reporting system that provides complete and comparative information on performance and costs is sufficient to motivate those concerned to make efforts to optimize their performance. After all, nobody wants to look bad in a performance comparison. But this is only the theory. The experience gained by the Bertelsmann Foundation shows that this is not the case in all public administrations. Even where there is complete reporting of performance and costs including a comparison with other organizations, changes are often put off or they have to be initiated with a great deal of effort. The lack of market forces means that the aforementioned incentive is also missing, because there is no need to succeed on the market. Taking no account of poor results, the management of an organization, e.g. council and administration leaders of a local government, can carry on as before. More often than not the people involved agree on certain reasons why in the concrete case things cannot be improved. The need for management is simply ignored. This kind of behavior can also be found in the private sector. It is only the optimization incentive provided by competition that keeps many commercial enterprises from behaving in the same way as public administrations.

Here a different module must be found which creates incentive effects in a similar way to the market. This can be seen in the fourth module of the working stages (presenting accounts/publicity work) developed by the Bertelsmann Foundation for the management process in the local government performance comparison:

Local government performance comparison:
4 x 4 concept

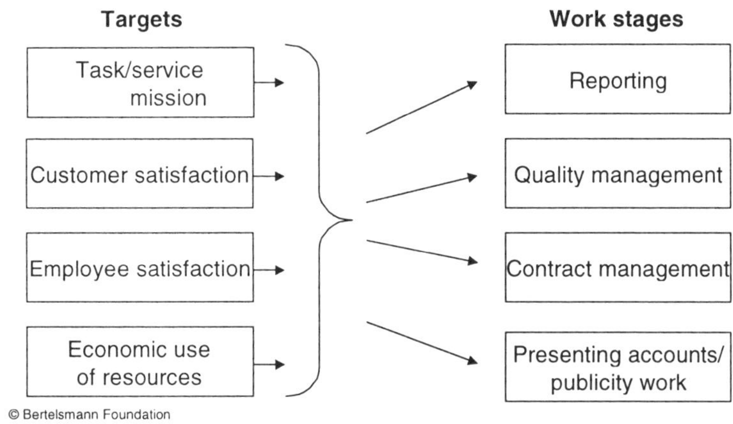

When the presentation of accounts is established as a public presentation of accounts within a performance comparison, the data assume a highly motivating function. Press reports and public discussion have an effect on those responsible in politics and administration that is similar to the effect of the market in the private sector. These factors decide on the rise or fall of elected representatives and senior administrative staff in the same way as positioning on the market decides in the private sector. A good result leads to public admiration and justified pride on the part of those responsible. But a bad result leads to public discussion, which achieves more among politicians and administrators than internal recommendations by experts or well-meaning reform proposals by employees can ever do.

This means that not just presenting accounts, but *publicly* presenting accounts is an additional essential element for the proper functioning of cost and results accounting in public administration, even if this is supplemented by a complete approach and by benchmarking. Only when the results are made public is the incentive function provided which can be compared to the function of the market as an implied element of CRA in the private sector.

Conclusion

Applied on its own, the CRA used in the private sector is not suitable for developing the management effect in the public sector that it is generally assumed to provide. The reason for this is the lack of market influences, which act in the private sector together with CRA to answer questions relevant to management. Merely transferring CRA to the public sector ignores the systemic link between CRA in the private sector and the market. This method remains a "blunt sword" when used in public administration without any replacement for the effects of this systemic link. In order to answer the questions relevant to management, three extra dimensions must supplement CRA for the public sector:

Graph 6

Local government performance comparison

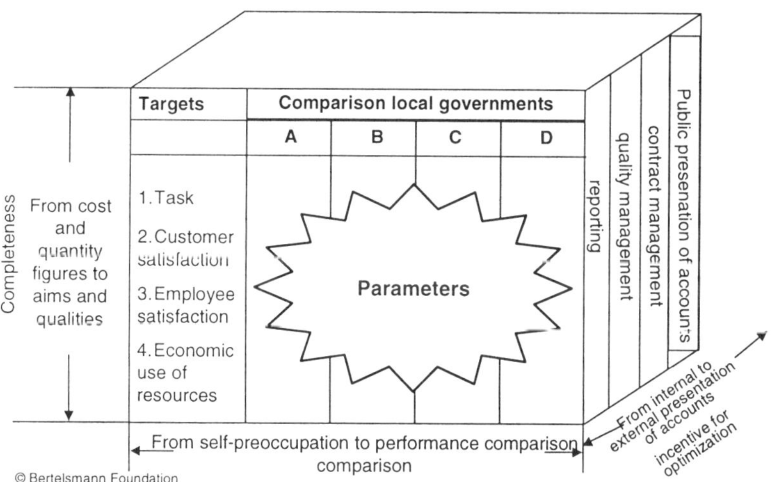

269

Only in this extended version is CRA similarly effective here to the CRA used in the private sector. Applied in this way, this method is suitable for providing a basis for all the instruments of New Management. It guarantees that the current modernization movement will not come to a standstill half way.

IV. Concluding Remarks

Franz Greß
Jackson Janes

As the reform of institutions, government, and governance in both countries has a long tradition, with a substantial number of commissions and task forces having already studied it, why add a new volume to the already long list of publications?

- First of all, we think it is always worthwhile to get first-hand information from scholars and practitioners on works in progress.

- Second, it highlights the parallel trends which have marked America and Europe in recent years.

- Third, governance reform is here to stay. It is rooted so deeply in an evironment of societal and technological changes of the transindustrial epoch that it cannot easily be derailed.

The transatlantic learning community is not a one-way street nor has it ever been one. To learn does not mean using a cookie cutter approach. It requires the understanding of social phenomena - facts as well as values - in their socio-historical context. Understanding can then be the base of fair evaluation and assessment. Learning means learning from differences, i. e. is to look from different angles at familiar subjects, which helps to overcome conventional wisdom and prejudices. As the USA and Europe are interconnected by structurally comparable civil societies sharing basic values, a comparative perspective has a sound base of communalities with which one can also decipher differences.

It is a challenging endeavor to edit a volume which focuses on changes of modern government structures in two countries with very different traditions. The concept of the "state" and its ambitious promotion during the Prussian-German era and finally its perversion in the Third Reich in the last century bares hardly any resemblance to the concept of government in a society which created its polity as the consequence of a war of independence from a colonial power, fought a bloody war about its basic values and their organizational consequences and needed nearly another century to develop a national government of significant weight.

On one side, one finds closeness to government. On the other, one sees relative statelessness. In contrast to the longstanding traditions of a subject culture in Germany, one recognizes in America a civic culture tradition of the classical liberal polity. The American orientation of trust in common sense and the importance of public preferences differs from the German custom of hierarchical top-down relations and protectionism. Which demonstrates at best a benevolent paternalism always tempted and overshadowed by authoritarian-bureaucratic features. Germany with some of its European neighbors still shares the experience of a path into modernity which is molded by the fact that public bureaucracy is historically older than democracy.

After the Second World War, re-education, the participation in the Transatlantic Alliance, and globalization in its various aspects facilitated changes in the structures and operations of German government and of the political culture along the norms and values of a Western style civic culture.

But by the second half of the 1970s the topic of governability had become prominent in Germany as well as in the United States. In the USA as a result of the defense and welfare shift and an activist federal bureaucracy, a mix of government overload and system underperformance developed which led to a decrease in authority. In Europe and Germany the vicious circle of bureaucratic weight and civic irresponsibility still had its impact.

At the beginning of the 1980s, U.S. President Reagan was able to identify goverment a part of the problem and not the solution, while the Californian taxpayers / voters had already sent a strong message with proposition 13. In Germany, the turn around from center-left to center-right (geistig-moralische-Wende) remained a vague ideological buzz word with minimal political impact.

Now, at the turn of the new century, it is impressive to see how strong the impact of the spirit and techniques of New Public Management has been in both societies. When President Clinton announced his "Reinventing Government" intiative in 1993, later called the "National Partnership for Reinventing Government", a project assigned to Vice President Gore, the aim was to strengthen the steering capacity and qualitative improvement of administration by using the entrepreneurial spirit of competition and customer choice to force improvement.

The principles of modernization enhanced in reinventing government quickly had its impact on the German discussion. They re-inforced the already ongoing discussion about deregulation, permit streamlining, and other features to move beyond command and control, by using incentives of various kinds, elaborated information strategies, mediation processes etc.

The reinventing government project in the United States obviously has lost momentum but the basics are still valid, i. e. to import business management methods into the public sector. The guiding line is: public goals should be achieved through market means wherever possible. But the approach is really more complex. It means focussing the public sector on defining public goals, marshalling public resources to achieve them, and finding the least bureaucratic, most decentralized means for achieving that purpose, whether it is through market incentives for businesses, through third sector non-profit organizations, through lower levels of government, states and localities, or even by a combination of all of the above in competition.

The reinvented government is one which does not deliver services. It regulates the services, it sets goals for them, with the intention to ameliorate collective problems. To overcome the bureaucratic systems created in the 1930s into the 1970s, and adapt them to the information age by empowerment of the people, one needs to ignore micromanaging and focus more on results and reward them. The catchwords is "steering rather than rowing" and this is not a simple process, as e. g. the competition between the charter school concept and school vouchers shows.

In both nations the reforms of governance are nourished from various sources. For a good part they are deficit driven; be it the scarcity of financial and operational resources and/or of resources of legitimacy (clearly visible in the distrust of public officials, *Politikverdrossenheit*) or the loss of social capital in America. Changes and adaptions are caused and facilitated by the emergence of a trans-industrial society in a global environment, accompanied by the explosive force of the information society which changes the nature of the public decisively.

Along with those secular trends go regional features like a strong economy in the case of the USA, the effect of Europeanization on top of the impact of globalization in the case of Germany.

This does not mean that the USA and Germany have identical patterns of reform, but there are tendencies to use very similiar positions and instruments. This is true for the New Public Management with all its features from benchmarking to public-private burden sharing and from empowerment to evaluation and it is true for the incorporation of the new information technologies. But it seems normal that the USA are a few steps ahead: The German "eGovernment-Initiative", begun in September 2000, promises to offer online access by the year 2005 to all services of the federal administration which are suitable for internet use (BundOnline 2005). At the same time, President B. Clinton launched a World Wide Web site called FirstGov (*http://www.firstgovs.gov),* a site with an Internet address which gives citizens access to government information and services 24 hours a day through a single online information portal which connects with one of the largest collection of Web pages, 27 million pages of information located on 20,000 U.S. government Web sites.

In federal systems like the USA and Germany, the balance between federation and the constituent parts is always in jeopardy. In both systems the feeling has arisen that a critical point in the intergovernmental relations has been reached - be it the ossification of the executive federalism, turning it into an unitarian state in disguise, or the sweeping transformations to federal preeminence since the 1960s and the continously growing cooperative character of U.S. federalism.

It is not by chance that in both systems, reform of intergovernmental relations is a centerpiece of the reform of governance as the time of inflexible hierarchies and remote decision making has lapsed. The National Performance Review, like its precedessors since President R. Nixon's New Federalism, endorsed the concept of empowerment of states and localities as a way of unravelling complex program requirements and allowing more flexibility by focusing on performance objectives of programs in order to create more efficiency. In Germany, reform of the relations between the federation and the *Länder* and between the *Länder* concerning the financial equalization system is one of the permanent leitmotifs of the German political and constitutional debate. The discussion about the quality of the changes in both countries is in full flare along the lines of "devolution revolution" vs. "restoring the federal balance" or "federalism of participation" vs. "federalism of substance" respectively. In both countries reinvention happens at all levels of government, much of it is along the lines of agency-to-agency reforms. The process provides enhanced government management and is part of the resurgence of the states, which began in the 1970s und prepared the way for a re-loading of burdens.

The public mood, at least among the elites, has changed in both countries considerably. Federalism has regained legitimacy. The misunderstanding that the story of progress and modernization is written only on Capitol Hill has been overcome. Dividing the job of governance has become an accepted commonplace. The question is: under what condititons? In Germany, the idea of implementation of minor competitive elements into the highly inter-locked executive federalism is present in political and scholarly arguments. The practical steps up to now have been modest, exept in the area of party-state federalism where the German *Länder* are real laboratories of (party-state)democracy by experimenting with all sorts of coalition governments.

As the reinventing process is on its way, questions still remain about its price: Government and citizens are more than ever related by a non-hierarchical relationship, fostered by a stress on services for citizens and sometimes even transforming into a customer-relationship attitude. At the same time political and bureaucratic powers are tending to become more distant and less participatory, especially in the German case where Europe-anization and international regimes are transforming responsible govern-ment with increasing intensity into an intransparent system of multi-level networking.

There is a tension between the type of government which embraces the entrepreneurial spirit, which subscribes to advanced information technology including the vision of a self-service government based on "instant democ-racy" of vote.com-world for everyone, based on on-line policy voting cen-ters on the one hand, and the type which is based on the idea of a common weal and the democratic concept of responsible government on the other.

And what is the price for the transformation of citizens into customers? Is the customer always right? And what are the customer's rights in compari-son to the rights of citizens?

Of course integrated services (one-stop shops), flat hierarchies, the intro duction of competitive components and all the other features resulting from New Public Management are important examples for the new spirit of re-form on its way from the classic administrative system to a civic culture administration. These changes will be helpful in everyday dealings with bureaucracy and will probably result in the cutting of red tape. Nevertheless it still is bureaucracy and not a miracle drug.

Governance in Germany and the USA is changing. That does not mean an Americanization of Germany or the Europeanization of the USA. The process is one of convergence caused and facilitated by globalization of the economies and the fragmentation of the societies rather than of mutual adaption. Politics has to manage these developments. It may be that the classic distinction between the European "Freedom-from" and the American "Freedom-to" has already lost much of its importance. Yet, the basic question still remains: What will safeguard and empower freedom most efficiently in the transatlantic community?

Contributors

Bernd Adamaschek
Bertelsmann Foundation, Division of State and Public Administration.

Arthur Benz
Professor of Political Science, Distance Learning University Hagen.

Robert J. Eger, III
Assistant Professor, Department of Political Science, University of Wisconsin-Milwaukee.

Franz Greß
Professor of Political Science, Center for North American Studies, Johann Wolfgang Goethe-University Frankfurt am Main.

Arthur B. Gunlicks
Professor of Political Science, University of Richmond, Virginia.

Merl M. Hackbart
Professor of Finance and Public Administration at the University of Kentucky, Lexington; Senior Fellow at the Council of State Governments.

Jackson Janes
Executive Director, American Institute for Contemporary German Studies (AICGS), The Johns Hopkins University, Washington DC.

Carola Kaps
Washington Correspondent of the *Frankfurter Allgemeine Zeitung (until summer 2000).*

John Kincaid
Robert B. and Helen S. Meyner Professor of Government and Public Service and Director of the Meyner Center for the Study of State and Local

Government at Lafayette College, Easton, Pennsylvania; Editor of *Publius: The Journal of Federalism.*

Klaus König
Professor of Adminstrative Science, Government and Public Law at the German Post-Graduate School of Adminstrative Sciences Speyer; Executive Director of the Research Institute for Public Administration at the German Post-Graduate School of Administrative Sciences, Speyer.

Richard Lehne
Professor of Political Science, Rutgers, The State University of New Jersey, New Brunswick.

Ursula Männle
Professor of Political Science at the Katholische Stiftungsfachhochschule München; Member of the State Legislature of the State of Bavaria (Christian Social Union).

William T. Pound
Executive Director, National Conference of State Legislatures (NCSL), Denver, CO.

Wolfgang Renzsch
Professor of Political Science, Otto-von-Guericke University Magdeburg.

Howard Rosen.
Minority Staff Director of the Joint Economic Committee in the 106th U.S. Congress, Washington, DC.

Klaus-Henning Rosen
Head of Department, Federal Ministry of the Interior, Berlin.

Volkmar Schultz
Member of the German Federal Parliament (Social Democratic Party); Chair of the German-American Parliamentary Group.

Karsten D. Voigt
Coordinator for German-American Cooperation at the German Foreign Office, Berlin.

Ernst Ulrich von Weizsäcker
Member of the German Federal Parliament (Social Democratic Party); Chair
of the Study Commission of the German Federal Parliament "Globalisierung
der Weltwirtschaft – Herausforderungen und Antworten".